Ionic colonnade under the green poplar trees, Aphrodisias

Author: Uğur Ayyıldız
Phone: +90 216 567 76 86
uayyildiz@tnn.net
web site: turkeytravelbook.com

Editor: Mary Ann Whitten

Published and Distributed by:
Kulube Basın Yayın Ltd. Co.
Noter Sok. Ziya bey Ap. 9/1a
Suadiye - Istanbul - Turkey
Phone/Fax: +90 216 360 09 24

Color Separation and Printing:
Mas Matbaacılık A.Ş.
Dereboyu Cad. Zağra İş Mrk. B Blok No:1
34398 Maslak - İstanbul
info@masmat.com.tr
Tel:(0212) 285 11 96

ISBN 975-93681-0-5

DISCOVERING
TURKEY
THROUGH THE LENS

UĞUR AYYILDIZ
OFFICIAL GUIDE - ART HISTORIAN

ACKNOWLEDGMENTS

I want to express my appreciation to the many visitors to Turkey whom I have guided and from whom I have learned as much as I have given, especially Liz Rawson and George Foster from London and Shamuel Shemes from Jerusalem, lovers of my country. Also the late Jane and Alfred Harris from Cleveland, who spent months on the bird's-eye-view drawings of Perge, Aspendos, Side, and Alanya, given to me long ago for publication. My deepest respect and love go to Mrs. McKillop of Salinas, California, the idol of my guiding life, with her ever enlightening letters and e-mails of her love of Turkey (we are celebrating her 98th birthday soon); dear Mary Ann Whitten, who spent long hours editing and proofreading the text; and, finally, Uncle Benjamin, for his kind support and encouragement.

All photographs are from my personal archive except the credits given below:

Keskin Color archive, pages 19A, 286
Net Publications archive, pages 12, 96, 100, 108B, 116
Ministry of Tourism and Culture collection, pages 42, 43,172B, 214, 359, 360A
Erdal Yazıcı, pages 321, 341, 365, 408
Military Museum, Istanbul, pages 8, 56C, 242A
Museum of Anatolian Civilizations, Ankara, pages 47B, 297A, 358A, 406B

The first rose in the colors of the Turkish flag: a hybrid developed by a hobby gardener in Yalova, Spring 2004.

CONTENTS

Preface 9
Geography 10
Regions of Turkey 10
Archaeology and History 40
The Heritage of Anatolia..............46
Timeline 52
The Turks 59
Turkish Language 60
Traditions and Customs................61
Turkish Cuisine.......................70
Shopping...............................73
Population.............................78
Transportation........................80
Touristic Excursions..................82
Economy 84
Education 85
Marmara Region 86
Istanbul...............................88
Edirne................................167
İznik-Nicaea..........................174
Bursa.................................176
Çanakkale 180
Troy-Ilion 183
Dalyan-Alexandria Troas..............186
Behramkale-Assos 186
Aegean Region 188
Bergama-Pergamum 190
Ayvalık 197

İzmir-Smyrna.........................200
Torba-Metropolis.....................204
Sart-Sardis 204
Manisa...............................208
Efes-Ephesus 210
Kuşadası 220
Priene...............................223
Milet-Miletus 226
Afrodisias-Aphrodisias 231
Pamukkale-Hierapolis 235
Laodikya-Laodicea....................238
Honaz-Colossae 238
Kütahya 239
Uşak 243
Bodrum-Halicarnassus.................245
Blue Voyage Destinations 253
Marmaris 258
Mediterranean Region 264
Fethiye-Telmessus....................266
Kınık-Xanthos........................270
Patara...............................272
Kaş-Antiphellus......................274
Kale-Myra............................280
Phaselis 284
Kemer 285
Antalya 288
Termessos............................295
Burdur and Isparta...................296

Yalvaç-Antioch of Pisidia 296

Perge-Aksu 299

Aspendos 302

Side..306

Manavgat Falls.....................................310

Alanya-Coracesion..............................312

Anamur and Silifke..............................316

Uzuncaburç-Olba-Diocaesarea 319

Kanlıdivane-Kanytelis..........................321

Kızkalesi-Corycos 323

Cennet-Cehennem 324

Mersin 325

Tarsus...326

Adana..330

Antakya-Antioch on Orantes...............333

Central Anatolia Region 340

Ankara..342

Boğazköy-Hattuşaş...............................348

Gordion..348

Konya-Iconium......................................359

Beyşehir 365

Göreme Region-Cappadocia................366

Nevşehir...394

Aksaray..396

Kayseri...403

Sivas...407

Southeastern Anatolia Region   410

Gaziantep...412

Şanlı Urfa-Edessa 416

Nemrut Dağı-Mt. Nemrut 424

Diyarbakır 428

Mardin 440

Eastern Anatolia Region.................446

Malatya...448

Bitlis...449

Van-Tuşpa 449

Erzurum..457

Ağrı Dağı-Mt. Ararat............................460

İshak Paşa Palace.................................462

Kars and Ani 467

Black Sea Region.............................474

Trabzon-Trebizond 490

Samsun-Amisos 500

Sinop..504

Amasya...510

Index..512

Suggested Tour Itineraries 525

ATATÜRK 1881-1938. Founder of the Turkish Republic

PREFACE

The publication of this book fulfills a desire I have had for a long time. In my forty-five years as a guide, I have traveled constantly throughout Turkey— sometimes with groups, sometimes with a single person, but always with my cameras. My earlier books on specific locations in Turkey were best sellers in many languages over several decades. My articles on various parts of the world, always with color illustrations, have appeared in Turkish magazines. I have lectured hundreds of times to my colleagues in the Guides' Guild of Istanbul and to innumerable large and small groups in several countries, and have participated in workshops organized by the Turkish Ministry of Culture and Tourism. While preparing this book, I traveled thousands of kilometers again with my wife, Inci, and Rodi, our Rottweiler, in order to update my slide collection, one of the richest in the Turkish tourism world.

Discovering Turkey through the Lens, my first comprehensive book written in English, presents brief information about Turkey's history and archaeology, and introduces the sights of interest. Here the reader will find facts on all seven geographical regions of Turkey, illustrated with more than 690 photographs, drawings, and paintings. All but a very few of the photographs are my own. This is the first book of its type, examining almost every corner of Turkey through the lens, and drawing on my experience as a freelance official guide and lecturer and as an art historian.

My hope is that this book will help the reader better appreciate and enjoy the richness of Turkey's natural beauties, historical sights, archaeological and other museums, as well as its hospitable people. I have enjoyed putting this book together and hope it will bring pleasure to its readers. The information serves as a guidebook while the traveler is in Turkey, and the extensive illustrations will be a permanent reminder of Turkey and the Turks.

UĞUR AYYILDIZ

Geography

Turkey is situated on a peninsula at the junction of two continents and at the center of the world map. The larger part of the country, Anatolia, lies in Asia; Thrace, which constitutes the smaller part (3%), is located in Europe. Anatolia is also close to the African continent, thus serving as a natural bridge between continents. It has a rectangular form 550km/342miles wide, 1600km/1000 miles long, and it is in the subtropical climate zone, midway between the Equator and the North Pole. Turkey is a mountainous country with an average altitude of 1131m/3700ft above sea level and covers an area of 814,578 sq km/ 314,250 sq miles, including the lakes. The country has 6000 km/3700 miles of shoreline along the Black Sea, the Sea of Marmara, the Straits, the Aegean Sea, and the Mediterranean, which surround it on three sides. On the land borders, it adjoins Greece and Bulgaria in the west; Georgia, Armenia, the Nahcivan section of Azerbaijan, and Iran in the east; Iraq and Syria in the south.

Turkey is divided into **seven geographical regions** according to differences in topographic characteristics, climate, flora, and rural lifestyle. The dominant plant growth in the country is Mediterranean and high-steppe flora. In addition to the variety in vegetation produced by the rainy climate in the Black Sea region, there are over 10,000 different species and alpine plants in the mountains. Animals such as lions, leopards and others that were part of the fauna of the country in past ages have disappeared or been reduced to limited numbers today. Hunting is now strictly controlled and reserved to certain areas, and endangered animal species are kept under protection in national parks and special regions.

The Marmara Region

The Marmara Region encircles the sea of the same name. The straits, Bosphorus and Dardanelles, separate the less rugged terrain of the Thracian region, where sunflowers are cultivated, from the fertile lands in the east. Istanbul is the most populous center in the country. Bursa is the second center in the Marmara region, famous for its historical monuments, the greenery of the surrounding area, Mount Uludağ winter sports area, and industrial centers. The largest industrial establishments in the country are located in this region, which also has the highest population density. Owing to environmental protection and planning, pollution of the Marmara Sea has been prevented. The straits are the sole outlet to the open sea for Black Sea countries.

Sokullu Mosque, 16ᵗʰC, Istanbul

Bursa, 19ᵗʰC drawing by Allom   Below: Sunset at Gallipoli

➟ Next page: Historical peninsula of Istanbul with Bosphorus and Asian side above

The Aegean Region

The Aegean Region has the longest, most twisting coastline of the country. The coastline is under the influence of the Mediterranean climate while the higher inner terrain differs considerably. Grape, fig, tangerine, olive, tobacco and cotton cultivation are important. It is a tourist's paradise with its beaches and famous archaeological sites. The islets to be observed west of the shores of the Aegean Sea are the rocky islands of Greece. İzmir is the commercial center for its vast hinterland. Annual camel wrestling in the countryside is still a famous spectacle of this region.

Temple of Artemis, Ephesus, Painting

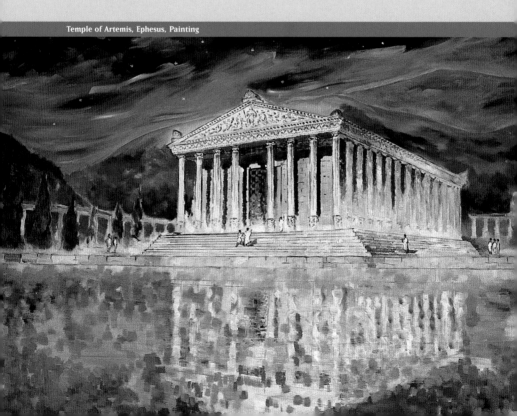

Exit from Odeon, Ephesus | Below: Manisa, 19th C drawing by Allom | Cascading formations, Pamukkale

The Mediterranean Region

The Mediterranean Region is known for its mild climate and the Taurus mountain range running parallel to the coast behind the plains. Fertile plains with completed irrigation systems are important for cultivating cotton, tobacco, and citrus fruits, and for greenhouse farming. Antalya's touristic reputation is based on the newest and most modern hotels in the entire Mediterranean, the cleanest beaches (a result of the importance given to environmental protection), the numerous magnificent archaeological sites, a seven-month swimming season, and its proximity by air to Europe. The beaches of Kemer display peerless natural beauties. The fertile Çukurova plain occupies the eastern part of the region.

A villager selling local handmade goods

← Previous page: Kuşadası shores

⇒ Overleaf: Konyaaltı beach and the Taurus chain, Antalya

Transhumance: villagers move to higher pastures, Beyşehir

Kemer shores, Antalya

Below: Four graces—three ancient, one modern—in Side museum

The Central Anatolia Region

The Central Anatolian Region is a high plateau with central plains surrounded by higher mountains. The capital, Ankara; the Konya plain known as the granary of the country; and the famous Göreme (antique Cappadocia) region are all situated here. The Salt Lake is in the central part of the region. To the east, Erciyes, an inactive volcano and the second highest peak in the country, rises beside the historical town of Kayseri. An inland climate with hot summers and cold winters is dominant in the region.

Stalactite decoration in Hunad Hatun complex, 13thC, Kayseri

Water well for flocks

Erciyas volcano and table-shaped hills, seen from south Nevşehir

Panorama of Göreme area

The Southeastern Anatolia Region

The Southeastern Anatolian Region is characterized by a range of mountains forming a bow-shaped boundary in the north, valleys that slope towards the Syrian border in the south, large plateaus, and an inland climate with low precipitation. The historical town of Diyarbakır is a lively trade center. Historic Şanlı Urfa and rapidly industrializing Gaziantep are other important cities of the region. The Southeastern Anatolia Project (GAP) has built dams, power stations, irrigation tunnels, and systems over the Euphrates and Tigris Rivers that cross the region from north to south. The electricity produced from the twenty-four dams and the amount of land irrigated in the arid summer

Detail from Zeugma floor mosaic, Gaziantep Museum

months are already making an
immense contribution to the
national economy.

Mt. Nemrut western terrace, Adıyaman

Black basalt city walls, Diyarbakır

Western terrace panorama, Mt. Nemrut, Adıyaman

The Eastern Anatolia Region

Eastern Anatolia, the largest region in the country, is covered with high mountains, and long, snowy winters prevail. Mountain ranges and extensive plateaus with valleys, rivers, and gorges squeezed in between constitute its topography. The largest lake in the country, Lake Van, and the highest peak, Mount Ararat (5165m/16941ft), are here. The region is connected to other parts of the country by highways, airports, and railways. The Caspian Sea oil pipeline traverses the region and reaches the Mediterranean.

⟹ Overleaf: Ağrı Dağı-Mt.Ararat in early April

Interior of the dome, Ulu Mosque, Erzurum

Wonderful skiing in red pine forests, Sarıkamış-Kars

Below: Urartu inscription and Old Van, view from citadel

The Black Sea Region

The high mountain ranges running along the Black Sea coasts and the narrow strip of shoreline form a region of breathtaking vistas decked year round in all tones of green. During the short summer season, the joy of swimming in the least salty seawater in the world can be experienced at its beaches. Trading ports and harbors for fishing boats are dotted along the coastline. The majority of Turkey's fish production is obtained from these waters. The eastern Black Sea region, which receives rainfall throughout the year, is a center for tea cultivation, while the central and western regions provide high quality tobacco and 70% of the world's hazelnut production. Along with interesting settlements and magnificent landscape, the eastern valleys descending steeply down to the sea have forests and Alpine plants with no equal in the world. The new highway, which will connect the Black Sea region to the Caucasus and the Caspian Sea area, and the oil pipelines that will reach the Mediterranean, will contribute greatly to the Turkish economy.

Alpine flora and Zigana area, south of Trabzon

An old bridge near Rize

Turkish flag? No, a 2ndC AD Roman decoration. Side theatre

Archaeology and History

Anatolia is the cradle of many remarkable civilizations. Its geographical position and geopolitical importance, its location at the crossroads of trade routes between East and West and sea trade routes between the Black Sea and the Mediterranean basin, the fertile lands sheltered by the surrounding rivers and mountain ranges, and the variety of climatic conditions have all made Anatolia attractive to civilizations throughout the ages. The results of hundreds of archaeological excavations and research projects carried out in Anatolia, which has been inhabited since prehistoric times, have produced striking results. In the last 100 years, finds from the earliest settlements, far exceeding museums' exhibition capacity, have required the rewriting of history books. Authorities agree that Western civilization and the roots of Western

Statue of Herodotus in his hometown, Halicarnassus

languages originated in this land. Excavations in Çayönü near Diyarbakır (8th millennium BC), Aşıklı Höyük near Aksaray (c.9th millennium BC), Çatal Höyük, Konya (7th-6th millennia BC), and Burdur, Hacılar (6th millennium BC) have uncovered some of the earliest known and richest village and city communities from settled civilizations in the Neolithic Age. With the participation and support of international universities and institutions, archaeological research in Anatolia will continue for many more years. The advanced culture of the Hatti civilization, the forebear of the Hittite Empire, was also uncovered in the excavations. Hittites used cuneiform writing by 1950 BC and created a centralized administration (1650 BC) for the first time in Asia Minor. Urartu in the east; Phrygia, Lydia, Lycia in the west; and the town of Troy and the

Neolithic Çayönü and earlier cave dwellings, Diyarbakır

Obsidian mirrors, 6th millennium, Çatalhöyük

later Ionian cities, foundation stones of the Hellenic civilization, all originated in Anatolia. Works from the period of the 3rdC BC (the Hellenistic period) of Alexander the Great and kingdoms founded by his generals are also very rich, beautiful, and important. The Romans adorned Anatolia from one end to the other with colossal monuments that continue to inspire admiration even in our day. Byzantium, the successor to the Eastern Roman Empire, diverged over time from Latin culture and continued for another millennium as an authentic Anatolian civilization in which Christian faith and Eastern-style pomp and tradition coexisted and the Greek alphabet was used. Byzantium disappeared into history after the conquest of Istanbul by the Turks in 1453. Beautiful monuments from the Turkish Seljuk and Ottoman periods survive today throughout the country.

← Mother Goddess Cybele giving birth, Çatalhöyük

Hatti bronze ritual symbol, Alacahöyük

Museum of Anatolian Civilizations Ankara

Lower city walls and entrance ramp, 2000-2500 BC, Troy II

The Heritage of Anatolia

For hundreds of years, Anatolia figured in mythology, holy books, and church records of Western civilization, all the way from the wooden horse of Troy on the west coast to Mount Ararat, where Noah's Ark landed, in the east. Anatolia pioneered many developments. It was the trade center of obsidian, the sole strategic weapon of the 6th millennium BC, soon exported throughout the entire Middle East. The earliest wine production, textiles, wall paintings, beer production, olive oil press, colonies, banking activities, and beauty contest, as well as the use of wheels, coins, metal ores, and the pottery wheel—all began in Anatolia. The Royal Road starting from the Aegean and stretching to central Iran with III stopover points was the first such route. The name Asia Minor was given by the Romans because Anatolia was, in many respects, a small replica of the Asian continent. The people living in these lands created three of the Seven Wonders of the Ancient World: the Temple of Artemis in Ephesus, the Mausoleum of Halicarnassus (Bodrum), and the Colossus, the giant statue adorning the entrance to the port on the nearby island of Rhodes. The Zeus Altar in Pergamum/Bergama, another Anatolian masterpiece, could easily have been included among the "Seven". Mother Leto gave birth to the pagan god Apollo and his twin sister Artemis on the banks of the Eşen River. The goddess Demeter; the god of wine and pleasure, Dionysus (Bacchus); and the great Mother Goddess Cybele, the oldest of them all, found their way from Anatolia, first to the Hellenic and then to the Roman world. Gods and goddesses had their homes on a number of mountains called Olympus such as those in Bursa (Uludağ), Edremit-Kaz Dağı (Ida), and Antalya-Çıralı. Natives of Anatolia included the Ionian Homer, poet of the *Iliad* and *Odyssey*, who lived in the 9[th]C BC; King Priam, his wife Hecuba, their sons Hector and Paris, their daughter Cassandra, and Aeneas, who escaped to Italy after the destruction of Troy and became the mythical founder of Rome. The myth of the Argonauts sailing in quest of the Golden Fleece toward the eastern Black Sea describes the currents of the Bosphorus and legendary cities along the shore. Xenophon of Athens (403 BC), the renowned army commander and writer, described local events, customs and traditions in *Anabasis: The Return of the Ten Thousand*, a first-person account which could be called the first travel book on Anatolia.

Among the Seven Wise Men of antiquity, Bias was from Priene, while the physicist-mathematician Thales and his student Anaximandros, who drew the first geographical map (6[th]C BC), the philosopher Anaximenes, and the physicist Anaxagoras were all

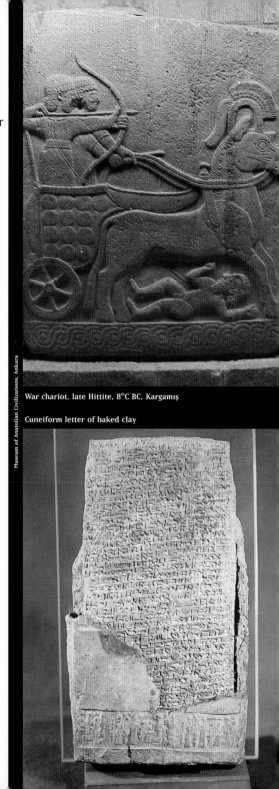

Museum of Anatolian Civilizations, Ankara

War chariot, late Hittite, 8[th]C BC, Kargamış

Cuneiform letter of baked clay

inhabitants of Miletus. Xenophon of Colophon, famous for his satiric poems (6[th]C BC), the mathematician and philosopher Eratosthenes, the well-known philosopher Herakleitos of Ephesus (5[th]C BC), and their contemporaries turned away from temples and gods to nature, exploring ways to a happier life by studying nature and drawing lessons from it. They became known in history as the enlightened **Natural Philosophers of Ionia**. Herodotus of Halicarnassus (5[th]C BC), known as the father of history; the philosopher Diogenes of Sinope, who roamed the streets of Athens in daytime with a lamp in his hand, seeking an honest man (4thC BC); Hippocrates of the island of Cos, the first physician (5thC BC); Strabo of Amaseia (1stC BC), famous for his 17-volume *Geography*; and countless other prominent architects, artists, musicians, and poets of the period grew up on these fertile lands and under these blue skies. The alphabet of Miletus was officially accepted by the Western Aegean world, the city-states of the Hellenes.

Western culture has preserved the stories of the Phrygian King Gordion and his famous knot; Midas, known for his long ears and golden touch;

Double-headed eagle, Hittite, 14[th]C BC, Alacahöyük city gate

Toy ox cart, 2ⁿᵈ millennium BC, Kültepe, Kayseri Museum

Croesus of Lydia, the richest king in history; Alexander the Great's encounters during his march to the East and to Asia; the epic struggle of the Great Mithridates of Sinope; and the king of Pontus, who waged the first national resistance in Anatolia fighting against the Romans. The Cilician Gates (Gülek Pass), a mountain pass that allowed access from the Taurus Mountains to Syria, was also famous. The first Christian church occupied a cave in Antakya (Antioch) and it was there that the believers were first called Christians. Later, the communities of the Seven Churches of Asia Minor spread into Western Anatolia. Hagia Sophia, the first and the most magnificent church, was built in Istanbul (6thC AD). The caravansaries of the Turkish world were the first in history, establishing a chain of castle-like inns from the western seaports to the east, each a day's distance from the next (13thC). Caravans could stay for three days with no charge. This was the very first service to encourage travel and commerce. Another early Ottoman heritage worthy of mention is the brilliant wit of Nasreddin Hoca. Edirne's Selimiye Mosque (16thC), the most aesthetically pleasing piece of architecture in the history of art, and the unique collection of the Museum of Anatolian Civilizations in Ankara are among the greatest treasures of Turkey's heritage. Topkapı Palace, Süleymaniye Mosque, and the university libraries of Istanbul hold the world's richest collections of Islamic manuscripts, books, and miniatures. The Ottoman Empire state archives are the most extensive in existence. The only imperial seafront palace, the Dolmabahçe (19^{th}C) in Istanbul, with its original furniture, carpets and upholstery, the world's largest crystal chandeliers, and its intact decor is the richest palace in existence. In June 2004 Dolmabahçe and Topkapı Palaces welcomed the forty-six presidents and prime ministers at the NATO Summit with banquets and great shows of Turkish folklore. Never before had so many leaders gathered at the same time in these historic buildings.

Anatolia was repeatedly shaken by waves of immigrations and invasions from both the West and the East. As their population increased, European and Asian peoples flooded into this land, the most prosperous of their times. From Vikings to Arabs, from Mongols to the barbarian tribes of Europe to Persians, invading forces landed on Anatolian soil. Threatened nations found shelter here; barbarian invasions put an end to existing civilizations; and the conquering peoples founded new civilizations by mingling with the native population. The Hittite Empire and the town of Troy were annihilated while at the peak of their powers by migrations of peoples from the west. Coming from the west much later, Alexander the Great put an end to the rule of the Persians. The kingdoms founded by his successors were conquered by the Roman Empire, starting from the end of the 2^{nd}C BC. Xanthos (Kınık, 5^{th}C BC) never surrendered to the Persians and was the first and only city in history where the men, not waiting to be conquered by the enemy, launched a suicide attack against the besieging forces after killing their families and destroying their town. In 1071 the Turks conquered Anatolia with a handful of warriors after the battle of Manzikert (Malazgirt). With the arrival of new immigrants, they settled in this new homeland and, by intermingling with the natives, created Turkey's population.

Instruments and belly dancing haven't changed! Musicians and dancers, basalt relief, Late Hittite, 8^{th}C BC Museum of Anatolian Civilizations, Ankara

EPOCH	ANATOLIAN EVENTS & LOCATIONS	NEIGHBORS
Paleolithic **c. 600,000 to** **13,000 BC.**	Artifacts of Homo erectus c.600, 000 BC. Neanderthal man. Cave dwellings. Nomadic life, hunting and food gathering, use of chipped stone, control of fire. Invention of arrow and hand axe, needlemaking. Dursunlu-Konya, Yarımburgaz-Istanbul, Karain, Öküzini, Belbaşı,Beldibi-Antalya, caves in Antakya and Şanlı Urfa provinces. No ice age in Anatolia.	Evidence of similar development in Syria, Lebanon, Mesopotamia, Palestine, and Egypt.
Mesolithic **13,000 to** **11,000 BC.**	Neanderthal man. Toolmaking: smaller cut stones, axes. Cave dwellings. Rock-carved figures at Eastern Anatolian sites. Hunting and food gathering. Rise of Homo sapiens. Man and dog become friends. Warmer climate.	Similar development in areas named above.
Neolithic **11,000 to** **c.6,000 BC**	Earliest settled villages: agriculture and food production, use of obsidian stone and pottery at late Neolithic. Advances in housing, domestication of animals. Social strata taking shape. Mother goddess Cybele worship and first cult buildings, statues, wall paintings. Trade with Middle East starts. Use of copper. Expansion of Central Anatolian language to west and east. Göbekli Tepe, Nevali Çori-Şanlı Urfa, Çayönü-Diyarbakır, Aşıklı Höyük- Aksaray, Çatalhöyük-Konya, and dozens more.	Earliest development in this age evolved only in Anatolia. Palestine, Jericho, Neanikomedia in Thessaly, 7th millennium BC.
Chalcolithic **c.5500-3000 BC**	Development of cities, rise of city-states with new systems of central organization and bureaucracy. Temples control trade. Use of clay seals. First multicolor pottery. Animal husbandry. Wider use of metals. Extension of caravan routes. Hacılar-Burdur, Fikirtepe-Istanbul, Beycesultan-Denizli, Can Hasan-Karaman, sites in Fertile Crescent between Euphrates and Tigris Rivers, and Halaf and Ubeyd cultures. First level of many tumuli (artificial settlement mounds). Yümükyepe-Mersin, Gözlü Kule-Tarsus.	Sumerian cuneiform writing c. 3000. Upper and Lower Egypt unite. Advance of Mesopotamian and Egyptian civilizations in trade and culture.

EPOCH	ANATOLIAN EVENTS & LOCATIONS	NEIGHBORS
Bronze Age 000-1200 BC	Troy I-VII, Hatti city-states, and Hittite Empire. Bronze objects. First four-wheel ox carts. Separate city-principalities. Fortified city of Troy I with megaron-plan houses. Use of gold and silver in palaces. Pottery wheel triggers mass production. High Hatti civilization (2500-2000 BC) adopted by Hittites (2000-1200 BC). Anatolia enters documented history with Hittite use of cuneiform writing from 1950 BC. Troy VI (1800-1240 BC), Trojan war. Early use of iron. Many Western Anatolian towns built in this period. Use of war chariots. Epoch ends with the destruction of Troy VII and Hittite Empire. Anatolia plundered by European (Sea) tribes. Dark Age begins. İkiztepe-Samsun, Aslantepe-Malatya, Alacahöyük and Boğazköy-Çorum, Kültepe-Kayseri	Pyramids built (c.2500), Assyrian traders in Hittite cities. Crete, Minoan Palaces of Knossos (200-1450). Gilgamesh Epic. Abraham lives in Harran c.1750. Moses, Exodus, 13th C BC(?). Hittite-Egypt Kadesh war 1285, first peace treaty 1270 BC. Assyrians rule in upper Mesopotamia. Invasion waves from west. Sea tribes struggle in Egypt.
Dark Age (Iron Age) 1200-750 BC	Central and Northwestern Anatolian nomadic or village cultures in former Hittite lands. Survival of some Aegean cities from the turmoil. Late (Neo) Hittites rule in Southeastern Anatolia. Newcomers, Aeolian and Ionian immigrations, settle along Aegean coasts.	Etruscans from Lydia settle in Italy c.900.

EPOCH	ANATOLIAN EVENTS & LOCATIONS	NEIGHBORS
Urartu State **860-580 BC**	Eastern Anatolian civilization. Strong warriors of highlands settle around Lake Van. Tuşpa (Old Van) becomes their capital. Many rock-top castles, irrigation systems, fine temple masonry. Thoroughbred Urartu horses gain wide reputation. Advanced metal objects exported as far as Italy. Assyrians invade in 580 BC. Urartu art objects, settlement mounds, acropolis-castles around Van.	Assyrians become a power in Mesopotamia.
Homer's Time **8th-7th C BC**	Mythological stories of Trojan war in the poetry of blind Ionian Homer and anonymous poets traveling to villages and palaces; poetic tales from the *Iliad and Odyssey*, gods and goddesses, rituals, heroism become basic parts of Aegean and Mediterranean culture.	Carthage colony of Phoenicians. Foundation of city of Rome 8ᵗʰC. Tower and hanging gardens of Babel.
Phrygia **750-300 BC**	After 350 years of nomadic life, branches of European invaders set up first political center in Gordion (legend of Gordion Knot) and expand over earlier Hittite sites in Northwestern and Central Anatolia. King Midas rules. Tumuli, rock-carved graves, unique-quality brass objects and pottery, wooden objects without use of nails, earliest mosaics.	First Roman census 566 BC. Achaeminian rule in Persia. Roman Republic 509.
Lydia **650-546 BC**	Rich kingdom founded on fertile lands of inner Aegean. First coins minted from electrum (gold and silver mixture). Ionian city-states and Lydian kings struggle. The "Thousand Tumuli", burial mounds of Lydian rulers, near Sardis. Sardis falls and Persian rule (546-333 BC) begins in Anatolia. As in the rest of the Aegean, Lydian region later ruled by Alexander the Great's generals and later by the Romans.	Destruction of Temple of Solomon. Kings Road from Persia to Sardis.

EPOCH	ANATOLIAN EVENTS & LOCATIONS	NEIGHBORS
Ionia h BC-1stC AD	Immigrants from Hellas mingle with natives, creating a new Anatolian culture through contact with the heritage of earlier high civilizations and Late (Neo) Hittites. Twelve major cities of Ionia form Panionian Confederation in 8thC. From 7thC Ionian culture influences Western Aegean architecture, society, and philosophy. Ionia's Hellenic language and way of life differ from those of Hellas. Ionian alphabet adopted by Athens. Persian dominance in Ionia with limited intervention in local affairs. Ionian cities join Delian Confederation in 478. Athens places imperialist pressure on Western Anatolia. Alexander defeats Persians in 332. Rebuilding of Artemision, one of the Seven Wonders of the World, begins. Pergamum Kingdom comes under Roman rule in 133. Roman Emperors spend more time in Anatolia and build cities of Imperial Roman taste. Ephesus becomes metropolis of Asia Minor with the Temple of Artemis and busiest harbor. Cleopatra and Mark Anthony married in Tarsus. Seven Churches of Asia Minor established in Aegean Region. Journeys of St. Paul.	Archaic and classical ages of Hellenic civilization. Persians in Hellas; wars at Salamis, Platea, and Mycale; defeat of Persians (479). Period of Pericles. Parthenon in Athens built with funds redirected from Ionian cities (447-432). Half-century of wars between Hellas city-states, e.g., Athens-Sparta. *Anabasis: The Retreat of the Ten Thousand* by Xenophon, 401-403.
Caria 7th-4thC BC	Carian fleets reach Eastern Mediterranean coast for trade. Starting from 6thC Caria ruled by Persian governors (Satrap). Herodotus, father of history, native of this land. Mausoleum, one of the Seven Wonders of the World, built in 4thC at Bodrum (Halicarnassus). Early 4th millennium BC Bronze-Age settlement, Pekmez Höyük, in Aphrodisias. Later towns of Caria adorned with Hellenistic, then Roman edifices such as temples, baths, official and commercial buildings, theatres, and stadiums.	Athens becomes a major naval power. Many famous philosophers, heroes, leaders (5th-4thC BC) executed; Socrates put to death in 399. Diogenes strolls in Athens with a lamp in daytime to search for an honest man!
Hellenistic Period 333-30 BC	Ionian cities moving to new sites; renovations and new edifices added to Pergamum and Ionian cities. Highest level of city and cultural life.	Alexander the Great on the march, 332-342. Rome becomes a major power

EPOCH	ANATOLIAN EVENTS & LOCATIONS	NEIGHBORS
Imperial Roman Era 30 BC-395 AD	Pax Romana brings peace and prosperity. Constantine the Great rebuilds Byzantium, new capital of Roman Empire (330 AD). Freedom of worship for Christians. First Hagia Sophia church opened in second half of 4^{th}C. Roman Emperors generously build up Anatolian cities. Roads and bridges built throughout Asia Minor. Roman Empire divides into two during reign of Theodosius I in 395.	Sasanid Empire in Persia. Jesus 4 BC- 30 AD. St. Paul's journeys in Asia Minor 42-60. Peter and Paul martyred in Rome. Jerusalem destroyed 70 AD. Jerusalem twice reduced to a field by Romans in 2^{nd}C AD. First Christian Ecumenical Council in 325.
Byzantine Empire 395-1453 AD	Fourth and last walls of Istanbul erected by Theodosius II in early 5^{th}C. Third Hagia Sophia, largest basilica, built by Emperor Justinian (532-537). Gradual cultural changes during his reign, e.g., Christianity and Greek language become dominant. Immigration of Christians from Holy Land and Egypt start with 7^{th}C Arab conquests. Fourth Crusade conquers Istanbul in 1204, bringing Latin plunder and rule until 1261. Byzantium becomes a regional principality.	Arabic calendar begins with Prophet Mohammed's move to Medina, 622 AD. Arab attacks in East destroy Turkic world. Khazar Turks (8-10thC) are converted to Judaism. Turkish rulers officially adopt Islam in northern Iran (late 10thC). First Crusade, 1096

Mehmet the Conqueror by Bellini
1480, National Gallery, London

Sultan Bayezid II welcomes the Jews of Spain in 1492
Modern painting

Atatürk and military lead
Painting Military Museum, Istanbul

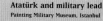
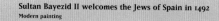

EPOCH	ANATOLIAN EVENTS & LOCATIONS	NEIGHBORS
juk Turk Era **1071-1243**	After the battle of Manzikert (Malazgirt) and defeat of Byzantium, Anatolia becomes a second Turkish motherland. Networks of caravansaries and bridges built on main roads from Konya, the capital. Turkish philosopher and mystic of Islam, Mevlana Celaleddin-i Rumi (1207-1273) begins his teaching in Konya.	Mongols put end to Seljuk power. Anatolia divided into Turkish principalities
Ottoman Empire **1299-1920**	Founder Sultan Osman followed by 35 family members on the throne. Fatih Sultan Mehmet conquers Istanbul in 1453 and moves the capital to this city. Admiral Piri Reis map of Atlantic shores, 1513. Süleyman the Magnificent (1520-1566), at the zenith of the Empire, orders an imperial mosque (Süleymaniye) from architect Sinan the Great (1550-1557). Sinan completes mosque of Selim II in Edirne (1569-1575), the most beautiful masterpiece of the architectural world. Decline and fall of Ottoman Empire. After First World War, Turkish independence wars begin under leadership of Mustafa Kemal, later known as Atatürk (father of the Turks).	Turkish navy saves and conveys crowds of Spanish Jews to Istanbul (1492). Selim I becomes Caliph (1517). Turkish conquests expand to Buda Pest in the west and Persian Gulf to the South. Mediterranean Sea becomes a Turkish lake during 16[th]C.
Turkish Republic Declared **1923**	Atatürk forms Grand National Assembly in Ankara, 1920. Republic of Turkey declared on October 29, 1923. On ashes of Ottoman Empire, Atatürk builds modern, Westernized, secular republic. Caliphate abolished. Massive reforms include alphabet, calendar, legal structure, women's rights, and more. Atatürk dies November 10, 1938; succeeded by İsmet İnönü. Turkey neutral in World War II. Multi-party elections, 1950, bringing in Democratic Party. Turkey joins NATO, 1952. President Özal introduces liberal economic reforms in 1980s. Golden Horn and Sea of Marmara saved from pollution in 2000s. Turkish candidacy for entry to European Union, possibly by 2010.	

Next page: Statue of Atatürk. On pedestal: "Peace in the Country; Peace in the World" motto from his famous Speech of 1933. City of Iğdır

YURTTA SULH
CİHANDA SULH

The Turks

Initially appearing on the scene of history around 1000 BC, the nomadic Turkish tribes founded the Hun Empire in the 2nd C BC. Stretching from the Great Wall of China to the Caspian Sea, the vast lands in Central Asia were the homeland of the Turks. The Turkish nation founded over 130 states, 16 of them empires, and moved slowly westward over a period of a thousand years, finally adopting Turkey as their homeland during the Seljuk and Ottoman Empires. After the 7th C, close contact and cultural exchange with the Arab world resulted in adoption of Islam first by the Turkish tribes dominating the border regions of Iran and then by the Turkish states. Thanks to their administrative skills and tolerance, the Ottomans ruled over three continents for 400 years. The Roman Empire is the only other example in history of centralized government maintaining control for such a long time over a vast area inhabited by communities differing widely in race, religion, and culture. The Ottoman rural areas were connected via roads, caravansaries, bridges, and forts.

People lived in prosperous towns where mosques adorned with domes and minarets were built beside churches and synagogues. All towns had medreses with both scientific and theological studies, hospitals, public kitchens and baths, and indoor toilets, while capitals like Istanbul and Edirne were enriched with palaces. Trade and industry were organized and controlled by guilds. It was in the 18th C that the empire's first attempts at Westernization started, and in the 19th C the empire fell into decline and finally disintegrated due to both internal and external forces. Although the Ottomans were not defeated in the battles in which they took part during World War I, the empire collapsed after the war. While its lands were being partitioned, the Turkish nation successfully fought a war of national liberation and founded the first republic in Asia under the leadership of Mustafa Kemal Atatürk, the national hero. Following the Lausanne Treaty, the declaration of the Turkish Republic on 29 October 1923 signaled the transformation to national consciousness. Atatürk defined a new path for the Turks: a secular republic with a Western lifestyle. When the great leader died in 1938 after fifteen years as president, his creation, the Republic of Turkey, had overcome many difficulties, embarked on industrial projects, built railways and ports, and implemented social reforms. The abolition of the Caliphate, adoption of the Western calendar and international measurement systems, the principle of secularism, the Latin alphabet, women's suffrage, dress reforms, and the unification of the disorganized educational institutions were indicators of a Western lifestyle. Turkey was neutral in World War II. The introduction of a multi-party system in 1946, the transition to a liberal economy in the 1950s, and membership in NATO were other initiatives of the parliamentary republic. Turkey's defense of the eastern borders during the Cold War years and its continuing strategic importance have entailed heavy defense spending, and, thus, some sacrifices in economic growth. To ensure stability and balance in the region, Turkey maintains strong, well-trained, and well-prepared military forces. Full membership in the European Union is a goal for the next decade.

Turkish Language

Leaders and alphabets of Turkish culture over the ages: Bilge Khan in Göktürk script (8[th]C AD), Bögü Khan in Uighur alphabet (8[th]C), Alparslan in Kufi characters (11[th]C.), signature of Mehmet the Conqueror (15[th]C), and Atatürk in today's Turkish

The Turkic language group, spread over a vast area on the European and Asian continents, is part of the Ural-Altaic language family and has many different dialects. The language spoken and written in the Republic of Turkey is called Turkish. The inscribed stone blocks of the Orhun and Yenisei regions, today within the boundaries of Mongolia, are the first written records of the Turkic languages (725-735 AD). The purity of the language used in these inscriptions by the rulers of the Göktürk state on political and social life demonstrates that Turkish had already been in use for many centuries.

Traditions and Customs

Variety creates a colorful mosaic of Turkish social life. In some rural marriages, men and women celebrate in different locations, but in a nearby village, they may join together in folkloric dances for days on end. The tradition of dying hands with henna during the ladies' "bride party" is popular in some regions. Depending on the family's wealth, city weddings may take place in a variety of venues from luxurious ballrooms to municipal wedding facilities. Some families may also have a religious ceremony at home in addition to the required civil ceremony. Local drum and pipe players or the wedding salon's orchestra and singers add to the guests' merriment. Belly dancers or folkloric dancers add more enjoyment and color. People never miss the chance to join in folk dancing. Turkey is the richest land for variety in folk dances, often winning the highest honors in international competitions.

Many other events are occasions for traditional celebrations. Between the ages of five and eleven, boys are the center of attention at parties celebrating their circumcision rituals.

Joining the compulsory military service is another joyful event; with the cheers of friends, boys depart to their place of duty. The Turkish national sport is wrestling. Every June, Edirne's famous spectacle is the centuries-old "oil wrestling" (since 1361). Football and basketball are the most popular sports in Turkey. Another favorite pastime is viewing the dozens of TV channels' shows, films, and series. Istanbul is a center of delight for night owls, and nightlife in summer resorts and larger cities is colorful.

When one is invited to a Turkish home, the customary gift can be flowers, baklava, or Turkish delight. In the countryside, the most common sweets are sucuk (prepared with grape syrup and whole nuts), pestil (mulberry or grape syrup paste), and helva (made from sesame seeds). Although the custom is not as popular as it was a few decades ago, many villagers still move to higher and cooler temporary settlements, with their cattle and sheep, in the early summer. This is a typical semi-nomadic way of life, transferring to a secondary, but more primitive settlement in higher pasturelands. In Eastern Anatolia this system still continues the old tradition of traveling with large tents made of goats' wool.

Other than prayers, the only ceremony in mosques is for funerals. In the courtyard of the mosque, crowds pay their last respects, pray, and accompany the coffin to the cemetery. Friday is the holy day of Islam. Mosques are full of men at the Friday noon service. Twice a year, huge congregations gather for morning services on the principal religious holidays. Though not required by Islam, visits to historic tombs of religious personalities (saints), with the hope of having wishes granted, are a common practice, especially in the countryside.

Bosphorus teashop   Tea served Turkish style   Simit, delicious sesame rings

Believers make wishes by tying fetishes to a (holy!) tree, Silifke

Below: Fishing for horse mackerel, a popular pastime, Golden Horn, Istanbul

Next page left: Shish kebab grill, Ürgüp

Next page right: Roasting whole lambs at a friend's party, İznik lakeside

Next page lower left: Sheep's intestines (kokoreç) on skewe Çanakkale

Next page lower right: Cracking wheat for bulgur, a village Adıyaman

Typical shoeshine stand, Beşiktaş

Street shoe repair on market day, Yalvaç

Backgammon is an exciting and popular game.

Copper cauldrons in a local market, Denizli

Traditional Turkish bath (hamam). Imperial Rome and the Turkish world shared this tradition.
Under a dome, there is a marble central platform heated from below, hot and cold running water to
individual marble basins, and scrubbing and massaging services available in separate sections for
women and men, or, in single baths, during separate hours for men and women. 19[th]c drawing

Pipe and drum for folk dances

Village and town ladies meet in their houses to help each other prepare for winter by making pickles, tomato paste, jams, or macaroni. Ladies' reception day is another custom. A certain day of the month is set aside for welcoming friends, who know that is the day to get together. Children are part of this social occasion.

Coffee or teashops (called kahvehane or çayhane in Turkish) are important social centers in the country. In every district and village, these men-only locations serve hot and cold drinks and are open from early morning till late at night. Men can chat on any and every topic, read daily newspapers, watch TV, play cards or backgammon, and drink endless cups of tea or coffee to while away the time. Young people learn from the stories and conversation of the old folks.

Dried beans cooked in sauce and a plateful of rice plus yogurt is the favorite meal for many. Kebabs wrapped in flat bread are a fast food available everywhere at any time and prepared mostly in kiosk-like small grills or at traveling pushcarts. Similar services also offer grilled köfte (meat balls) or kokoreç (a sandwich with sheep's intestines roasted on a skewer). There are 24-hour restaurants specializing in tripe

soup (served with garlic and vinegar) in all major centers. At open-air spectacles one can observe the fine art of cracking open shells with the teeth, eating the kernel of baked and salted watermelon, melon, pumpkin or sunflower seeds, and spitting out the shell.

← Turkish delights: belly dancing and silk carpets

Flag salesman

Turkish Cuisine

This is one of the leading cuisines in the world for the most discriminating palates. In a typical Turkish restaurant, bread is always served fresh, never toasted. Since butter, oil, and tomato paste are used in abundance in various dishes, butter and ketchup are not served separately. The main dishes are vegetables cooked with lamb, mutton, or veal. Rice, various savory pastries (börek), bulgur, dry beans, and a rich selection of vegetables cooked in olive oil are served as side dishes.

Meatballs, shish kebab, döner kebab, or other varieties of kebab with spices, yogurt, or aubergines can be tasted in special kebab houses. An out-of-this-world oriental taste is spicy, pizza-like lahmacun. Truly tasty sweet pastries, baklava and the like, can be enjoyed in small shops, many of them engaged in this line of business for a couple of generations. Because of the fishing ban between May and September, the best selection of delicious fresh fish is found during the other months of the year. The two best-known national drinks are of milky color. **Rakı**, the one with alcohol, is a strong drink that turns to white when water is added. The other is the refreshing **ayran**, made by diluting yogurt. Rakı can be served both as an aperitif with dried fruits or melon and white cheese, with various mezes, and/or during meals; it should not mix with other drinks. The homeland of wine and beer is Anatolia. Among those of similar quality, Turkish wines are quite satisfactory in taste, variety, and price. The well-known Turkish coffee is offered at every opportunity in small cups, and can be prepared with or without sugar. The saying that "a single cup of coffee is remembered for forty years" dates back to the 16[th]C when Turks first became acquainted with this drink. Turkey is also a paradise of fresh and dried fruits.

Döner on the spit

Kebabs with ayran

↓ Baklava with pistachio nuts

Fish shops in late autumn, Istanbul

Olives for every taste, Spice Bazaar, Istanbul

Shopping

Shopping centers in large cities usually provide fair-priced, good-quality domestic goods. Weekly markets in different districts of town offer the cheapest and most colorful choices. Turkey plays a leading world role in textile and glass. Cotton, wool, silk, and leather clothing are beautiful and inexpensive souvenirs.

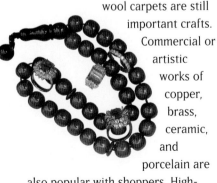

Handmade jewelry and traditional handmade silk or wool carpets are still important crafts. Commercial or artistic works of copper, brass, ceramic, and porcelain are also popular with shoppers. High-quality trademark items are very economical compared to their European equivalents. Turkish delight, baklava, helva, pastırma (beef pastrami), dried nuts and fresh fruits are delicious products many travelers enjoy taking back home. The best-known old center for jewelry, carpets, and souvenirs is the Covered (Grand) Bazaar and its nearby shops in Istanbul. It is strictly forbidden to take antiques out of the country. In major cities, there are many modern malls with hundreds of shops.

A silk Hereke prayer rug with 17^{th}C design

Above: Spice Bazaar

Below: a side street in the Grand Bazaar, Istanbul

Handmade carpets, jewelry, meerschaum items and pipes, brass and copper objects

Preparing and weaving wool carpets in the village

Hereke and Kayseri silk carpets are of the finest quality

Population

In 1997 Turkey became the second-most-populous country in Europe with 62.8 million inhabitants. The 2005 population is estimated at around 70 million. It is believed that the population growth rate of 1.7% in 1995 will fall to 1.2% in the 2010s and to 0.8% by the year 2020, yet Turkey will be the most populous country in Europe, increasing its population to 83 million. The population is 98% Muslim and over 60% dwell in urban centers. The average life expectancy was 67 years in 1995 and is expected to rise to 73 in 2020. With the youngest population in Europe, Turkey is a large potential workforce for the future. In addition to the dominant Turkish language, some forty-five ethnic groups' mother tongues also exist in Turkey, including Kurdish, Caucasian, Laz, Georgian, Albanian, Greek and Armenian languages. State broadcasting in some local languages has started.

The Turkish population is mostly below 20 and all children look healthy

Crowds visiting the Princes' Islands, ferry station, Büyükada, Istanbul

Transportation

The very first maintained road in history was constructed in Anatolia (5^{th}C BC). Turkey, lying at the crossroads of continents, is located on the Silk Road and forms a natural bridge between Asia and Europe. Modern trans-European motorways are being constructed along the old routes. The road in the south connecting the Middle East to Europe, and the Black Sea coastal motorway that will extend to the Caucasus will make immense contributions to national commerce and tourism. The existing roads, constructed and maintained by the State Highways Administration, are of average quality. In highway transportation, Turkey has the largest fleet of well-organized, busy TIR trucks engaged in transportation from Europe to

No motor vehicles, only phaetons, on the Princes' Islands. Four generations of phaeton drivers in one family, Heybeliada

Central Asia and to the deserts of Arabia. Bus transportation is fully developed; fast and comfortable buses are available in all parts of the country. Although regular passenger and freight trains are in operation nationwide, the best, newest, and most frequent trains operate between Istanbul and Ankara. Besides being the largest in the Middle East, Turkey's airline fleet is the youngest and the most rapidly developing one in Europe. To relieve Istanbul's heavy traffic, plans are under way for a third bridge and a huge tunnel to connect the Asian and European sides of the Bosphorus; an additional underground metro system, connecting to the seaports, is under construction.

Istanbul passenger ship terminal at the city center

Bosphorus Bridge from Asian side

Touristic Excursions

The unrivaled beauty of the land, the celebrated warmth of the people, and the myriad charms of Turkey welcome visitors. Anatolia has been a focal point for religious tourism since the earliest times in history. Such holy places as Artemis temples in Ephesus and Sardis, Didyma's temple of Apollo, and others, which were the most magnificent examples of their type, drew visitors from all over the Aegean world. Istanbul has always been a focus of attraction throughout the ages. This interest reached its peak after the development of group tours and the beginning of railway services from Europe, including the famous Orient Express. Tourism is one of the engines of the national economy.

Steam engine train tours are available in Turkey

Since its port is located right next to the city center, Istanbul is the most convenient sightseeing city for cruise passengers. Cruise lines often visit Turkey's coastal sites in order to show the marvelous regions to sightseers. Turkey offers rich archaeological sites of incomparable beauty, natural wonders, warm hospitality, crystal-clear seas, and sunny beaches. There are high-standard hotels in all tourist centers. In addition to Turkish Airlines, most major airlines connect Turkey with the rest of the world. Comfortable buses, a great majority made in Turkey, also carry tour groups all over the country on the well-organized highway network. Turkish travel agencies and tourist guides are internationally renowned for their knowledge and long years of experience. Many travelers, who learn to appreciate Turkey during tours or private excursions with rental cars, return again and again to spend their holidays in this land as

vast, varied, and colorful as a
continent. Easy-to-use, low-cost
communication facilities are
available throughout
the country. National and
international festivals, fairs, and art
events contribute to tourism all year
round. The exquisitely rich
performances of Turkish folk dance
groups can be enjoyed in festivals
and special programs.
(Please see pp. 525-528)

Above: Kaş on the Mediterranean. Below: Istanbul harbor

Economy

Turkey serves as a contemporary model for the other countries in the region with its cultural wealth, rich history, unique geographical position, dynamic and well-educated young population, and, most important of all, its secular, parliamentary Republican system. The Turkish nation has attained a high position among major world powers through the economic and political achievements of the Republican era. Turkey today has one of the world's twenty largest economies and one of the top ten emerging markets. The Middle East peace process, coupled with the potential of the countries of the Caucasus and the Black Sea, will make Turkey a focal point of social, cultural, and political solidarity between the West and Muslim countries. Textiles are the number one export industry, and developed countries are among the principal buyers. The production and export of motor vehicles and medium-tonnage ships are steadily on the rise. Turkey is one of the few countries self-sufficient in most natural resources and in agricultural products. Liberal and competitive free-market conditions prevail. There is a rapid rate of development because of the strengthening economy, growing industry, and increasing urbanization. In addition to the hydraulic and thermal power stations in the country, imports of natural gas and electricity from abroad are increasing the energy capacity. Pipeline projects will transport oil from Azerbaijan and Kazakhstan and natural gas from Turkmenistan to the Mediterranean through Turkey. These pipelines will also be a solution to the extremely dangerous traffic congestion on the Bosphorus and Dardanelles. The Southeastern Anatolia Project (GAP) is the largest electricity and irrigated-farming project in the history of the country. With the work on GAP reaching its final stage, there will be an ongoing, multifold increase in national development, and the growth in products and services will contribute to the economic importance of Turkey.

Education

Eight years of education is obligatory in elementary schools. This education and a three-year high school or vocational education is free of charge at state schools. There is a nominal fee for university education and scholarships are available. In addition to public schools, private fee-charging high schools and universities also provide education, often with a foreign-language curriculum. Private donations for new school buildings make a significant contribution to national education.

23 April, Children's Day: primary school kids in folkloric costumes

Next page: A quiet beach on Marmara Island, Sea of Marmara

Marmara Region

Istanbul

Maps: Inside back cover

Attracting travelers for centuries as a world center, Istanbul is a metropolis where Eastern and Western civilizations meet. Contemporary Western and traditional Eastern

Panoramic views of the peerless Bosphorus, a blending of sea and land in pleasing harmony, provide magnificent natural beauty all year round. In no other city do natural wonders and human masterpieces blend so elegantly and gracefully. The classic one-day tour will offer the visitor the opportunity to see the masterpieces of the city such as the Hagia Sophia Museum, Süleymaniye

lifestyles exist colorfully side by side. Modern buildings and artworks mingle with masterpieces of the classical Turkish, Byzantine, and Roman periods, sometimes looking as if they are leaning on each other. Istanbul, the largest city in Turkey, is the country's busiest commerce, import, export, industry, entertainment, and educational center. The climate is mild.

Mosque, Sultan Ahmet (Blue) Mosque, the Roman Hippodrome, Topkapı Palace, and the Covered Bazaar and its vicinity. Other tours cover the European and Asian shores of the Bosphorus, including Roman, Byzantine, and Turkish monuments. At least three or four days are necessary to really get to know Istanbul. A visit to Istanbul may also provide a Western traveler the opportunity to step on Asian soil for the first time; there are tours from the European to the Asian side by boat or over the bridges that connect the two continents. The historical city of Istanbul, built on seven hills, has an ideal location on a triangular peninsula flanked on three sides by the Sea of Marmara, the Bosphorus, and the harbor of the Golden Horn, an extension of the Bosphorus. Haliç

to settle opposite the "land of the blind". After setting sail and searching for such a land, they came at last to the Istanbul peninsula. Delighted with the natural beauties lying in front of them, they recognized the advantages offered by the bay called Haliç. They also noticed the colony settled on the opposite side of the Bosphorus. Byzas thought, "Those people must

(the Golden Horn) has played an important role in the city's development as a world metropolis. Around 650 BC a sea tribe living in a town called Megara decided to leave their settlement and look for a new homeland under the leadership of Byzas. According to the customs of the period, before any such undertaking, an oracle had to be consulted. The oracle advised Byzas

have been blind if they could not appreciate such an ideal place for a settlement", and founded Byzantium, present day Istanbul, on the peninsula. Archaeological excavations at the tip of the Golden Horn and on the Asian side of the city have uncovered other settlements dating back to the 3rd millennium BC. Following its foundation, the gradually growing and developing city-state became the center of the Roman Empire and of the world from 330 AD onward. In the next 1600 years, it was the capital of three world empires, namely the Roman, Byzantine and Ottoman Empires. One hundred and twenty emperors and sultans have reigned in Istanbul. All through its history, this old city continued to expand westward on the peninsula. The land walls were rebuilt three times, each time farther to the west. The existing walls were built in the 5[th]C AD and resisted many attacks until they surrendered to Sultan Mehmet the Conqueror's army in 1453. The city started to change under Ottoman rule. New settlements flourished on both the Asian and European sides of the Bosphorus since there was no threat of any enemy reaching the capital of this powerful empire. The Galata hills opposite the Golden Horn became richer as well. The silhouette of the city underwent a striking change: the crown jewels of Istanbul, the domes and minarets of the imperial mosques, began to dominate the skyline. Despite expansion outside the city walls since the end of the 19[th]C, the main roads and squares retain their 4th and 5[th]C locations.

Entrance to the Bosphorus: domes and minarets of Istanbul, seen from the Asian side

Silhouette of the city in morning haze

Throughout history, the city has had different names such as Byzantium, Constantinople, Konstantiniye, and Asitane. The hills on both sides of the Bosphorus are covered with woods. The shores are adorned with magnificent palaces, mosques, summer residences of embassies in the Ottoman Empire, and two Turkish fortresses. Pleasant places for dining and drinking, restaurants offering seafood and mezes, and nightclubs line both shores. On a boat cruise along the Bosphorus, the first remarkable sight is undoubtedly the Bosphorus Bridge. This first bridge, built in 1973, and its later twin, the Sultan Mehmet the Conqueror Bridge built in 1988, have greatly helped the flow of traffic.

About one-third of the population resides on the Asian side. Places worth visiting on the Asian side include the pretty mosques and historical Karaca Ahmet Cemetery in Üsküdar, Leander's Tower, and the Selimiye Barracks (where the founder of modern nursing, Florence Nightingale, worked when it was used as a military hospital during the Crimean War). The twin hills of Çamlıca offer the most panoramic view of Istanbul. Among the crown jewels of Istanbul are the Princes'

Islands, comprising nine islands and islets. There are many marvelous old mansions, summerhouses, cottages, and restaurants on the four bigger islands, which can be reached by regular boat services or special boat tours. Horse-drawn carriages are the only means of transportation on these islands. The Marmara Sea, the smallest sea in the world, is connected to the Black Sea via the Bosphorus, and to the Aegean Sea via the Dardanelles. It is rich in fish and sea flora.

The Hippodrome and Sultan Ahmet Square

The first of the seven hills on the promontory was the most important and dynamic part of the city throughout its history. The important buildings and monuments of the Roman era were built in the vicinity of the Hippodrome. Very few remains of these works have survived to the present day. The Imperial Palace, known as the "Great Palace", used to spread over an area extending from the Hippodrome down to the seashore. Like many of the other monuments in the city, it lost its importance with the Latin invasion in 1204. The Hippodrome has reached our day with its ground level raised by 4-5 meters and only three monuments remaining: the Egyptian Obelisk, the Serpent Column, and the Walled Obelisk. In the Turkish era, traditional festivals, ceremonies, and performances were sometimes organized in this square. To the west of the Hippodrome, the Palace of İbrahim Paşa, opposite Sultan Ahmet Mosque, is the sole remaining example of the rich private palaces of the 16thC. This elegant building is open to visitors as the Museum of Turkish and Islamic Arts.

The Egyptian Obelisk (The Obelisk of Theodosius I)

Proclus, one of the administrators of the city, erected the obelisk in 390 AD, during the reign of Theodosius I. It is the oldest monument in the city and has been considered magical in every period. The obelisk rests on four bronze blocks on a Roman base decorated with reliefs. These depict the emperor, his children, and other prominent persons watching the races from the imperial box, as well as the movements of the spectators, musicians, dancers, and chariot races. The 15thC BC obelisk measures 25.60m/78ft including the base.

The Walled Obelisk

Built of roughly cut stone, this imitation obelisk stands at the southern side of the Hippodrome. Its exact date of construction is unknown. It is named after the Emperor Constantine Porphyrogenetus who had it repaired in the 10thC. The Fourth Crusaders plundered the bronze plates decorated with golden lettering that once used to cover its surface.

Below: Royal box and spectators

Egyptian Obelisk of fine quality pink granite

The Serpent Column

This is one of the oldest monuments in Istanbul. The heads of the three intertwined serpents used to form the legs of a gold cauldron. The thirty-one Hellenic cities, which defeated the Persians in the 5thC BC, melted the bronze items they had captured to create this unique monument. The eight-meter-high column was originally erected at the Temple of Apollo in Delphi. It was brought to Istanbul in 324 by Constantine the Great and erected in the middle of the Hippodrome.

A 16thC miniature of Hippodrome area, showing an imperial parade

The Cistern of a Thousand and One Columns

It is located to the west of the Hippodrome. Of the 224 original columns, 212 are still standing. The brick vaults of the cistern, surrounded by thick walls, and the plain column capitals are interesting. Since renovations, the cistern has included areas for shops.

The German Fountain

The octagonal, domed fountain at the entrance to the Hippodrome was a present from Emperor Wilhelm II to the Sultan and the city of Istanbul (1898). It was made in Germany and installed on the site. It is a beautiful fountain, but does not blend well with the ancient monuments surrounding it.

The Museum of Turkish and Islamic Arts

The Palace of İbrahim Paşa (16thC) has functioned as the Museum of Turkish and Islamic Arts since 1983. Built on arches, the building surrounds three sides of a central courtyard. Rare works of Islamic art are on display in the hallways and rooms. The stone, baked clay, and metal objects; ceramic ware; and handwritten books are some of the most valuable examples of their period. The carpets exhibited are magnificent examples of 13th-20[th]C handmade Turkish carpets. This matchless collection is the richest of its kind in the world. The finest examples are the 13[th]C Seljuk carpets. The floor below is the ethnographic section where scenes of everyday Turkish life and objects in daily household use in past centuries are on display.

Sultan Ahmet Mosque (The Blue Mosque)

This imperial mosque is another example of classical Turkish architecture and is the only mosque originally built with six minarets. Although it is popularly known as the "Blue" Mosque, its real name is Sultan Ahmet Mosque. Built between 1609-1616, the mosque used to be part of a larger complex. There is an outer courtyard, and the inner

The Cistern of a Thousand and One Columns, 19[th]C drawing of it as a workshop

courtyard and the edifice itself are elevated. From the gate opening to the inner courtyard, one can view the domes, rising above one another in perfect harmony, over the symbolic central ablution fountain and the surrounding porticoes. Entering through one of the three gates opening to the mosque interior, one encounters the rich and colorful ornamentations of paintings, tiles, and stained glass that complement the exterior view. The interior has a centralized plan with the main and side domes rising on four large columns that support broad, pointed arches. The walls of the galleries surrounding the three sides of the interior chamber are decorated with over 20,000 exquisite İznik tiles. The areas above the tiles and the inside of the domes have painted decoration, but blue was not the original color. During the last renovation, completed in 1990, the darker color of the interior decorations was painted again in its original light colors. The dome covering the interior space, illuminated with 260 windows, is 23.5m/76.5 in diameter and 43m/141ft high. Its market building, repaired and reconstructed in recent years, is situated to the east of the mosque.

Blue Mosque interior, and overview of Blue Mosque from Hagia Sophia

Vakıflar Carpet and Kilim Museum

The Directorate of Foundations (Vakıflar) has a very rich carpet and kilim collection. Selected samples from this collection are exhibited in Sultan Ahmet Mosque. Carpets are displayed in the section next to the Sultan's loge, and kilims in vaulted lower galleries of the mosque.

The Mosaic Museum

The market of the Sultan Ahmet Mosque was built over the remains of the former Byzantine "Great Palace" of the 4th-6th centuries AD. The mosaic pavements that were unearthed at the lower end of the market decorated the floor of a large hall. They are done in the style of the Antakya (Antioch) School of the Roman Age. Mosaics found in other districts of the city were carefully moved here.

Tiger hunting mosaic found on the site of today's museum

Hagia Sophia Museum

Hagia Sophia, considered one of the Eight Wonders of the World, occupies a prominent place in the history of art and architecture as one of the rare works of this size and age that have survived to our day. Hagia Sophia, called Ayasofya by the Turks, is erroneously known as Saint Sophia. Hagia Sophia means "holy wisdom". Although no churches were built during the reign of Constantine the Great, some sources maintain that he built the first Hagia Sophia church. The first, smaller-scale, wooden-roofed church was constructed around 350 AD, during the reign of Constantius, the son of Constantine the Great. This church burned down during riots in 404, and a second basilica replacing it was inaugurated in 415. During the bloody uprising of 532 that broke out at a chariot race in the Hippodrome, tens of thousands of inhabitants of the city were killed and numerous buildings were destroyed. Hagia Sophia was also burned during this so-called "Nika" revolt, directed against Emperor Justinian.

When Justinian finally suppressed the revolt, he decided to build a house of worship "the like of which has not been seen since Adam, nor will it be seen in the future". This largest church of Christendom, whose construction started in 532 over the remains of the previous basilica, was completed and inaugurated in 537. The architects were Anthemios of Tralles and the mathematician Isidoros of Miletus. The basilical plan had been applied since ancient times, but the construction of a gigantic central

dome over a rectangular plan, as in the Hagia Sophia of Justinian, was attempted for the first time in the history of architecture. During the reign of Justinian, Hagia Sophia emerged as a manifestation of Byzantine refinement and pomp, and in later periods, it became a legend and a symbol of faith. The outer appearance is not elegant; it was built as a shell, without much care for proportions. In contrast, the interior is as splendid and captivating as a palace; it is a gigantic "imperial" structure. Despite its uniqueness and magnificence, the structure had some vital faults. The most important problem was the enormous size of the dome and the pressure it exerted on the sidewalls. The architectural elements necessary for transferring the weight of such a dome to the foundations were not fully developed at that time. The outward-leaning sidewalls witnessed the collapse of the original low dome in 557. The second dome constructed was much higher but reduced in diameter. The eastern half of this dome also collapsed twice, in the 10th and 14th centuries.

Vast sums were spent in all ages for the upkeep of Hagia Sophia. The Turkish conquest of the city in 1453 led to its immediate conversion into a mosque and saved Hagia Sophia from collapsing. Among the major restorations at later times were the buttresses built by the Turkish architect Sinan in the 16thC, the restoration by the Fossati brothers in the mid-19thC, and the repairs, including the fortification of the dome with iron bands, after 1930. With modern, portable scaffolding erected under the dome, restorations will be easier in the future. The three different color tones of the dome mosaics indicate three different restoration stages. After serving two different religions believing in the same god—916 years as a church and 477 years as a mosque—Hagia Sophia was converted into a museum in 1935 on Atatürk's orders. With its height and diameter, it was the largest dome of its age, and it is still one of the largest domes in the world. Due to the restorations, the dome is no longer perfectly round. Its diameter measures 31.87m/101ft from north to south and 30.87m/104ft from east to west, and its height is 55.60m/182ft. Four winged angels with covered faces decorate the four pendentives, which support the dome. There are altogether 107 columns on the ground floor and the galleries. Befitting the principal church of a great empire, the altar, the ambo (pulpit), the ceremonial objects at the section in front of the apse, were all plated in gold and silver and decorated with ivory and jewels. The

Latin invaders tore all of these down and carried them to Europe, together with some architectural fragments. In the half dome of the apse, the Virgin with the Christ Child on her lap and, on the right side, the Archangel mosaics, can be seen. The huge leather medallions, 7.5m/23ft in diameter, hanging from the walls at gallery level, and the calligraphic inscriptions on the dome remind us of its use as a mosque. A ramp gives access to the upper galleries. The magnificent interior looks completely different when seen from these galleries surrounding three sides. In the northern wing, there is a mosaic panel, and, in the southern wing, there are three panels, each with three figures. The large mosaic panel seen while leaving the inner narthex is from the 10th C. Figures with distorted perspective represent the Virgin and the Christ Child in the center, and on the two sides Constantine the Great offering a model of the city and Justinian offering a model of Hagia Sophia. The huge bronze exit doors, partially embedded in the floor, are from the 2nd C BC and were probably brought from a pagan temple in Tarsus. In the courtyard of the museum, there are Turkish works of art of various periods. These include the tombs of several sultans, a school, the clock house, and the ablution fountain.

The Basilica Cistern

This is the largest and most magnificent covered cistern in the city. The ceiling of this forest of columns is made of brick and is cross-vaulted. The name of the cistern comes from a basilica that was once located nearby. It was built during the reign of Justinian I (527-565) to supply water to the palaces in the vicinity. Its 336 columns are arranged in 12 rows of 28 each, and the cistern measures 170m/322ft by 70m/211ft.

The cistern's forest of columns

Archaeological Museums

The Tiled Pavilion, the Museum of the Ancient Orient, and the Archaeological Museum are all located in the first courtyard of Topkapı Palace and are collectively called the Archaeological Museums. In the museums, there are collections of 60,000 archaeological artifacts, 75,000 cuneiform tablets, and 760,000 ancient coins.

Statue of Marsias, Roman hall

The Istanbul Archaeological Museum

The museum, founded by the painter and archaeologist Osman Hamdi Bey, was opened in 1891. On its centennial in 1991, a large, modern section was added and the entire museum was rearranged for new and more extensive displays. Facing the entrance is the huge and formidable statue of the god Bes. To the left are halls where ancient statues are exhibited. These matchless, well-preserved statues dating from the archaic period to the Roman era line the beautifully arranged, attractive exhibition halls. Again to the left of the entrance, there is a room dedicated to Osman Hamdi, and then halls containing the artifacts he personally unearthed in the royal necropolis of Sayda (Sidon). The first three sarcophagi belong to the family of Saydan King Tabnit. A matchless Lycian sarcophagus and the Satrap sarcophagus are also in this room. The next section contains the world-famous Sarcophagus of Alexander the Great and the Sarcophagus of Mourning Women, both dated to the 4th C BC. The four sides of the first sarcophagus, which was erroneously thought to belong to Alexander the

Sarcophagus of Mourning Women, c.350 BC.

Below: So-called sarcophagus of Alexander the Great, late 4thC

Great, are decorated with reliefs depicting scenes of the war between the Macedonians and the Persians, as well as hunting scenes. On the side wall of the new annex, the facade of the temple of Athena in Assos has been reproduced in its original dimensions. The section on "Local Cultures of Istanbul" is housed in the first hall where magnificent works uncovered in the tumulus excavations and artifacts from various ages that were found in the vicinity of the city are exhibited in a pleasing modern setting. The room containing Byzantine works of art is also located here. Another section is called "Istanbul through the Ages". The upper floors contain showcases displaying contemporary artifacts, an exhibition called "Anatolia through the Ages and Troy", and a chronologically arranged display of works from Palestine, Syria, and Cyprus under the title "Civilizations of Anatolia and Neighboring Countries".

relics from ancient Anatolian civilizations, comprise a unique and beautiful collection. Hatti, Hittite, and Urartu finds are other works of art in the exhibition.

Entrance to Museum of the Ancient Orient

The Museum of the Ancient Orient

This is the first building to the left of the entrance to the Archaeological Museums. Artifacts brought here from Egypt and the Middle Eastern countries that were under Ottoman rule before World War I, as well as

The Tiled Pavilion

This interesting two-story building opposite the Archaeological Museum was the first pavilion of Topkapı Palace, built by Mehmet the Conqueror. This summer pavilion, dating back to 1472, is an example of early Ottoman architecture influenced by the Seljuks. There is a long inscription on the entrance wall. Here, 13th-19thC Seljuk and Ottoman ceramics and tiles are exhibited in chronological order. 16thC tiles from İznik are important works in this museum.

An oil lamp and 16ᵗʰC tiles from the Tiled Pavilion (below)

Beautiful monumental fountain of Ahmet III, 18ᵗʰC.   Hagia Eirene has fine acoustics.

Topkapı Palace

Topkapı is one of the oldest and largest palaces in the world, and has been a museum since 1924. The palace is a complex surrounded by 5 km/3 miles of walls and occupies an area of 700,000 sq m at the tip of Istanbul's historic peninsula. The Palace, used as the Sultan's residence and the center of administrative affairs, was the heart, the brain, and the very center of the Ottoman Empire. Thirty-six sultans ascended the throne, and from the 16thC, they were also the caliphs, religious leaders of the Islamic world. The first and outermost courtyard of the palace is entered through the so-called Imperial Gate (Bab-ı Hümayun). The monumental fountain seen outside the gate is a precious example of 18thC Turkish art. As soon as one enters the courtyard, the Hagia Eirene comes into sight; this 6thC Byzantine church is now the main concert hall of the Istanbul International Music Festival. The main entrance to Topkapı Palace Museum is the second gate, the Gate

Bird's-eye view of Topkapı Palace. Painting

of Salutation (Bab-üs Selam); passing through this gate, one enters the second courtyard, which was allocated to administrative affairs of the state. To the left of the courtyard, there is a weapons collection and the council hall where cabinet meetings were held. The only comprises 400 rooms scattered around smaller inner courtyards. It was altered and enlarged over the years. This place was the private residence of the Sultan, his mother, brothers and sisters, wives, children, and other members of the family, as well as the servants and eunuchs. In

Topkapı Palace, Hagia Sophia and Blue Mosque, seen from the Bosphorus

tower in the palace premises was the Tower of Justice, so called because it was the venue of the state court of justice. The tower was also used to keep the entire city and the port under observation, and its only entrance is from the harem. The harem section of Topkapı Palace the Ottoman Empire, there was no empress. The power to rule the harem belonged to the Sultan's mother.

Overleaf: Miniature of a banquet, 16ᵗʰC, Topkapı collection ▥➡

The Kitchens and the Porcelain Collection

On the right side of the second courtyard are the palace kitchens with twenty long chimneys. One section was kept in its original condition while others were turned into exhibition halls for porcelains and tiles. Some of the over 12,000 pieces of Chinese and Japanese porcelain in the palace collection are on display here. Outstanding porcelain and glassware produced in Istanbul are also displayed in chronological order. The building opposite houses the collection of silverware and European porcelain.

One celadon and two blue-and-white pieces, Chinese porcelain collection

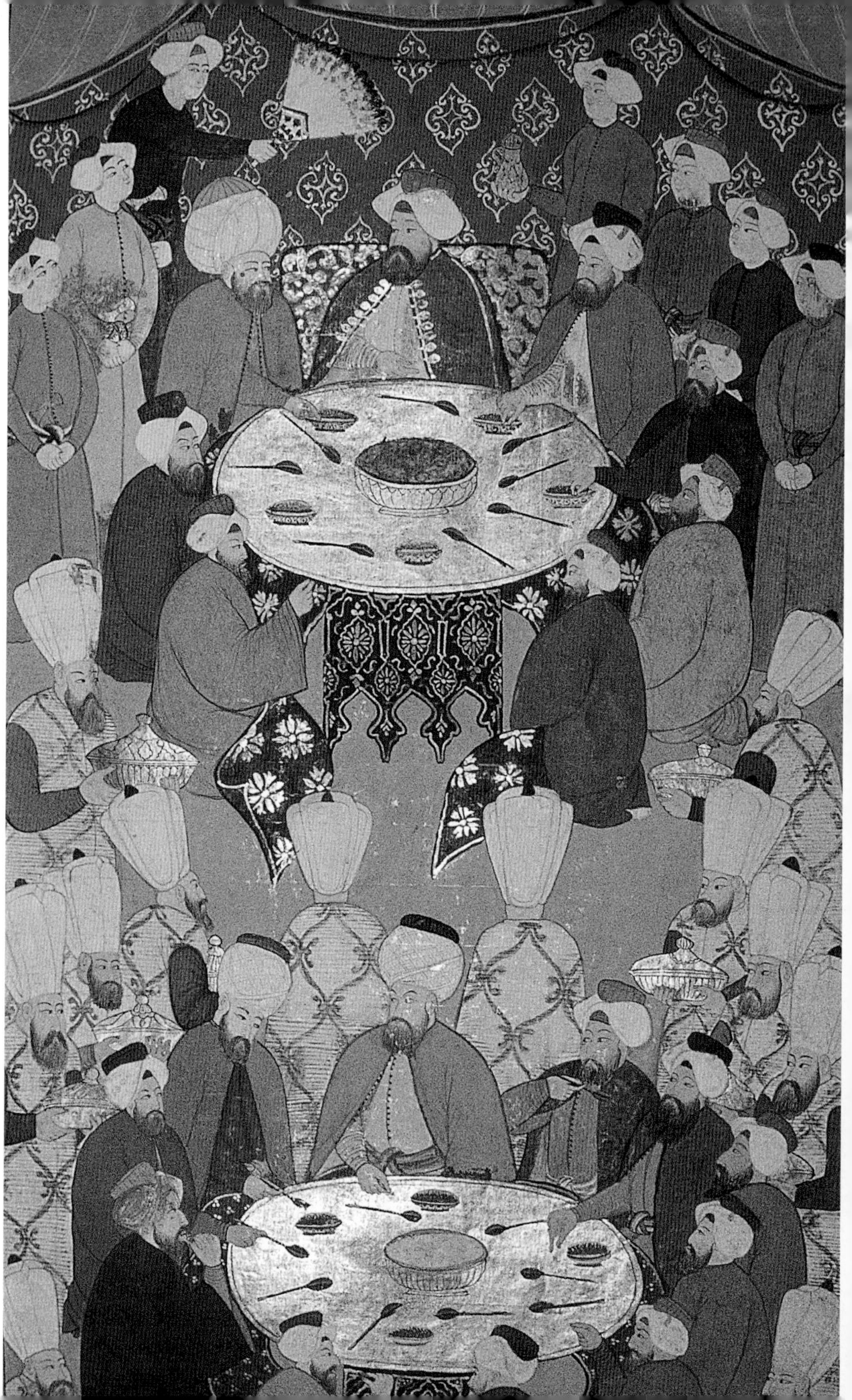

The Third Courtyard

Entrance to the third courtyard, the private domain of the sultans, was through the Gate of Felicity (Bab-üs Saadet). No one could enter this courtyard without special permission. The throne room, the imperial university, the treasury, and sacred relics of Islam surround this courtyard. Sultans'

clothing from many ages is also on display. The library of Ahmet III in the center of the courtyard is an exquisite and harmonious example of Turkish Baroque architecture. The treasury section is the richest collection of its kind in the world. All the pieces exhibited in the four rooms are originals. Masterpieces of Turkish artists from different centuries, as well as priceless pieces from the Far East, India, and Europe are exhibited in a modern setting. In a section requiring an additional admission fee, the first room contains four

Sultan Selim III and palace notables in a ceremony, c 1800.　　Above: Spoon Maker's 86-carat diamond

114

thrones used in different periods of the Ottoman Empire: one pure gold, one embellished with unique enamel and precious stones, another of ebony inlaid with ivory motifs, the last inlaid with tortoise shell and mother-of-pearl, with the sultans' aigrettes and pendants decorated with rare stones and large emeralds. In the second room, beautiful handmade Russian, Chinese, Iranian, and Indian works and imperial medals are displayed. In the third room, unique works of jade, zinc, and rock crystal; a 16th C ceremonial helmet; and two large candelabras, each made of 48kg/106 pounds solid gold, are displayed. In the fourth room, amidst the ceremonial swords, daggers, and imperial jewels, are the Topkapı Dagger, symbol of the palace; the Spoon Maker's diamond; the ornamented suit of armor of Mustafa

A 19th C drawing

Helmet inlaid with precious stones and gold

Ceremonial jug

III; and a golden cradle embellished with precious stones. The balcony connecting the third and the fourth rooms offers a breathtaking view of the entrance to the Bosphorus and of the Asian shore. In the room opposite the treasury, there is a very rich collection of pocket, wall, and table clocks. Passageways connect the third courtyard to the fourth where pavilions are set amidst gardens. The terrace beside Bağdat

Fruit Room in harem

Kiosk is the best place to get an overall view of the Golden Horn, the Galata district, and the wonderful skyline of old Istanbul with its domes and minarets. At the edge of the terrace, there is a gold-plated bronze baldachin as well as the Circumcision Room, the entrance wall of which is decorated with tiles. The interiors of these pavilions have rich decoration.

➡️
Next page: 18ᵗʰC dagger, symbol of Topkapı Palace

18ᵗʰC throne of enameled gold, set with precious stones

Çemberlitaş (The Column of Constantine) and The Goths' Column

When the capital was transferred from Rome to Istanbul / Constantinople in 330 AD, this column was erected in the center of a large oval-shaped square on the second hill of the city. Today it rests lower than its original height and was formerly topped by a statue of Constantine the Great as the sun god. Fires and erosion have cracked the porphyry blocks of the column, which was therefore reinforced with iron hoops. The marble capital dates

to the 12thC and the supporting lower section, to the 18thC. It was believed that a small chamber under the column housed sacred relics of early Christianity. In the outer garden of Topkapı Palace, at the entrance to Gülhane Park from Sarayburnu, the oldest Roman monument (3rdC AD) in the city, the Goths' Column, stands intact among the tall trees surrounding it.

The Squares of The City

Beyazıt Square, built in 393 during the reign of Theodosius I, was the largest square in the city. There was a gigantic triumphal arch in the center decorated by bronze bullheads, hence the name "Forum Tauri" (Square of the Bulls). The present-day name of the square derives from Bayezid Mosque, which was built in the 15thC. The mosque, neighboring the always crowded and lively Covered Bazaar, used to have a complex of surrounding buildings, but only the medrese, the baths, and some of the shops remain today. To the north, the campus of the University of Istanbul now occupies the ground on which Mehmet the Conqueror built his first palace. The monumental gate of the university and the fire lookout tower in the garden are from the 19thC.

Eminönü Square, at the southwest end of the Galata Bridge, is one of the liveliest centers in the city and leads to the Yeni Camii (New Mosque) and Spice Bazaar. **Taksim Square** opens to the most famous street of Istanbul, İstiklal, ending at the Tünel. Hotels, the subway station, the **Atatürk Cultural Center**, and a park surround Taksim Square. Other districts like Üsküdar, Kadıköy, Sarıyer, Şişli, and Ortaköy have smaller charming squares.

Monument of Mehmet the Conqueror.   ➠ Atatürk Monument, Tak

Main street of Covered Bazaar

Below: Sports fans celebrating in Sarıyer, Bosphorus

The Covered (Grand) Bazaar

The oldest and largest covered bazaar in the world is situated in the heart of Istanbul. Resembling a giant labyrinth with approximately 60 lanes and more than 3,000 shops, this bazaar should not be missed. Almost a city in itself, the covered market developed over time. The bazaar consisted originally of two 15thC buildings with thick walls and a series of domes. In later centuries, the neighboring streets developed and were covered; new additions were made, turning it into a trading center. The so-called main street of the bazaar is lined with jewelry shops, and a side lane opening to this street is allocated to goldsmiths. Prices vary and bargaining is customary in these small shops. The Spice Bazaar by the Golden Horn is another covered market on a smaller scale.

Domes and minarets at sunset

Süleymaniye Mosque

The silhouette of Istanbul is adorned with domes and minarets. The largest and most imposing mosque of the city is the Süleymaniye. The aesthetic supremacy of its interior and exterior, and its perfect proportions have captivated visitors for centuries. The Süleymaniye Mosque is an architectural masterpiece. Sinan, the grand master of architecture, built this mosque and the large complex surrounding it between 1550-1557. The beauty of the exterior of the mosque is best appreciated from a distance. This imperial edifice can be seen in all its magnificence from Galata Tower on the other side of the Golden Horn. The spaciousness, unity, and exquisite decoration add to the imposing view of the interior. The 53m/173ft high central dome with

a diameter of 26.50m/86.5ft rests on four pillars called elephant feet. The most attractive features of the interior are the extremely colorful, original 16ᵗʰC stained glass windows with Turkish motifs in the wall of the mihrap. Decorated with beautiful tiles, the tombs of Süleyman the Magnificent and his wife Roxelana are in the cemetery of the mosque. A small and extremely modest grave is located at one corner of the complex. This is the tomb of the architect Sinan the Great, who lived to be ninety-nine years old and was for fifty years the esteemed and respected chief architect of the empire, a diligent and productive architect who left over 400 works behind him.

Great architect Sinan and two of his works: Mosque of Süleyman on the hill and Rüstem Paşa mosque with a single minaret

Süleymaniye Mosque has perfect proportions outside and inside. The dome overlooking the entire interior has European-style 19thC painting.

Right: Minber, on the southeastern wall, has balanced decoration.

Above Right: Bronze baldachin at the fourth court's terrace of Topkapı Palace with view of Süleyman's Mosque on the third hill.

Far right: 19thC drawing of Golden Horn scene

Valide Mosque and The Spice Bazaar

Also called the Yeni (New) Mosque and completed in 1664, this was the last imperial mosque built in the classical style and is situated in one of the centers of the crowded city life, next to both land and sea traffic. The **Spice Bazaar**, second-largest covered market in the city, was part of the mosque complex. Other surviving parts of the complex are the tombs and the magnificent fountain. On the mosque side of the L-shaped Spice Bazaar, there are cafes and a popular flower market; fish, vegetable, and grocery stores occupy the other side. All of the shops inside the bazaar used to sell spices, but over time, some have turned into grocery stores, dried fruit shops, gift shops, or jewelers. It is a favorite site in Istanbul with its animated and distinctive atmosphere.

One of the colorful shops in the Spice Bazaar
Opposite: Valide Mosque at busy waterside location

Rüstem Paşa Mosque

This mosque with a central dome and a single minaret arises amidst the rows of shops and warehouses near the Spice Bazaar. The architect Sinan built the mosque in 1561 for Grand Vizier Rüstem Paşa. The facade and the small but attractive interior are decorated with some of the finest examples of İznik tiles.

The Golden Horn

Because of Istanbul's geographical position, the Golden Horn, a natural and extremely secure harbor, has played an important role in the development of the city. The inlet divides the European shore into two. It is approximately 8km/4.5 miles long with the widest part at the entrance from the Bosphorus. Two streams drain into this inlet at its far end. There are no tides or currents

One of the 16ᵗʰC İznik tiles in Rüstem Paşa mosque   **Interior of Orthodox Patriarchate, Fener**

here. The name "Golden Horn" is both a symbol of fertility—because of the fertile lands on its shores, the abundance of fish in its waters, and the fresh water of the streams—and a reference to its shape. The harem section of Topkapı Palace gives a bird's eye view of the Golden Horn. In the 1980s over 4,000 buildings on the shores of the Golden Horn were demolished, the businesses moved to new centers outside the city, the shores turned into parks and gardens, and wastewater treatment plants constructed with vast canal systems and filter stations. In Balat

Elegantly dressed boy at Eyüp Mosque before circumcision

Upper Golden Horn and Haliç Bridge

**Monument models from
Miniaturk Park, upper
Golden Horn**

Above: Hacı Bektaş complex,
Nevşehir

Below: Mausoleum of Atatürk,
Ankara

Next page above: Altar of Zeus
Pergamum

Below: Malabadi Bridge,
Diyarbakır, and Mağlova
Aqueduct, Istanbul

Miniaturk Park models: Mardin today

Below: Selimiye Mosque, Edirne

Above: Artemision, Ephesus; Mausoleum, Bodrum

A weekend in the park

there is a small Bulgarian church made of cast iron, and farther along, in Fener, is the church and complex of the **Orthodox Patriarchate**. On the opposite shore, the large building in Kasımpaşa is a naval construction dating to the 19thC. The **Koç family**, founders of one of Turkey's most successful holding companies, converted an old eight-domed foundry, which had produced ship anchors, into a museum for model ships, machinery, and nautical equipment. The **Aynalıkavak Kasrı** in this district is the only surviving pavilion of the palaces on the Golden Horn and is open to visitors as a musical instrument museum.

"Miniaturk Park", a well-organized presentation of Turkey's most famous monuments in miniature, is an interesting new attraction for visitors at the upper Golden Horn. The park is open daily from 10^{00}-19^{00} and Sundays 10^{00}-21^{00}. There are exhibition rooms and restaurants in the park. A former slaughterhouse in this district was restored and converted to a large culture center.

Tomb of Eyüp with fantastic tile decorations and many visitors, especially on Fridays

Eyüp Sultan Mosque

The mosque and mausoleum of Eyüp Sultan, located at the far end of the Golden Horn, is a sacred site for Muslims. Eyüp-el-Ensari was a standard bearer of Mohammed and died here during an Arab siege of the city in the 7th C. His grave was discovered at the conquest, and a mausoleum and the first mosque in Istanbul were later built on this site. When the original mosque was destroyed in an earthquake, the present one was constructed in its place in the 1800s. The walls of the mausoleum in the courtyard are covered with tiles from different periods. Cemeteries occupy the vicinity of the mosque and the neighboring hills. The famous Pierre Loti Café is on the slopes of this district, and can be reached by cable car. At the entrance of this district a huge building, originally a fez-making factory (Feshane), is used for temporary exhibitions.

The Kariye Museum (St. Savior in Chora)

The word chora means "outside the city, the countryside". It is likely that a small church built here before the erection of the 5th C Roman city walls gave its name to the later churches built on the same site. The small present-day edifice dates to the 11th-14th centuries. Its attractive exterior, as well as the mosaics and frescoes inside, are considered masterpieces of the Byzantine "renaissance". Mosaic panels in the two narthexes at the entrance depict the lives of the Virgin and Christ in the chronological order described in the Bible. Religious subjects were depicted in frescoes in the side chapel. In time, the Chora monastery and church gained importance when imperial palaces were constructed nearby. Master artists under the difficult conditions of the 14th C made these rich and meticulous decorations. The famous scholar and statesman Theodore Metochites built the side chapel, the exonarthex, and had the church decorated in the 1320s. The mosaic panels were created by a group of artists. The museum is located in a charming district with old wooden houses, hotels, and cafés.

Mosaic of the Dormition; frescoes of angels; and side chapel

Tekfur Palace

Roman and early Byzantine palaces were situated in the center of the city, near the Hippodrome. The **Blachernae Palace** complex, spread over a wide area adjoining the city walls and extending down to the Golden Horn, was in use from the 7th-8th centuries until the conquest. The only surviving pavilion of the complex is the Tekfur Palace (12thC), built adjacent to the city walls. ➡

Church dome and mosque minaret side by side, Üsküdar

The City Walls

City walls surround the triangular promontory on which old Istanbul is located. The walls on the western part, which are approximately 22km/14 miles long, date back to the 5thC. After its foundation, the city of Byzantium expanded toward the west, and new city walls were erected three times, each time extending farther, making the peninsula easily defensible. In the direction of the Balkans, the terrain to the west is quite flat, but the gigantic walls ensured protection on the land side. A single, sturdy wall also defended the shores of the Golden Horn and the Marmara. The land walls start from the seashore and, after crossing hills and valleys, join the sea wall on the banks of the Golden Horn. The land walls are 6.492km/4 miles long. Behind the moat and the first row of walls and battlements rises the higher main wall with ninety-six towers. Most of the gates have survived to our day in their original form. Through continuing restoration and renovation work that began in the 1980s, the area near the walls has been improved, restored in parts, and some areas are now public parks.

Roman city walls, 5thC: fine example of Roman military construction

Yedikule (The Seven Towers)

The most impressive gate in the walls was the **"Golden Gate"** near the Sea of Marmara. This imperial ceremonial gate was placed like an arch of triumph between two marble towers. Victorious armies, the emperor, and his entourage entered the city through this gate. With the addition of five towers during the Ottoman Period, the seven towers were turned into an inner fortress. Over the ages, it was used as a treasury, a storehouse, and later as a prison for ambassadors. Today this interesting castle and the "Golden Gate" towers serve as a venue for summer concerts and other cultural activities.

The Military Museum

It is the second richest of its kind. The former military academy, where **Mustafa Kemal Atatürk** was a student, was renovated to create this 22-room museum, which can exhibit only a small part of the total collection of 50,000 objects. On certain days, a **Janissary Band** ("Mehter") gives concerts on the museum grounds.

Mehter band preparing for a parade

Galata Tower

Built in the 14th-15th centuries on the site of an older tower, the Galata Tower offers a spectacular view of the Golden Horn, Old Istanbul, the entrance to the Bosphorus, and the Asian shore. An elevator takes visitors to the top two floors of the tower, now open as a restaurant and nightclub. From these floors and the panorama terrace one can get the best view. In this wonderful location, visitors can enjoy colorful Istanbul nights with belly dancers, folk dance groups, and singers. Hezarfen Ahmet Celebi, the first flying man, used handmade wings to go from Galata Tower to the Asian shore in the 17thC. From Galata Tower to Taksim Square, a promenade through the Beyoğlu district and İstiklal Avenue is a nice and easy stroll to observe 19thc Istanbul. Shops, restaurants and amusement centers create a lively city atmosphere.

Galata Tower overlooking entrance to Golden Horn and Bosphorus

Boğaziçi (The Bosphorus)

The Bosphorus is approximately 30 km/19 miles long, with the Anadolu and Rumeli fortresses facing each other at its narrowest point. Here the width of the strait is about 800m/2625ft. Known in modern Turkey as "Boğaziçi", its name in the ancient world was "Bosphorus" (Bull's Pass). On the surface, the Bosphorus flows like a river from the Black Sea to the Marmara, with the current getting much stronger and truly dangerous around the fortresses. Below the surface current, there is another current flowing in the opposite direction. These currents have always constituted a danger for ships crossing the strait. The Bosphorus is like a narrow valley with an average depth of 50m/160ft and a maximum depth of 110m/360ft. Because of the currents and the differing temperatures at various depths, the Bosphorus is a paradise for fish. One of the most beautiful sights in the world, the Bosphorus is a strait winding between two continents and joining two seas. The

Dolmabahçe Palace and five-star hotels along the Bosphorus

Black Sea is connected to the Aegean through the Bosphorus and the Dardanelles. Each season brings a different beauty: in spring it is adorned with the purple flowers of the Judas trees. The first bridge across the Bosphorus was completed in 1973, and was followed by the second, Fatih (Mehmet the Conqueror) bridge in 1988. An underwater tunnel and a third bridge are planned and should be completed by 2010.

➠
Next page: View from Greater Çamlıca Hill: Bosphorus Bridge and modern Istanbul

Fine view from Üsküdar

Dolmabahçe Mosque, Ritz Carlton, and Hilton Hotel

Fatih Bridge and Rumeli Hisar

Ortaköy Mosque

▪▶ Far right: Historical event: the first aircraft carrier to pass through the Bosphorus.
To get permission, the ship had no equipment, but was pulled by tugboats (2001)

Old waterfront houses

The Anatolian Fortress

Situated on the Asian shore of the Bosphorus, this fortress was built by Sultan Bayezid in 1390-91. Together with the Rumeli Fortress on the opposite side, it ensured full control over the traffic in the Bosphorus. This small fortress creates a picturesque scene with its green surroundings and the old wooden houses leaning against its walls. Passing the fortress, a little farther up the Bosphorus, is the Kanlıca district, famous for its seaside cafés and yogurt. The Asian tower of the Fatih Bridge also rises here.

The Rumeli Fortress

Istanbul had been besieged many times before Mehmet the Conqueror took the city in 1453, but it managed to defend itself with the help of the Roman city walls. The Rumeli Fortress was built before the 1453 siege opposite the earlier Turkish fortress on the other shore to stop any reinforcements or help coming to the city from the Black Sea. This military building was completed in the amazingly short time of four months in 1452. This largest and strongest fortress of the Middle Ages lost its strategic importance after the fall of the city. During the annual Istanbul Festival of Arts, the interior of the fortress is used as an amphitheatre. It is best viewed from the Asian shore or from the boats operating on the Bosphorus.

Cruises on the Bosphorus

An excursion on the Bosphorus is both a must and a joy for those visiting Istanbul. The ideal way to see the beauties of the Bosphorus, by night or by day, is by boat. The scheduled ferryboats leaving from Eminönü are one option. Hotels or tour agencies organize tours, or one can hire a private boat. On such a tour, following a zigzag course towards the Black Sea, one sees the European shore on the left, and the Asian shore on the right. Leander's Tower is situated off the shore of Üsküdar, and on the opposite bank is Dolmabahçe Palace. A 1704m-long suspension bridge rests on two huge towers, one in Ortaköy on the European side and the other next to the Beylerbeyi Palace on the Asian shore. One can see the old monuments together with the modern bridge. The wide building with two towers on the Asian shore after the bridge is the Kuleli Military School (19[th]C).

Rumeli Hisar

Dolmabahçe Palace

Dolmabahçe Palace, a blend of European architectural styles, was built between 1843-1856 by Karabet Balyan, the court architect of Sultan Abdülmecid. The Ottoman sultans had many palaces throughout the ages, but Topkapı was the official residence until the completion of Dolmabahçe Palace. This three-story palace, built on a symmetrical plan, has 285 rooms and 43 halls. Beautiful, well-kept gardens surround this seaside palace. In the middle is a large ceremonial hall that is higher than the side wings. The entrance section of the palace was used for the sultan's receptions and meetings, and the wing behind the ceremonial hall was used as the harem. The palace has survived intact with its original decorations, furniture, silk carpets, and curtains. It surpasses all other palaces in the world in wealth and magnificence. Its walls were covered with the paintings of famous European artists of the period. Ceilings and walls were decorated by using about five tons of gold. All the

Full view of Dolmabahçe Palace from the Bosphorus

Largest ceremonial hall in the world

↓ Sultan's reception room

furnishings in the important rooms and halls are in different shades of the same color. The ornate wooden floors have different designs in each room, and they are covered with the famous silk and wool carpets of Hereke, some of the finest examples of Turkish art. Rare handmade artifacts from Europe and the Far East decorate every room in the palace. Brilliant crystal chandeliers, candelabras, and fireplaces add to the lavish décor. The ceremonial hall is the largest of its kind in the world. A 4.5-ton colossal crystal chandelier hangs from the 36m/118ft high dome. The hall, still used for important political meetings, receptions and balls, was previously heated by an oven-like system under the floor. Central heating and electricity were later additions to the palace. Long hallways lead to the harem, where the bedrooms of the sultan and the quarters of his mother, other ladies of the court, and the servants were located. The separate wing used by the Crown Prince now serves as the Museum of Paintings and Sculpture and is entered from Beşiktaş. In the Republican era, Atatürk resided in Dolmabahçe Palace when he visited Istanbul. The most important event to take place at the palace was Atatürk's death in 1938. Before his body was taken to Ankara, it was laid in state while the public poured in to pay their last respects. All the clocks in the palace still show the time of death of this great Turk. Dolmabahçe Palace, the world's only seaside imperial palace, is open to visitors on several days of the week and is one of the "must-see" places to visit in Istanbul.

Yıldız Palace

This complex of pavilions and gardens, surrounded by high walls, is scattered over a large area of hills and valleys overlooking the Bosphorus. This second-largest palace in Istanbul is separated into various sections, each serving a different purpose. The greenhouse and theatre in the harem section are attractive examples of their kind. The staff dining room to the right of the entrance was later used to exhibit a weapons collection. Today exhibitions and concerts take place here. The Yıldız Palace Museum and the Municipal Museum of Istanbul are also in this complex. The beautiful large gardens and pavilions of Yıldız Palace now serve as a lovely city park, and Şale Pavilion, another beautiful palace-museum, is part of these gardens, whose entrance is near the Çırağan Palace.

Yıldız Palace main building ⬇ Şale Kösk

Çırağan Palace

The best sites along the Bosphorus and the Golden Horn were reserved for the palaces and mansions of the sultans or other important persons. Most of these, however, have disappeared over time. One of them, the large Çırağan Palace, burned down in 1910. Court architect Sarkis Balyan had built the palace, replacing an earlier wooden palace, for Sultan Abdülaziz in 1871. Lavishly decorated rooms complemented the exterior columns, superior examples of stonemasonry. Çırağan Palace was connected to Yıldız Palace by a bridge, and high walls surrounded it on the land side. After remaining in ruins for many years, the palace was renovated and turned into a five-star waterfront hotel with several new additions.

Çırağan Palace and Hotel

Leander's Tower

This is a small and attractive tower built on an islet at the entrance to the Bosphorus. It is a famous symbol of Istanbul. Used in the past as a watchtower and a lighthouse, it now serves tourism with a restaurant/bar and a balcony offering a gorgeous panoramic view of Istanbul. Western sources have erroneously attributed the tower to Leander, who drowned as he was trying to swim to his lover, Hero. Actually, this mythological story took place in the Dardanelles. According to another story, an emperor once dreamed that his daughter was going to die of snakebite and put the girl in this tower to ensure her safety. Nevertheless, the tragedy could not be averted and a snake hidden in a fruit basket bit the girl.

Üsküdar

This district behind Leander's Tower provides the best view of Istanbul and the entrance to the Bosphorus. At sunset, the fascinating silhouette of the city and at night the illuminated monuments appear in all

Next page: Kadıköy and Princes' Islands from Lesser Çamlıca Hill

their glory. Üsküdar has a pier for crossings to the European side. The 16thC mosque in the square, the monumental fountain in the center, the miniature Şemsi Paşa Mosque, and the medrese on the shore, the latter two built by Sinan, are fine examples of Turkish architecture. The historical Karaca Ahmet Cemetery and behind this the two Çamlıca hills are on the slopes of Üsküdar.

Kız Kulesi (Leander's Tower)

Kadıköy

There are no buildings of historical significance in the beautiful district of Kadıköy on the shores of the Marmara. It has been one of the fastest growing districts in Istanbul for the last twenty years. Many monasteries were built on the site of ancient Khalkedon, and the early Christian Ecumenical Council met here several times in the 5thC. Once adorned by 6thC AD royal palaces, Fenerbahce peninsula, the district's lovely seaside park, is popular for promenades. Baghdad Avenue (Bağdat Caddesi) is famous for the shopping opportunities it offers. On the Üsküdar side of the district, there is the Haydarpaşa Railway Station, completed in 1906 in the Prussian architectural style. This was the first (or last) stop of the Istanbul-Baghdad railway. Cemeteries and monuments for the British and French soldiers who lost their lives in the Crimean War are situated next to the large military hospital. Selimiye Barracks, a huge 18thC building known as Florence Nightingale Hospital, is nearby.

Souvenir photo at Atatürk statue, Kadıköy

Selimiye Military Barracks

Below: Haydarpaşa Railroad Station

Beylerbeyi Palace

Beylerbeyi, where the Asian tower of the Bosphorus Bridge sits, is a pleasant district known for its palaces since the Byzantine era. Sultan Abdülmecid built Beylerbeyi Palace between 1861-1865 on the site of another wooden mansion on the shore. The exterior and interior decoration is a blend of Eastern, Turkish, and Western motifs. The three-story building is divided into two sections, the harem (for women) and the selamlık (for men), and has twenty-six rooms and six halls. The original furniture, carpets, curtains, and other fixtures have been preserved in good condition. At the back of the building there is a large pool, as well as terraces and stables, the latter a very good example of its kind. This palace-museum is open to visitors throughout the year on certain days of the week.

Sadberk Hanım Museum

One of Sarıyer's most interesting mansions, a three-story building, was chosen as the locale of a beautiful museum of ethnography founded by the Koç family. Later the building next door was bought and added to the museum to display the rich archaeological collection. This modern and impressive exhibition is in chronological order and contains pieces from the Neolithic age and Hatti, Hittite, Urartu, Greek, Roman, Byzantine, and Seljuk periods.

Kilyos

This small and charming village on the Black Sea coast is famous for its sandy beaches stretching as far as the eye can see. The roads running through the Belgrade Forest and from Sarıyer join just before reaching Kilyos. The forest road passes alongside aqueducts and reservoirs. The village is 25km/17miles from the city center, and hotels, guesthouses, and restaurants serve visitors during the summer months.

Şile

This is a lovely resort town on the Black Sea coast, 50 km/35miles from Üsküdar. A motorway winding through the forests reaches the famous, extensive beaches of Şile. The small fishermen's harbor, the ruins of a Genoese fortress, and the famous lighthouse are worth seeing. To the west of the village the beaches extend uninterrupted, and to the east there is a series of small, sandy bays. The summer months are quite lively and crowded.

Kilyos Beach

Interesting rock formations at Kerpe, east of Şile

Şile's lighthouse, Turkey's largest

Famous eastern beach at Şile

The Princes' Islands

The group of nine islands in the Sea of Marmara is known as the Princes' Islands and is only an hour away from the city. There are regular boat and sea bus services to four of the islands from the entrance of the Golden Horn and from Kabataş Pier. The four larger islands, grouped close to each other, are covered with summer residences, villas, and pine groves, and are famous for their beaches and picnic areas. The islands are crowded between May and late September, but sparsely populated at other times. The residential areas have developed mostly around the piers and on the sides of the islands facing the city. The only means of transport is the horse-drawn phaeton. During the summer season, and particularly on holidays, the bays and beaches attract private yachts and motorboats. As the boat or sea bus approaches **Heybeliada**, two large buildings catch the eye. Between the twin hills of the island, the upper building of the Naval High School can be seen, and on top of the other hill, in the middle of pine groves, is the Orthodox seminary, which will reopen soon. Hiking paths encircle the hills, offering routes through the pine groves and beautiful vistas. The restaurants and the cafés on Heybeli are lively even in the winter months. Renovated and modernized in 1995, the Halki Palas Hotel, dating back to the mid-19thC, is open the year round. The largest and the most famous of the islands is **Büyükada**. It takes two hours to go around the island in a phaeton, but the shorter tour of the island, which takes only one hour, is more interesting. The Yörük Ali public beach is in a wonderful cove on the side overlooking Heybeli. Next to it is the Dil promontory, a favorite spot for picnickers. In contrast to the heavily populated residential areas near the pier, the southern part of the island is quite deserted. Boats often visit the coves on this side. On the higher slopes of the island, there is a dilapidated old hotel from the 19thC, perhaps the largest wooden structure in the world, trying to remain standing until the day it will be restored. The area around the pier is colorful and bustling with restaurants, cafés, and shops. Four hotels cater for guests in the summer months. The island's beautiful houses, well-kept gardens, and extraordinary views make an unforgettable impression on visitors.

Kınalıada

Below: Heybeliada, with Halki Palace Hotel in the woods

Water Sports Club, Heybeliada   Above: View of Büyükada   Panghia Kamariotissa Byzantine church, Heybeliada

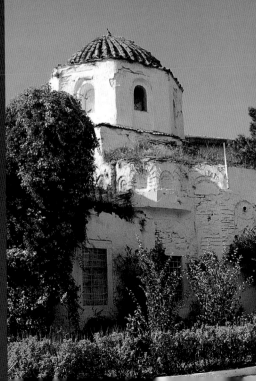

Phaeton (horse carriage) and the charming gardens of Büyükada

Edirne

This quiet Thracian city with outstanding masterpieces of Turkish monumental architecture is extremely close to the Greek and Bulgarian borders. Edirne is the "gateway" to Turkey for European tourists arriving by train or driving. It is one of the principal cities in the province of Thrace and a major center for trade and commerce. There is an active university life as well. Lying between three rivers, the site was ideal for defense from invaders. The Thrak tribes were the earliest settlers of the region. The foundation of "Hadrianopolis" dates to the first half of the 2ndC AD and the name itself preserves the memory of the Roman emperor Hadrian. Fortified by Theodosius with a new circuit of walls, it was a sort of outpost for nearby Istanbul-Constantinople. Under Turkish rule, the city became the second capital of the Ottoman Empire, for about a hundred years, until 1453. The archaeological treasures here are the **Eski Camii** (Old Mosque) of the early 15thC; the **Üç Şerefeli Camii** (1477), a pioneer in Turkish architecture with its large central dome flanked by lesser ones; the mosque complex built by Bayezid II in the 1480s as a school of medicine; and the hospital, baths, soup kitchen for the poor, hans, covered markets, and caravansaries. For well-informed art historians, the most beautiful edifice ever erected is Edirne's **Selimiye Mosque**, built for Sultan Selim II by Sinan, the master of classical Turkish architecture, between 1569-1575. Soaring above the city with its four elegant minarets, this crowning work of Sinan rises up on a square plan. Then the square plan turns into an octagon supporting the drum of the dome. The columns, the unique supporting system of the dome, are either within the walls or just next to them, giving the interior a striking unity. The proportions of the interior and exterior are sublime and matchless. A perfect harmony surrounds the viewer. The dome is 42.25m/138.5ft high and 31.22m/102ft in diameter. Marvelous tiles complement the high-quality marble and woodwork. The original decoration on the inside of the dome has been restored. Works of art from the Turkish-Islamic period are exhibited in the medrese, and a shopping arcade borders the other side of the courtyard. A 225km/157 mile express highway connecting

Istanbul to Edirne makes it easy to visit even if only for this one masterpiece, the Selimiye Mosque. On an island of the western river just outside the city, there are still some remains from the tower of the **Sultans' Palace**. Since the 14ᵗʰC, in the palace gardens, oil wrestling has been performed. It is thought to be the oldest continuing tradition in the world. This traditional Turkish event, taking place every year in July, carries on an age-old ceremony and draws many spectators from all over the country. The riverside monuments of the Balkan Wars, the old bridges still in use on the rivers,

the well-preserved and charming old houses, the historic train station and the only tower surviving from the citadel are other places of interest. Edirne is also famous around the country for its cheese production. Hotels include the interesting Caravansary Hotel, a 16ᵗʰC building, and a few modest hotels.

Marvelous exterior of Selimiye Mosque and interior of the dome

Right: Tower of Justice, last remains of Edirne royal palace

Below: Lightweight oil wrestlers

Opposite page, top: Sesame seeds and oil are an important product of the region

Opposite page, below: Villagers in their colorful horse cart ready to be photographed

İznik -Nicaea

Settled since early times, Iznik is surrounded by a green belt of olive trees, vineyards, and orchards on the eastern side of the lake bearing the same name as the town. Iznik is worth seeing for its Roman and Byzantine city walls with three original gates still in use. The small but beautiful **Yeşil (Green) Mosque,** the **Nilüfer Hatun İmaret** (today the Archaeological Museum),

the **Hagia Sophia Museum** at the crossroads in the town center, and the ruins of the Roman Theatre are the highlights of the visit. The town is situated in ancient Bithynia. Lysimachus, the famous general of Alexander the Great, after conquering the town in 301 BC, named it after his wife, Nikaia. The Arabs, Crusaders, Byzantines, and Ottomans stormed its walls. The regional Roman governor of Bithynia, Pliny the Younger (111-113 AD), wrote to Trajan for advice on what to do about the Christians in his province. This was the first official mention of the new religion in the Roman

Iznik tiles, first half of 16th C, Selim I Mosque, Istanbul

Empire. Nicaea was the meeting place for the first (325 AD) and the seventh and last (787 AD) Ecumenical Council meetings. The last meeting took place at Hagia Sophia church, built by Justinian in the 6th C, and decisions were taken against Iconoclasm. When the Crusaders captured Constantinople in 1204, Nicaea became the capital of the Lascarid Principality until 1261. The Byzantine family tomb, unearthed intact outside the town in recent years, is quite interesting with its colorful wall decorations. İznik was the home of the world-famous 16th C Turkish tiles and ceramics, some of whose workshops have been unearthed. The majority of the grapes of local production are exported fresh to European countries. Lakeshore restaurants and a few standard hotels are available for visitors. İznik can be visited within a few hours on an Istanbul-Bursa tour.

Triple entrance in city walls, Iznik

Bursa

Also named "Beautiful" or "Green" Bursa, the fifth biggest city of Turkey lies on the lower slopes of Mt. Uludağ, an extinct volcano. With a naturally irrigated fertile plain, the city is especially famous for its juicy, sweet peaches and candied chestnuts. Facilities include historic spas and a ski center. Since the 16thC it has been the center of silk production in Turkey and now of the textile industry. Towels are the most famous among the textiles produced in Bursa. It is also the most important center for car manufacturing. All the early Ottoman Turkish monuments and edifices are in perfect condition. The "must see" places include the **Ulu Mosque** at the city center, the colorful **Covered Bazaar** next to it, and the building complexes at the upper terraces of the city. Named after its founder, the local king Prusias, a small settlement was founded by the slopes of ancient **Olympus (Mt. Uludağ)** in the 3rdC BC. Developing in time, it became an important center during the Byzantine period. The most glorious

days of the city were during Ottoman times when it functioned as the capital. Because of the numerous monasteries built between the 7th and 14th centuries, the mountain was named the Monks' Mount. Ulu Camii (the Great Mosque), built in 1400, has twenty small domes placed over twelve pillars. One of the domes in the middle, covered with a glass pane, and the ablution fountain placed underneath are peculiar to this mosque. The rich calligraphy on the walls and the wooden minber are the other outstanding features. On the east terrace of the city, **Yeşil Camii** (the Green Mosque), together with the nearby **Yeşil Türbe** (Green Mausoleum) and the medrese (today the Museum of Turkish-Islamic Arts), were built in the early 15thC. The mihrap wall of the mosque, the interior of the Green Mausoleum and the sarcophaguses there are adorned with beautiful tiles decorated in relief. Restored in the 19thC, the mausoleums of the founders of the Ottoman Empire, Sultan Osman and his son Sultan Orhan, are situated on the high terrace of the city where a clock tower stands. On the upper terrace, beneath hundred-year-old trees, lie the **Muradiye Mosque** (15thC) and medrese, together with the twelve beautifully decorated mausoleums of the Sultan and the

imperial family members. The best examples of old Turkish houses are in this district. Other city highlights are the remains of the Roman and Byzantine city walls; historical spas; the mausoleum of the main characters of Turkish shadow theatre, Hacivat and Karagöz; the Archaeological Museum in the Cultural Park; the forests of the **Uludağ National Park**; and the luxurious hotels at the mountaintop during the skiing season. A cable car runs from downtown up this mountain, the world's richest source of wolfram ore. İskender kebab, the delicious trademark of Bursa, is served at its best in the restaurants where it was invented. The city has a number of hotels and thermal hotels of all qualities. Daily tours from Istanbul can be made via boat or fast ferry to Yalova.

Previous page: Reading the Koran in Ulu Mosque, Bursa

Below: General view of downtown Bursa and lower slopes of Uludağ

Opposite page, top left: Green Mausoleum, 15thC

Opposite page, top right: Interior ablution fountain, Ulu Mosque

Opposite page, bottom left: Mausoleum in Muradiye complex

Opposite page, bottom right: An old mansion in Muradiye distri

Çanakkale

Çanakkale is a small, quiet city on the Asian shores of the Dardanelles. University students and passengers arriving on the frequent ferryboats are lively additions to the town. The Gallipoli Peninsula, across the strait, is filled with memories of World War I. At the entrance to the strait, the **Unknown Soldiers' Monument**, the largest of its kind, commemorates the Turkish soldiers who fought bravely and died for their independence. Ironically, this strait witnessed the very first world war (!): the Trojan affair some 3,150 years ago. The city is a cruise stopover harbor for visits to Troy. At the narrowest point of the strait, two Turkish fortresses were built in the 16th C. During World War I, the Allies attempted to cross the straits of Çanakkale, a first assault in their efforts to reach the Black Sea and bring reinforcements to Russia. On 18 March 1915, they attacked from the sea with a force never seen

Anzac Day at the Unknown Soldiers' Monument

before. The Turkish minefield and the bombardment from heavy artillery placed on the hills were a complete surprise, and some large units of the fleet sank to the bottom of the water. The Allied fleet had to withdraw. Later in the land campaign, a violent battle was fought and, under the command of Mustafa Kemal, the Turkish forces drove back the Allied forces—the British, French, and Anzacs (Australian and New Zealand troops)—at the beginning of 1916. Every year in the early spring, the grandchildren of these soldiers, who fought, died, and were buried in this land alongside the Turkish soldiers, come to commemorate their ancestors and attend the "Dawn Ceremony" at the Unknown Soldiers' Monument. **Gelibolu (Gallipoli)** Peninsula is a national park. The Çanakkale Archaeological Museum is small but rich in its exhibited artifacts. The area's hotels are open throughout the year. Sardines and other seasonal fish from the strait are delicious. Along with agriculture, especially fruit and olive production, stockbreeding is carried out in the rural areas. The 32km/20mile road leading to Troy passes through fertile lands. Istanbul is four hours' drive from Çanakkale.

View of silted harbor from Troy

◀▪▪▪
Previous page: Turkish Unknown Soldiers' Monument at tip of Gallipoli peninsula

Troy-Ilion

Despite its famous past, the ruins of the city look quite ordinary. City walls with fine masonry, a narrow passage, demolished walls, marble pieces scattered around catch the eye at first sight. A fertile plain surrounds the mound, and from over the ruins, today's shoreline can be seen in the distance. The site was known from the poems of a blind poet, created with his fantastic imagination about intrigues of

mythological gods, war and love stories, and heroic adventures. The castle-like site described in Homer's epic, the *Iliad*, turned out to be Wilusa, mentioned in Hittite sources. On this westernmost hill of Anatolia, a settlement was established in nine layers to control land trade and sea passage through the ages. Certain features of Anatolian dress, hairstyle, weapons, and navigation equipment, as well as a group of major gods, found their way to the islands and the Aegean world. Troy was both the front line and a vital trade center influencing Western civilization. Thus for this important city of its time, the most celebrated legends were created, and in the citadel protected by high walls, the **Homeric** heroes, the king and his family, were created in the poet's imagination. Paris, the youngest son of the king and the queen, was left in the mountains because of an oracle's bad omens and brought up by a shepherd there. He grew up to be a shepherd on the same mountain, Mt. Ida (Olympus). The events of his life proved the omen true. According to the myth, at a wedding in Olympus a golden apple marked "for the most beautiful" was thrown in the hall, arousing a controversy among the gods. All the goddesses claimed that the apple was sent for her and the feast turned into a fight. Zeus, believing that he had found the best solution to the problem, recommended that the nearest mortal judge a contest among Hera, Athena, and Aphrodite. Each of the goddesses promised something to Paris in order to get the apple: Athena promised victory in every war; Hera, kingship of the world; and

Aphrodite, the most beautiful woman in the world. Paris "naturally" gave the apple to Aphrodite. But the most beautiful woman, named Helen, was the wife of a king. Paris fell in love with Helen and abducted her to Troy, starting a ten-year war between the Trojans and the Achaeans. The Achaeans gave a wooden horse, a copy of which can be seen today at the entrance of the site, to the Trojans as a "gift." Their soldiers, hidden inside the wooden horse, came out at night, slaughtered all the Trojans, and demolished their rich city. The city thus paid a high price for Paris' love of a woman. The works of the blind poet Homer, composing his poems around 400 years after the war, were first heard in the houses of nobles in the western provinces of Asia Minor. A long world war was sparked by a great love story. Homer of Ionia created the cultural bases of the Western world for the next few millennia. These poems were written down for the first time in the Greek language in Athens in the 6thC BC. Modern archaeology enlightens history with its finds and now sees the war as an economic struggle, tending to see the rest as poetry. The German Heinrich Schliemann, while listening to the stories read by his

Recent excavations, 2002-2003

clergyman father, dreamed of finding the treasures of King Priam, which were said to be in a city named Troy. To his ability to learn many languages, he added some financial resources and cooperation from the Ottoman court, and with Homer's book in hand he started his journey in the ancient Troad at the age of fifty. When he found a hill corresponding to the war scenes and two creeks watering the plain, and realized that this place was so close to the Hellespont, he was convinced that he had found the right spot for his dream to come true and started digging in 1870. Today's archaeology calls his work "butchery." Schliemann, thinking that he had found the city, ruined the settlement with the trenches he dug, but finally found a treasure. The next day, he smuggled the treasure to Athens, first exhibiting it there and later in Berlin. After World War II, the treasure disappeared. In recent years, it was announced that the Trojan treasures were in Russia. A mere handful of Anatolian treasure, which has nothing to do with King Priam, awaits the day it can return to its homeland. The excavations were continued first by Dörpfeld and then, 1932-1939, by an American team led by Blegen. Since

Protective covering for Troy II city wall remains

1988, Professor Korfmann from Tübingen University, Germany, and his excavation team have conducted excavations and research in Troy. There was a continuous settlement in Troy from 3000 BC until 400 AD, in nine main layers and over thirty habitation levels, each established on top of the previous.

Troy I is dated between 3000-2500 BC. Five megaron-like, long, narrow houses with stone foundations and sun-dried mud brick walls formed this first layer. A wall 90m/295ft in diameter encircled them. At Troy II, the settlement was a little bigger, built to higher standards, and lasted until 1800 BC. The treasure thought to be Priam's was unearthed at this layer, a thousand years earlier than the time of the king. Over the other layers are the strong fortifications of Troy VI (1800-1275 BC). During the city's most prosperous age, an earthquake destroyed it. In the next layer, the houses of Troy VII were rather primitive. Relying on the heavily destroyed finds of this layer, archaeology dates the "probable" Trojan war to this period, around 1240 or 1200 BC, and suggests that the Wooden Horse must have been a gift by the winning side to the "Earth Shaker" Poseidon, who destroyed the walls. Troy VIII was formed in the Hellenistic Period (330-30 BC). The altar and the sacred well seen on the return route of the walking path are from this era. In the Roman period, all the early settlements were destroyed and the Athena Temple was enlarged. First the Persian Emperor sacrificed a thousand bulls here, and then Alexander the Great and the Roman Emperors made many offerings and sacrifices at this temple. The small marble theatre and a bath were built during the Roman Period, and the ninth settlement, Troy IX, continued until the 400s AD. There has been little research outside the city walls, where the ordinary people lived.

On the highway to İzmir lies another 3^{rd}C BC shore settlement, **Dalyan-Alexandria Troas**. Very little of this ancient city can be seen among the fields. Biblical tours frequently visit this place for the memory of St. Paul's two visits. On the side of the asphalt road, the Baths of Hadrian and the remains of the silted-up harbor on the coast are of interest.

Behramkale-Assos was another famous city of this province. The acropolis on a high and dominant hilltop overlooks the sea and Lesbos Island. The restored Athena temple, well-preserved city walls (3^{rd}C BC), the village, lively small harbor, nearby hotels, and beaches are popular with vacationers.

Overleaf: Temple of Athena, Priene

Above: Harbor of Alexandria Troas. Below left: Assos acropolis, Temple of Athena, 6thC BC. Right: well-preserved city walls

Aegean Region

Bergama-Pergamum

Bergama, 100km/62 miles from Izmir and 30km/19 miles from the cruise ship port of **Dikili**, is an attractive place to enjoy rich archaeological remains after driving through fertile farmland. At the top of the city, there is an acropolis like an eagle's nest with fantastic views and fine remains. Called Satan's Throne in the Bible, it was one of the Seven Churches of Asia Minor. Along the old road winding down the hill, the remains of the middle city can be seen. In the lower city are an interesting museum and the **Red Court**, the largest building in Asia Minor from antiquity. During the 3rd and 2^{nd}C BC, at the time of the Pergamum Kingdom, the flourishing cultural, religious, and artistic way of life was different from that of any other city. It was in the Pergamum acropolis, for the first time in history, that a library, temples, and a main theatre—all of them available to the public—were erected next to each other at the side of a large palace. Although historical mention of

19^{th}C drawing of the Temple of Serapis by Allom

Right: Recent restorations at Temple of Trajan

Pergamum has not been found before the 4thc BC, some archaeological finds can be dated to earlier settlements. A general of Alexander the Great, Lysimachos, who ruled the western part of Anatolia, chose the hill of Pergamum, a site far away from the sea and easy to defend, as the hiding place for a considerable treasure. Philetairos, a faithful captain, preserved the treasure, took possession of the city when Lysimachos died, and founded the Pergamum monarchy (283 BC). During the reign of Eumenes II, Pergamum led the Hellenistic world in the fields of economy, arts, science, and culture. He was the king responsible for developing political relations with Rome. Attalus III, lacking natural heirs, bequeathed the kingdom to Rome in 133 BC. Under this new power, the city enjoyed another period of development. Later Mark Anthony presented Cleopatra the city's rich library, but the 200,000 books of incalculable value were eventually destroyed in a fire in Egypt. The word **parchment** is a version of the name Pergamum, where it was first used for scrolls. The Byzantines encircled Pergamum, the seat of a diocese in the Christian period, with new city walls. Turks conquered the province in the first half of the 14thC.

Archaeological excavations began in the second half of the 19thC by the railroad engineer Carl Humann and are still conducted by German teams with excellent results. Right after entering the **Acropolis** through the original entrance, one's first view to the right is the palace, and opposite is the huge courtyard of the Temple of Athena. Straight ahead are the remains of the famous library. The ruins of the Temple of Trajan, built by his successor, the Emperor Hadrian, occupy a large vaulted terrace in a dominant location. This must be the site of an earlier temple of the Emperor Augustus, and early Christianity described it as Satan's place. At the edge of the small **Temple of Athena**, on the slope of the hill, stands the huge Theatre, the steepest of its kind, with eighty rows of seats for 10,000 spectators. It is fully open to the natural scenery. The stage, made of wood, was erected only on the days of performances, where audiences witnessed great tragic and comic performances. At the end of the promenade, at the path passing over the stage, are the remains of Dionysus' Temple. Situated at the other end of the path is the kingdom's most important temple, the **Altar of Zeus**, constructed in 190 BC, during the reign of Eumenes

Top: Colonnade of Acropolis.

Below: Steepest ancient theatre

Top: Altar of Zeus in Berlin Museum

Below: Detail of altar relief

II following a victory over the Galatians. Fragments found in the 19thC excavations were taken to Berlin where the altar was reconstructed in original size in a special museum. Today, only the foundation of the altar can be seen on the terrace. In the lower city are the imposing remains of the so-called Red Court or Red Basilica, originally a Serapeion dedicated to Egyptian gods, built under Hadrian (2^{nd}C AD). The best-known healing center of antiquity, **Aesculapium**, is nearby. This pre-Roman temple in honor of Aesculapius, the god of medicine, was expanded by the Romans and used for both healing and worship. The ruins of the 2^{nd}C AD complex include a few re-erected columns and traces of the library, a circular temple originally covered with a dome, and rooms destined for baths. Its small theatre seated up to 3,500 spectators and is still used for summer performances. The tunnel connecting the sacred spring to the temple is below the center of the courtyard.

Empty site of Altar of Zeus, pining for its return

Top: Acropolis viewed from the colonnaded street | Below: Sacred tunnel of the Aesculapium

Ayvalık

Sea and land, as well as hills covered with forests surround the town in great harmony. The center of Ayvalık is at the shores of a colorful bay. Famous for olives and olive oil production, Ayvalık also has a few 19thC churches and beautiful beaches. Boat tours and seafood restaurants are readily available in town and on **Cunda Island**. Known as Satan's Table, the high hill across the bay is a picnic spot famous for the striking sunset panoramas.

Panorama of Ayvalık

Next page: Twilight view of Ayvalık Bay

View of Izmir from Kadifekale

İzmir-Smyrna

The third largest city after Istanbul and Ankara, Izmir was founded at the crescent of a large gulf of the Aegean Sea. From the top of the hill (Mt. Pagos) on which the medieval fortress of Kadifekale stands, there is an enchanting view of the bay. Less interesting remains of the Agora are from the 2ndC AD. Archaeological research on the **Bayraklı** district of the city tells us that the first settlement on the soil of Smyrna can be dated to the 3rd millennium BC, the same age as the first level of Troy. Smyrna adopted some of the cultural and religious models of the Hittite civilization. The settlement dating to the 10thC BC was destroyed by the Lydians around the 7thC BC, and the city was rebuilt in the second half of the 4thC BC, with the support of Alexander the Great. At one time part of the dominion of Pergamum, it was eventually included in the territories controlled by Rome and was embellished with majestic new buildings. Today's Izmir was the ancient Smyrna, one of the Seven Churches of Asia Minor. Ottoman rule started in the 15thC. This flourishing commercial center has long attracted European traders for export and import. At the end of World War I, Izmir was entrusted to Greek control,

Shopping district

from which it was released by the victorious effort for national liberation under the leadership of **Mustafa Kemal Atatürk**. From the earliest days, its role in trade has been vital for the wide hinterland. While most ancient cities' old harbors silted up over time, the one in Izmir is still in use. Sites to visit are the fortifications of the citadel, the remains of the Agora on a lower terrace, and the interesting Archaeological Museum. The city's landmark, a small but attractive clock tower, is near the 19thC mosque at the old harbor. The city was reborn on the ashes of the one burned during the war of Independence in 1922. The center of that catastrophe was later converted to a huge park, now the site of the Izmir International Fair. The downtown shopping center, "Kemeraltı", is a typical and colorful local bazaar. After an easy hour's drive to the west of Izmir, swimming fans arrive at colorful **Çeşme**, famous for its lovely beaches, beautiful 16thC castle, and lively nightlife. It is only a ten-minute drive to one of the world's most important centers of windsurfing, **Alaçatı**. Çeşme's harbor is an important and busy seasonal port for export and for ferry services to Italy. Its location, mild climate, sandy beaches, and plentiful hotels make it an ideal center for touring.

Landmarks of Izmir: clock tower and charming mosque in main square

Famous Çeşme beaches

Torba-Metropolis

A 2nd millennium BC hilltop settlement was replaced by a 3rdC BC city. In Metropolis, most of the ruins belong to the Hellenistic period and some to the Roman era. The excavations, started about fifteen years ago and still going on, have resulted in some rich finds. This city, on the busy ancient Smyrna-Ephesus road, was a rich settlement. The fertile plain, marble quarries, and wine and olive production brought wealth to Metropolis. Interesting excavated parts of the city include the stoa, theatre, bath, gymnasium and latrines, acropolis, and terrace houses. When researchers complete the excavations, this will be another essential place to visit in the Aegean region.

Sart-Sardis

Called Sart in Turkish, the ruins of Sardis are an hour away from Izmir. The drive passes through the farmland of the world-famous Smyrna raisins. The site includes the remains of one of the largest pagan temples of the ancient world, one of the earliest synagogues in the world, and the facade of the gymnasium, the largest restored ancient building in Anatolia. The first-ever coins were minted here at the end of the 7thC BC. The city was the capital of the Kingdom of Lydia. The richest of all rulers, King Croesus, lived here, losing his throne in 546 BC to the Persians. The first paved road in history, the **Royal Road**, started from Persia, and ended in Sardis. In the Revelations of St. John, Sardis was addressed as one of the **Seven Churches of Asia Minor**. Starting from Izmir (Smyrna), Biblical tours visit Sardis, nearby Philadelphia (Alaşehir), and Thyatira (Akhisar) in the same day. The other churches—Pergamum (Bergama), Ephesus (Efes), and Laodicea (Pamukkale-Denizli)—

are in the vicinity. The "Seven Churches of Asia Minor" refers to the early communities of believers, not actual church buildings. There were no churches because worshippers were heavily persecuted and prayers were conducted secretly. The Lydians were famous for their skill in politics, trade, and the economy. For some 120 years, Sardis was ruled by semi-mythical kings and became a major power in western Anatolia. The source of their wealth was gold mined from the River Pactolus, which still runs by the city. Following its capture by the Persians under Cyrus, the glorious city guarded the western frontier of the huge Persian Empire.

Remains of Temple of Artemis, Sardis

After the conquest by Alexander the Great, the city had an important position in the Hellenistic world and continued this major role through the Roman and Byzantine ages. Of the once splendid upper acropolis, there are now only a few Byzantine remains. Of note is the **Gymnasium**, dating from the Imperial age (3ʳᵈC AD), with a successfully restored huge colonnaded two-story facade and inscription that mentions Caracalla. Attached to the courtyard is a contemporary **synagogue** in which fine wall decorations and noteworthy mosaic pavements have been uncovered. **The Temple of Artemis** is still fairly well preserved.

This temple, third largest of its kind, was built on the site of an earlier Altar of Cybele, the Mother Goddess, who was the chief deity of Anatolia from the Neolithic age. Construction of the temple we see today began in the early 300s BC. This was followed by a second phase in 175 to 150 BC; the last but never completed phase took place during the 2ⁿᵈC AD. The columns have exceptionally fine Ionic capitals. Next to the temple are the remains of a small Byzantine church. Other remains of the past worthy of mention include the baths, a 3ʳᵈC BC theatre, a Hellenistic cemetery, and the so-called House of Bronzes (6ᵗʰC AD).

Synagogue, Sardis

Top: Gymnasium, Sardis

Below: Roman remains at Akhisar-Thyatira

Manisa-
Magnesia ad Siplus

Less than an hour's drive from Izmir, settled on the lower slopes of a high mountain and spreading over the large plain with modern districts and important industrial zones, Manisa houses several splendid examples of Imperial Turkish architecture. The Sultans' Mosque and complex gifted by Ayse Sultan, mother of Süleyman the Magnificent (16ᵗʰC), is an important example. Every April, a festival is held near the complex in honor of mesir macunu, a sticky elixir once reserved for the imperial family, but today thrown from the roof of the mosque to the public waiting below. The Muradiye Mosque was designed by the architect Sinan the Great, and the adjacent medrese (16ᵗʰC theological school) today houses Turkish ethnographical artifacts. The former soup kitchen, now the Archaeological Museum, has a rich collection of Sardis and Lydian burial mounds. The region's numerous vineyards produce small, seedless Smyrna grapes, dried for export. Sipil Dağı National Park to the south is the location of famous "crying rock" of Niobe. Also on this mountain is one of the farthest-west Hittite rock carvings (13ᵗʰC BC) showing the Mother Goddess. The ruins of ancient Sardis, once the capital of the Lydian kingdom of Croesus, lie on the Sart Cayi (Pactolos River) bank. The Temple of Artemis, a restored gymnasium, and the synagogue confirm the city's past splendor. In the village of Birgi, the Çakır Ağa Mansion is a fine example of traditional Turkish architecture. Two of the Seven Churches of Asia Minor, Akhisar (Thyatira) and Alaşehir (Philadelphia), are in Manisa Province.

Remains of Byzantine basilica, Alaşehir

19ᵗʰC drawing of Manisa by Allom

210

Efes-Ephesus

Visiting Ephesus is an easy stroll on fantastic marble-paved Roman roads. The busy harbor of Kuşadası is only 16km/10miles away. Ephesus was the harbor for pilgrims coming to visit the Artemis temple. It was always an important banking center, and its political leaders, who preferred to side with strong rulers like Lidyans, Alexander the Great, and the Romans, governed mostly in peace. Ephesus, at its height, witnessed the visits of St. Paul and the Virgin Mary, who is said to have spent her last years here under the care of St. John the Evangelist. Ephesus, one of the Seven Churches of Asia Minor, was called the Metropolis of Asia under the Roman Empire. Recent archaeological excavations that found three early native settlements have revised our knowledge and taken the history of this site back to the third millennium BC. The Hittite name for this city, "**Aphasa**", changed to Ephesus. Ionia was the ancient name of western Turkey, the motherland and the cradle of Western civilization. From the 5th C

Colonnaded main avenue to lower city, theatre and harbor

BC, Persians controlled the whole region but left the cities independent in their way of life. The city-state of Athens collected large sums of money from the Ionian cities, promising help against the Persians, but reneged on the agreements, spent the money to construct the Athens Acropolis, and later attacked the Ionian cities to gain more. These attacks from East and West ended after the arrival of the victorious Macedonian, Alexander the Great. During the rule of Alexander the Great's generals, Ephesus and sister cities like Pergamum, Smyrna and Metropolis were rebuilt, beginning another period of prosperity. For Ephesus, as for the rest of the Roman Empire, the 2nd and 3^{rd}C AD were the last period of greatness. The city was abandoned by the 6^{th}C; the site was later used as a marble and ready-made column quarry. Archaeological work started in the late 19^{th}C, and has continued almost nonstop since then. After the entrance to the museum grounds, the first sight is the great courtyard of the State Agora. To the left are remains of the monumental main fountain, and opposite is the Odeon, a formerly roofed-over small theatre

19th C drawing of Ephesus ruins by Allom

that was also used for official meetings; to the west are the remains of Prytaneion, the town hall buildings, and a small temple in which the perpetual fire of this autonomous city burned. To the left the huge supporting terrace of the Temple of Domityanus and the large arch of Polio Monument can be seen. Remains of an altar in the center and the monument of Memmius next to a fountain are the other edifices. The view ahead is amazing: a huge marble road **(Street of the Curetes)**, flanked by the remains of once-colonnaded and covered sidewalks with shops, statue bases, a few temples, and, at the end of the street, a restored monumental edifice. The early 2^{nd}C AD Trajan Fountain is the first edifice on the right. A few steps farther is the well-preserved large complex of a Roman Bath named after Scholastikia (400s AD), who restored it. It is connected to the ancient public latrine, one of the favorite "take my picture" stops. A small but picturesque temple dedicated to the Roman Emperor Hadrian is next to the bath. An inscription dates it to the early 2^{nd}C AD. From the opposite side of the

Top: Hadrian's temple

Below: Public latrines, favorite photo spot

Temple of Hadrian, the interesting complex of the so-called "houses on the slope" faces onto the Street of the Curetes and to the sea. These houses for the wealthy are terraced onto the slope and are distinctive for their considerable decorations, elaborate (up to five-story) plans, and full comfort, including running water, baths and toilets and even private temples. The beautifully restored **Library of Celsus** was built at the time of Hadrian and put into service with a rich collection of scrolls. The double arch on the right side of the facade was a gift to the city by two former slaves. This is the gate to the largest agora of antiquity. This commercial agora, surrounded by many shops, served the harbor of Ephesus, one of the two leading Mediterranean trade centers in the imperial Roman period (Alexandria of Egypt was the other). Ephesus' theatre, the largest of antiquity, has come down to us in a wonderful state of preservation and is still used for festival performances. Originally dating to the 3rdC BC, this theatre, with a full view of the harbor and open sea, was altered and extended a few times in the Roman era and could seat about 24,000. This was the location of St. Paul's struggle with the

Library of Celsus and double-arched entrance to commercial agora

silversmiths of the city. From the exit steps of the theatre, the long colonnaded street ahead, the **Arkadiane**, has a great view. The high walls at a distance to the west belong to the Harbor Baths and to the **Church of the Virgin Mary**, where the 3rd Ecumenical Council meeting was held in 431 AD. The remains of the Stadium and the Vedius Gymnasium stand to the east of the road, beyond the modern parking lot. The House of the Virgin is a restored, pretty 7th C Byzantine chapel on the slopes of a forested mountain. The fame of the chapel began when this building matched the description of a dream by an Austrian peasant, Catherine Emerit. The Vatican has accepted this traditional belief. Another Christian site closer to the ruins is the Grotto of the Seven Sleepers, containing graves and sarcophaguses. The town of **Selçuk** is the Ephesus of our days. There is an attractive medieval fortification on the dominant hill of the plain and a huge basilica on the lower hilltop, which was also fortified. This domed basilica (6th C.), built with a donation from the Byzantine Emperor Justinian, was earlier than his Hagia Sophia basilica in Istanbul. Below the hill, the high

Largest theatre of antiquity, still in use during festivals

Goddess Cybele, after ten thousand years, continued to be worshipped as Artemis in the Ionian and Roman worlds

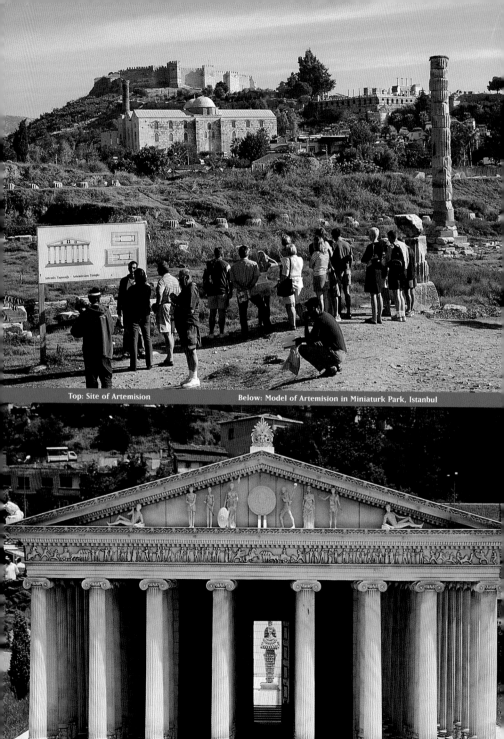

Top: Site of Artemision   Below: Model of Artemision in Miniaturk Park, Istanbul

Gigantic Domitianus statue in Selçuk Museum

River God and a warrior at rest in Selçuk Museum

building with two domes is the Isa Bey Mosque (1375 AD), a fine example of distinctive Turkish Seljuk art. Just a few hundred meters farther ahead a moat with a single re-erected column is the excavation site of one of the most beautiful of the Seven Wonders of the World: the **Temple of Artemis** or **Artemision**, the first and largest monumental temple built entirely with white marble. The remains are unfortunately very few and scattered around on the site. Fine Roman copies of Goddess Artemis statues in the Selçuk Museum give an excellent idea about the look of the originals. The archaic Artemision was erected in the mid-6thC BC atop an earlier local temple. When this monument became surrounded by swampy grounds and was allegedly burned by a lunatic, a second Artemision was immediately erected on the same site (324-250 BC) with the same dimensions but on a higher base. Acting like a bank, the Oracle was responsible for the safekeeping of money and valuables entrusted to the temple. After the spread of Christianity, the temple was deserted and suffered from devastation by nature and by man, who used its ready-cut stones for other construction.

Statue of Virgin Mary at house near Ephesus said to be her last residence

Kuşadası

This lovely and busy summer resort town has a picturesque location overlooking the Kuşadası gulf, which stretches out towards the Aegean. Kuşadası is the "number one" port for all cruise companies in the Aegean. Ships line up in the harbor, mostly for a single day, and visitors start their tours to Ephesus, Priene, Miletus, and Didyma, the fantastic remains of ancient Ionian cities. Kuşadası offers many good hotels, holiday villages with crystal clean beaches, restaurants for different tastes, and a wealth of great shopping possibilities for Turkish-made goods. The Greek island of Samos is a stone's throw away. In front of the harbor, now connected to the mainland by a breakwater, rises Kuşadası (the island of the birds), an islet with a well-preserved fortification. In the center of town, the other 17[th]C fortification is one of the oldest hotels in the world still in use. Less than an hour's drive to the south of Kuşadası, a few miles after **Davutlar** town, there is the fantastic National Park with protected fauna and flora and four beautiful beaches, like a botanical garden with two climates, canyons, and a few leopards. The first beach is sandy, the others have smooth pebbles, and all have old trees right on the shore, turning the beaches into a heavenly place. The Kuşadası marina is another **Blue Cruise** departure harbor for discovering the Turkish turquoise coasts. Experienced world travelers find it difficult to name another place as beautiful as the fully unpolluted "Blue Flag" shores of Aegean and Mediterranean Turkey.

Davutlar beach

Kuşadası shores and harbor.

Below: Town center

Small but attractive Women's Beach, legendary trysting spot for Zeus, Kuşadası. Below: The (almost) unequaled Dilek National Park

Priene

Situated next to Güllübahçe village, Priene is on a terrace dominating the plain that was silted by the **River Meander**. There was an earlier city, with a safe harbor, on the plain below. At the beginning of the 6thC BC the philosopher **Bias**, considered one of the

View of the plain from Priene

Seven Sages of Antiquity, lived in that Priene. The upper city was established by 350 BC with a fine grid plan. It was not large, but politically was the most important city of Ionia because it maintained the sacred **Altar of Poseidon**, symbol of the twelve cities of the **Panionian Confederation**. Next to the main temple of Athena was a sanctuary dedicated to Alexander the Great, considered a divine being. This prosperous commercial city declined under Roman rule as the harbor began to silt. Priene was a diocese seat in the Byzantine period, and a basilica was erected next to the theatre. After climbing partly over the original steps, visitors arrive at the first outstanding edifice: the well-preserved, fantastic Theatre, a unique early example with a seating capacity of 5,000. Although some stage parts were added in the 2ndC AD in the Roman era, the 4thC BC Hellenistic period features remain the principal ones. The altar of Dionysus, god of spectacle and enjoyment, and the special seats for local dignitaries are intact. Beyond the theatre, in the most dominant location, the 350 BC Temple of Athena rose with grandeur and perfect proportions. The architect was **Pytheos**, creator of one of the Seven Wonders of the Ancient World, the Halicarnassus Mausoleum in the town of Bodrum. Four of the columns have been re-erected. The Agora in the center of city, with the small temple to Zeus and well-preserved official buildings, is surrounded by porticoes on three sides. This was the busiest place for shopping, strolling, and official affairs. The **Bouleuterion**, the Senate house with 640 seats, and the **Prytaneion**, office for the executive committee, are next to the main entrance. The lower Gymnasium, house blocks, water system pipes, partly preserved city walls, fine early stonework, and the view of the rocky Acropolis, almost hanging over the city, are remarkable points of interest. It is possible to see Miletus across the fertile plain, which was once the deep bay.

Charming theatre

Below: re-erected columns of Athena Temple

Hellenistic walls.

Below: Well-preserved Bouleuterion

Milet-Miletus

Miletus, the leading 7-6thC BC trade center with over ninety colonies along the Black Sea, Aegean, and Mediterranean, was established on an isthmus in a strategic bay with easy connections to the rich hinterland. Under the ever-shining Ionian sun, the residents of Miletus gathered information about the knowledge, experience, and traditions of existing and ancient societies from Mesopotamia to Egypt and mingled them with heritages of Asia Minor. Discounting the importance of multiple deities, countless temples, and various myths, the Ionian philosophers, following the path of their own understanding and studying Mother Nature, developed a system of understanding as advanced as today's modern ideas. World famous sages such as **Thales, Anaximander**, and **Anaximenes** were natives of Miletus. Knowledge gained from Turkey's archaeological digs, international research, and

Ilyas Bey Mosque, 1404

institutional studies are changing our information about the backgrounds of Western culture. The world is just starting to understand the millennia-earlier Anatolian foundation stones of the Western way of thinking. Miletus is another silent ancient ruin, with little still visible from its golden age of the 7th and 6thC BC. The Persians razed the city in 494 BC. The local architect **Hippodamos**, using his own invention of grid city planning, rebuilt the city. It remained an important metropolis till the late days of the Roman Empire. The silting of the last harbor slowly ended the city's fame and colorful history. St. Paul visited Miletus on his third missionary journey. **Balat** was the Turkish name of the village that existed on the ruins. Next to the ancient harbor, now the parking lot, stands the best-preserved edifice of the site. The Theatre, set against a hill, was originally built around the 4thC BC and was enlarged in the Roman period to a seating capacity of 15,000. The fortification at the top was a Byzantine work; the 14thC AD Turkish caravansary in front of the theatre was built with re-used stones. Another important Turkish masterpiece is the small and charming İlyas Bey Mosque of 1404 AD. The

Sanctuary of Apollo Delpinion was the principal place of worship in the city. Other important remains include the Bouleuterion from the second half of the 2ndC BC, the southern Agora (market place) built in the Hellenistic age, and the 2ndC BC Stadium for 15,000 spectators. The Baths of Faustina were named after the wife of Marcus Aurelius, who donated them in the 2ndC AD. The bath complex is well preserved. The monumental gate leading to the Agora was removed and re-erected in the Berlin Museum. A small local museum displays artifacts from the site.

Top: River god as a fountain

Below: Theatre and silted ancient gulf

Fantastic 2ndC AD monumental southern gate of Miletus agora in Berlin Museum.
This and other treasures in world museums must be homesick.

Didim-Didyma

In antiquity a Sacred Way connected Miletus to the Temple of Didyma and its port. The road was flanked party by statues of the Brancihds oracle family and of reclining lions. Research revealed the existence of a small archaic temple, far earlier than the foundation of the colossal place of worship dedicated to Apollo. At Didyma, as in many other centers of Asia Minor, the Ionians replaced local cults with their adapted forms of worship. The statue of Apollo can be compared to religious motifs of Hittite and other Anatolian originals. The first temple was burned by the Persians at the beginning of the 5[th]C BC, but when Alexander the Great conquered Anatolia in 332-333 BC, construction of the beautiful new temple began immediately. The Temple of Didyma was the largest after the Artemision of Ephesus and the Temple of Artemis in Sardis. Although

A passage to the inner court

the Romans continued work on this Didymaion, it was never completed. Still-standing columns, the original walls, two very interesting vaulted passages to the inner courtyard, and the small town around the temple make the visit unforgettable. Among the numerous decorations found in the temple are capitals ornamented with heads of griffins and bulls. The Medusa heads, which were part of a frieze on the architraves, are examples of 2[nd]C AD sculpture. Next to safekeeping people's valuables and attracting pilgrims, the main function (and income of course) of the temples was soothsaying. Believers could climb the steps and give their offerings and written questions about fortune and destiny to the oracle standing on the higher terrace of the entrance. After a session with the prophetess Pytia, who sat on a tripod next to the statue of Apollo while chewing laurel and inhaling the smoke of burning leaves, the oracle deciphered her whispered statements and handed back the divine response. This reliance on soothsayers was common for people

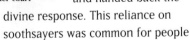

from all levels of society, from royalty to villagers.

The main road passes through the Meander plain and follows the shores of Bafa Lake to the nearby **Heraklia** ruins. Before reaching Milas, the road continues by the ruins of **Euromos** city. The impressive **Temple of Zeus** (2ndC AD) is well preserved in a romantic setting.

Below: Entrance facade of the temple

Remains of columns.

Medusa head

Afrodisias-Aphrodisias

The ruins and the natural setting of Aphrodisias are as colorful as the name. The extremely well-preserved Roman stadium and the fantastic museum are striking. The ancient name of the region was Caria. The ancient town's position on a 600mt/1800ft-high plateau was strategically important. Beginning in 1961, New York University supported the excavations and, thanks to Prof. Dr. Kenan T. Erim's lifetime efforts, an archaeological treasure of Turkey was reborn. Settlement on the site goes back to at least the 3rd millennium BC. Its greatest prosperity was in the Roman period. In this city-state and throughout the region, Aphrodite, an adaptation of the earlier Anatolian deity Cybele, was worshipped as the goddess of love, nature, and fertility. Byzantines later named the town Stavropolis (the Town of the Cross). The turmoil and wars of the 12th and 13th centuries left the site in ruins. The tour of the site is an easy walk. When the **Sebastion**, the ceremonial way richly decorated with reliefs on large marble slabs, is restored, it will be a beautiful addition to Aphrodisias. This colonnaded street, dedicated to the cult of emperor worship and greatly ornamented with sculptures by local artists, is the first sight among the ruins. The Agora was at the other end of this portico. The shiny, white marble, 8,000-seat Theatre, uncovered in the 1970s, adjoins the acropolis, the artificial mound of the prehistoric settlements. To the north, surrounded by re-erected columns with a gigantic central pool (or, others believe, a competition track) is the 1stC AD Tiberius Portico. The Baths of Hadrian, next to the portico and the agora, were built in the ring style of Roman baths. Nearby is the Odeon, the small and formerly roofed-over theatre. The remains of the Bishops' Palace and some Byzantine churches lie between the Odeon and the **Temple of Aphrodite**. Thirteen

of its Ionic columns are still standing. The temple was erected over an earlier pagan sanctuary in the late Hellenistic period, and because of the Emperors' great respect for Aphrodite (Venus of the Romans), the city was favored with imperial support and protection. In the late 5thC AD, the temple was converted into a Christian church by removing its cella walls and rebuilding toward the outer side of the columns. With this alteration and addition of an apse, the building was transformed into a basilica. A series of earthquakes in the 4thC and especially in the 7thC, plus the damage of time, had little effect on the still-standing and best-preserved edifice of the city: the **Stadium**. It is huge, large enough for 30,000 spectators on 22 tiers to enjoy athletic events. The latest restoration is the Tetrapylon, the attractive 2ndC AD monumental gateway to the Temple of Aphrodite. At the front of the Tetrapylon is a lone grave, that of Prof. Dr. Kenan T. Erim, who spent all his time and gained his fame through his archaeological studies and contributions at this site; when he died in 1990 he was buried here. The Museum displays a sensational collection of masterpieces of the local artisans' works, sculptures, and reliefs. The art objects of the Aphrodisias school of sculpture were exported to many cities.

Top: High reliefs from the Sebastion ceremonial colonnade.

Below: Agora and Bath of Hadrian.

Temple of Aphrodite.

Below: Fantastic 30,000-capacity stadium, Aphrodisias.

Pamukkale-Hierapolis

Pamukkale is a wonderland. Its petrifying springs have created an extremely unusual landscape in which many ancient monuments remain. Once situated right by the springs, crowded hotels have been cleared off the site and removed beyond the historic boundaries. Standing below a 100mt/320ft-high plateau, this amphitheatre of snow-white cliffs with tiers of basin formations is magical and looks as if someone painted the whole cliff. The scene faces a fertile valley and the Taurus mountain range at the horizon. The scenery is one of the Seven Natural Wonders not only of Turkey but of anywhere in the world. Pamukkale in Turkish is a literal description of the landscape: "Cotton Castle". Warm waters have excessive calcium oxide and other mineral salts. While pouring down over the cliffs, this bubbling, cascading water leaves travertine deposits behind, forming a white covering to create the fairy panorama. Sections not receiving enough running water take

Terrace formations in Pamukkale

on darker colors. Next to those unique formations, the Roman and Byzantine ruins are numerous, including Turkey's best-preserved necropolis (city of the dead). From the earliest days, temples with an oracle cult were a fashion in Asia Minor. Healing possibilities of sacred springs in the area have always attracted settlements. The earliest records of the town do not go beyond the Hellenistic period. Eumenes II of Pergamum Kingdom became the ruler of the region. After 133 BC, the Romans brought a period of prosperity, but the town's golden age was in the 2nd and 3^{rd}C AD. The ancient fame of the region's well-treated wools continues in the famous towel and textile manufacturing at Denizli. While wandering in the travertine formations, visitors are not permitted to wear shoes, but the basins are not slippery and the scenery from the top of the cliff is unforgettable. The central Roman Thermal Baths are fairly well preserved. The larger rooms are covered with barrel vaulting and have statue niches in the travertine walls that were once faced with marble. The two larger rooms of this huge complex now serve as the site's

View of the cliff and plain from the top of the terrace

small local museum. The main pool, now enclosed in a building housing a café and shops, is original and considered the most interesting of its kind. Cluttered with ancient columns from the Roman street, the waters bubble at body temperature, and the blossoms of nearby oleander trees scent the air, creating an unforgettable ambiance. Behind the pool stands the entrance to the poisonous source of the thermal spring next to the remains of the Temple of Apollo and monumental city fountains. A well-preserved 2^{nd}C Roman Theatre leans against the hillside overlooking the entire city and the plain. With future restorations the theatre can be re-erected almost completely. In situ stage decorations depict scenes from mythological stories. Situated above the theatre hill, the **Martyrium of St. Philip** is an important Byzantine edifice dating to the early 5^{th}C AD. This octagonal building had facilities to accommodate pilgrims. The arch dedicated to Emperor Domitian and the addition of a Byzantine gateway adorned the Colonnaded Roman Road extending in the hub of the city. Toward the west is another large Roman Bath that was converted to a church in the Byzantine period. The Necropolis of Hierapolis covers the northwest of the city limits. This vast cemetery's tombs and

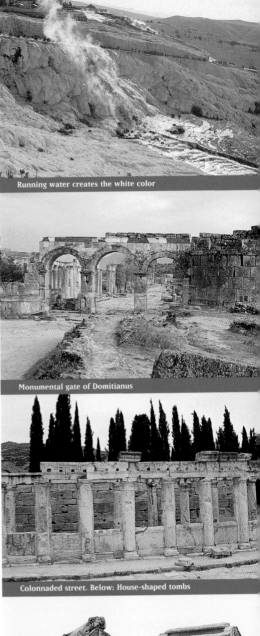

Running water creates the white color

Monumental gate of Domitianus

Colonnaded street. Below: House-shaped tombs

Theatre

sarcophaguses, in various shapes, date from late Hellenistic to early Christian epochs. House-shaped monuments are the most common. Karahayıt village, famous for its rosy-colored small formations and good thermal hotels, is only a few miles away.

Laodikya-Laodicea

St. John named this site as one of the Seven Churches in the Book of Revelation. Some excavation has started. A fountain, stadium, theatres, some walls, and aqueduct remains are visible. The site is interesting for Biblical tours and is less than ten miles from the famous Pamukkale-Hierapolis.

Honaz-Colossae

The Letter to the Colossians mentioned in the New Testament makes this place important to Christian history. The site is a mound surrounded by gardens and farming fields. Since it was not excavated there are no remains to study. Most tourists are those with Biblical interests. The visit can be a half-day round trip from nearby Denizli or Pamukkale (Hierapolis).

Kütahya

Founded on the western slopes of a vast plateau in the Inner Aegean, Kütahya has an acropolis surrounded by city walls. Today the town spreads down from the hillside with modern sections and industrial zones. The view from the citadel is amazing. Since the 18ᵗʰC, Kütahya has been an important tile production center. Today, handmade products of fine quality are created at many workshops and factories. The old houses, some of which have survived to our day, and the town's historic mosques attract the attention of visitors. Famous for its tiles and museum, the town of Kütahya has reasonably good hotel facilities. The inner Aegean part of the country produces, under strict official control, the best opium for the pharmaceutical industry. **Afyon** (which means "opium"), another historical city of this region, has a castle, rich Phrygian rock-cut burial chambers, and temples. A very significant ancient site, **Aizanoi**, is

Medieval citadel walls of Kütahya

located in the small town of **Çavdarhisar**, west of Kütahya. A beautiful Roman temple, the **Temple of Zeus** (2ndC AD), is erected on a small mound. Dedicated to the Mother Goddess and Zeus, it is one of Anatolia's best-preserved monuments. During excavations on the terrace, settlement layers from the 3rd millennium BC were unearthed. The region was a sacred place of the Anatolian Mother Goddess. The walls of the temple, the columns, and the architrave blocks

have reached our day with their original appearance. To the west of this attractive and elegant monument, an Acroterium, a decorative building block (the head of a woman in high relief), lies on the ground. The stadion adjacent to the stage building of the theatre has no equal. Other significant structures are a bath complex, two Roman bridges still in use over the creek that passes through the village, and by the mosque, a round building, known to be the earliest example of a stock exchange. A paved Roman road with colonnaded sidewalk is also here.

Previous page: Temple of Zeus, Aizanoi-Çavdarhisar

Painting of Atatürk before final Independence battle

Façade of Aizanoi Temple

(Military Museum, Istanbul)

Uşak

There are 4000 BC settlements in the area, but within the city limits the only historic buildings are a few old Turkish mosques. Uşak handmade carpets of 16-17thC were exported in great quantities to the palaces, mansions, and churches of European countries. The production of handmade carpets is enjoying a revival in our day. The **Karun Treasury** of local Lydian art objects at the Archaeological Museum is very interesting. These artifacts, 363 unique silver pieces from the burial mounds nearby (7th-6thC BC), were smuggled to the USA in 1966 and displayed at New York's Metropolitan Museum. After decades of great effort, Turkey was able in 1993 to bring the Karun Treasury back where it belongs.

During the Independence War, the Uşak region was Atatürk's headquarters.

Sole example of adjacent theatre and stadium, Aizanoi

Opium poppies can be pink, violet, or white

Top: Ruins of Herakleia. Below: Gümüşkesen Mausoleum, Milas

Tower of St. Peter's Castle, Bodrum.

Temple of Zeus, 2ⁿᵈC AD, Euromos

Bodrum-Halicarnassus

The native inhabitants of the area were Lelegs and Carians. From the middle of the 6ᵗʰC BC, Halicarnassus was under Persian domination and in the first half of the 4ᵗʰC BC the city became the capital of the Carian kingdom. According to **Herodotus** (5ᵗʰC BC), the father of history and a native of Halicarnassus, Dorian colonists founded the city. **King Mausolus** who reigned for years and

was succeeded in 353 BC by his sister-wife, Artemisia, was entombed in the first monument of such magnificence commemorating a loved one. The architect responsible for the Mausoleum was Pytheos. Although earthquakes damaged the edifice, it was still standing as late as the beginning of the 15ᵗʰC, when the Knights of Rhodes built Saint Peter's Castle using stones from the remains for the construction of their fortress. The Turks conquered this last stronghold on the coast of Asia Minor in 1522. The British Museum houses the finest pieces of the Mausoleum, smuggled out in the mid-

19th C. Several fragments are on display at the site. The well-preserved 2nd C AD tomb (Gümüşkesen) in the nearby town of **Milas** seems to be a smaller copy of the famous **Mausoleum**. Situated on a small peninsula, the **Castle of St. Peter** is an extremely well preserved, magnificent architectural complex,

Bronze statue of a boy

one of the best of its kind, and houses one of the great museums of our time, containing displays of the findings of diver-archaeologists.

Remains of a theatre can be seen on the hillside at the north. On the Bodrum peninsula there are ten or more smaller holiday resorts, each on a beautiful bay with its own characteristics. Life is never boring in such an atmosphere for visitors of any age at any time of year. Bodrum is famous for holiday villages and top-quality hotels as well as its charming small boutique hotels. Distance to the airport is twenty miles.

Site of the Mausoleum

Right below: Ancient Theatre, Bodrum

Model of Mausoleum, Miniaturk Park, Istanbul.

Statues of Queen Artemisia and King Mausolus in British Museum.

St. Peter's Castle and marina, Bodrum

Marina promenade

Below: a Blue Cruise anchorage bay

Construction of a typical Bodrum yacht

Below: Beaches on western end of Bodrum peninsula

Shores and bays of Blue Cruise

Below: Breathtaking vista of Ölüdeniz (Dead Sea) beach

MUĞLA

Gökova İskelesi

Köyceğiz

Ö ᴢ ᴄ ᴇ ğ ɪ ᴢ G.

Ortaca

Bodrum

Gökova Bay

Marmaris

Datça

Dalyan

Knidos

Boz Büyük

Mediterranean Sea

Feth

Blue Voyage Destinations

A unique pleasure only on the shores of Turkey!

May to October is the high season for "Blue Cruise" pleasure trips, a Turkish seventh heaven. Private or chartered yachts sail the southwestern shores of Turkey. Enjoying the delightful natural beauty together, couples and friends share the trip, many returning over and over again. Such scenic surroundings can be witnessed only along Turkey's Mediterranean and Aegean shores. Swimsuits on, free of hassles and worries of any kind, visitors can be sure pleasure is guaranteed. In some small bays the water reflects the green of the trees, in others the blue of the sky. Roman theatres, medieval castles, rock-cut tombs, and ancient walls are common sights along Turkey's coasts. In most places, the green forest reaches the rocky heights of the Taurus Mountain chain that rises from the sea and fills the whole northern horizon. Bodrum and Marmaris are ideal departure or arrival marinas for the yachts touring the turquoise waters and green shores of Turkey. Preferred by many experienced world travelers and ranked as the most beautiful and without equal for sea and natural surroundings, the "Blue Voyage" pleasure cruises revel in Mother Nature's special gifts created only for Turkish shores. The pleasure will not be spoiled by disturbing waves, strong currents or tides, hurricanes, Riviera- or Caribbean-style crowds, pollution, dangerous jelly fishes or sharks, or monotonous rocky Aegean-island scenery. These magical, pleasing and ever-changing surroundings offer enchanting panoramas impossible to find anywhere in the world with this mild climate and pleasant sea temperature. "Blue Cruise" boats travel about half a day and enter one of the small pool-like bays for swimming or strolling in the woods. Nights are spent in the same anchored spot under the clear sky filled with brightest stars hanging over the hills and trees.

Even kids and dogs enjoy a Blue Cruise!

Three different coves in Gökova Bay

Left: Stuffed mussels are delicious!

Below: Village women near Milas planting tobacco seedlings

Right: Fisherman in Bodrum repairing nets

Bottom: Some villagers still use old-fashioned plows, Yatağan

Marmaris

Surrounding hills reflect their green onto the circular bay connecting to the open sea by a beautiful and entrancing strait. While town and marina cover the upper bay, shores are beaches or woods. Sailboats and yachts of different flags and sizes cruise around the inlet. Occasionally a cruise ship may anchor in the bay. The modern marina is another essential port for "Blue Cruise" yachting on Turkey's turquoise waters and offers regular connections with the nearby Greek island of Rhodes. With many hotel choices and a long tourism season, Marmaris is a favored holiday resort. The small castle in downtown is the only historic monument. **Gökova Bay** to the north and the Datça Peninsula to the west offer one of the world's most marvelous lacework-style sea and land combinations. The green color of the woods melts into the blue with great harmony. Gökova Bay, less than twenty miles north of Marmaris, has boats for daily tours, including to **Sedir (Cleopatra) Island,** famous for its unique snow-white small beach. To the west at the tip of the peninsula stand the ruins of **Knidos** with its two harbors. This city was famous for the Temple of Aphrodite and the nude statue of the goddess by the great artist **Praxiteles** (4^{th}C BC). A visit to the few remains is easier by sea. From Marmaris daily tours to **Dalyan,** extended tours to Fethiye and on to Antalya and Alanya can easily be organized.

Dalaman, a few miles from Dalyan, is the nearest international airport at less than two hours' driving distance. The quiet farming town of Dalyan is famous for the ruins of ancient **Kaunos** in a very romantic setting next to typical Lycian rock-cut tombs. Environmentally concerned visitors can view the protected *Caretta caretta* turtle nests on the long, sandy beach. For excitement in Dalyan there are boat trips on the meandering river to the turtle beach. This river trip, partly among the reed beds, gives the best view of the hillside Lycian rock-cut tombs. Thermal mud therapy is another option in Dalyan tours.

View of Marmaris Gulf from western hills.

Below: Shore and hotels in Marmaris

Downtown Marmaris

Below: A cove in Gökova Bay, 25 km north of town

The unique snow-white beach of Sedir (Cleopatra) Island, Gökova Bay

Hisarönü Bay, west of Marmaris, a favorite Blue Voyage stopover

Opposite page, below: Caretta caretta turtle beach near Dalyan

Above: Lycian rock tombs and Dalyan River

Ruins of Kaunos

Mediterranean Region

Fethiye-Telmessus

Fethiye is well known for its large-capacity hothouse vegetable farming and citrus fruit production. Over twenty rock-cut Lycian monumental tombs, dating from the 4thC BC, are the historical heritage from ancient Telmessus. The small local museum displays archaeological findings. Sheltered Fethiye Bay, with its wooded islands and forested surrounding mountain ranges, is another Turkish paradise. Cruising by yacht is the only way to enjoy this gift of nature. **Göcek** town, at the center of the bay, is an ideal marina for one-day or longer seafaring. Though Fethiye is a popular holiday resort and a port for yacht cruising, the most famous beach in Turkey for guidebooks and posters is only eleven miles from downtown. At the bottom of a steep mountain slope, the vast beach stretches toward the west and turns into the shape of a long sandy hook with tropical lagoon colors. **Ölü Deniz** ("dead sea") is a small inlet with a very narrow entrance. The view is extraordinary and during the long season this unique beach and a full range of nearby hotels and pensions are favorite locations. While some prefer the sea and sun, there are many paragliding enthusiasts who jump from the high mountain, flying down to the beach.

Lycian tomb on a Fethiye street

Right: Water sports, as well as mountain trekking, paragliding, jeep safaris, and fine hotels are available everywhere in the Ölüdeniz (Dead Sea) area, only 17 km from downtown Fethiye.

Below: Lycian rock-cut tombs in Fethiye

➠
Next page: The Dead Sea's fascinating long beach and silent cove

Kınık-Xanthos

There are hundreds of ruins all over Turkey, but Xanthos is one of the important symbolic sites. Many ruins extend around the hillside high above the valley. **Lycia**, an indigenous Anatolian civilization of the past, enjoyed a long period of prosperity. The defense of Xanthos, the capital of the independent Lycian confederation, was an historic model of heroic courage, first against the Persians (545 BC) and then the Romans. In both battles the men of the city enclosed all their women, children, servants, and property in the acropolis and set it on fire; when the enemy made the final attack the defenders all died fighting for independence. Only 80 families— those who were away—survived. To the north of the Lycian acropolis, a well-preserved Roman theatre and three pillar-tombs are the focal point of the ruins. Almost all figurative pieces excavated in the 19ᵗʰC are in the British Museum and a few in

Lycian tower tombs

Istanbul's Archaeological Museum. The base of the famous Nereid Monument, the Harpy tomb, and the 5ᵗʰC BC Inscribed Pillar are important features still at the site. On the Roman acropolis there is little more than the remains of a Byzantine basilica. The **Letoon**, three miles west of Xanthus, was the official sanctuary dedicated to Leto, mother of twins: the goddess Artemis and the god Apollo. It is most interesting that Asia Minor was the birthplace of the children of the Greek god Zeus and his favorite mistress, Leto. Three side-by-side temples (3ʳᵈ-2ⁿᵈC BC) have been excavated as well as a fine Hellenistic theatre and a monumental fountain. Excavation finds are in the local museum. Fertile farming land surrounds both sites. The River Xanthos is good for boat safari adventures in spring.

Opposite page, top: Pillar inscribed in Lycian language and remains of Byzantine basilica, with Agora and Roman theatre behind.
Below: Three temples in Letoon

Patara

Mountainous Lycia's key cities and official temples were erected in the valley of the Xanthos River (Eşen Çay today), which gave its name to the capital. The Xanthos ruins, Letoon sanctuary complex, and Patara main harbor are close together along the river. All can be visited by the Fethiye-Kalkan road and from the marinas of these towns. Patara was one of the busiest ports of Asia Minor. Over the ages, the river connected to this rich hinterland silted the prosperous harbor into a marshland.

Today Patara is famous for its over-18km/11mi-long golden beach, Roman remains, and village with pleasant facilities. The theatre hill—partly covered by dunes—once had a lighthouse. There is a fine panorama of the shoreline and the former harbor from this spot. Patara was the landing port for St. Paul on his third missionary journey and for Emperor Hadrian on his visit to the region, and was also the birthplace of St. Nicholas (c.300 AD). The temple of Apollo, pride of the city, has not yet been found. A well-preserved triple-arched triumphal gate (c.100 AD), two baths, small but important temple remains, Hadrian's granary storage, and a large necropolis are other noteworthy parts of the site.

Monumental entrance to Patara

Partly buried theatre

Below: The endless beaches of Patara

Kaş-Antiphellus

On the "Blue Cruise" route, the mountain range extends parallel to the sea and toward the east as the pine forests become mixed with Mediterranean flora. This is also visible while driving over the fine, scenic roads. The town of Kaş is situated on a rocky slope partly covered with bush and scrub and has a narrow, flat waterfront. A small marina, a few standard hotels and pensions, enjoyable nearby bays, and small islands for yachters' pleasure are the attractions. Ancient remains include the ruins of Antiphellus, a 4thC BC Lycian sarcophagus in the middle of town and more just at the outskirts, and a small pre-Roman theatre with fine masonry. Across the harbor, less than two miles away, is the tiny Greek island of Meyisti. There are no suitable beaches within the city limits, only rocky coastline. To the west, on the way to the seemingly endless sandy beaches of Patara, the small developing town of Kalkan sits on a rocky terrace high above the miniature bay. Daily boat tours from Kaş convey visitors eastward to a different world: Kekova island and sunken city. The island and land create a lake-like strait, with Kale and Üçağız village on land and shipyards and a Byzantine basilica on the island (the basilica's standing apse, landmark of the island, unfortunately collapsed recently). It is most interesting to sail in the blue waters, viewing the Lycian edifices and sarcophaguses, a scene reminiscent of sunken Atlantis. By road or boat from Kaş or on "Blue Voyage" yachting tours, this site is a "must" stop. Strolling on the ruins or rocky land, climbing to the well-preserved medieval castle, swimming in such colors next to sunken masterpieces, and viewing the Taurus mountain chain at the horizon is an exciting experience. The village pensions and fish restaurants are modest and colorful. Along the road to the east there are many less known ancient ruins.

Opposite page, top left: Roman theatre in a charming location

Top right: A public beach near Kaş

Below: Rocky shores of downtown Kaş

General view of town and harbor, Kaş.   Below: Harbor market, Kaş

Ancient names of the region's cities and towns. Painting

Opposite page, top: Yacht harbor
near Kale-Myra

Below: Kekova Bay and Islands can
be visited only by boat

This page, right: Lycian tombs

Below: Necropolis and sunken city
on Kekova Bay

Kale-Myra

Demre was the town's old name. In the middle of very rich farmland and famous for citrus fruit growing, ancient and modern settlements are side by side. Greenhouses for early-season vegetable production, the farmers' main source of income, cover half the plain. The historical remains are unequaled. Below the rocky acropolis and above the well-preserved Roman theatre, harmoniously carved out of the mountainside, are impressive tombs of rulers, their family members, and other local dignitaries. Lycian rock-cut tombs (5thC BC) resemble the timber dwellings of those days. The city was another port for the voyages of **St. Paul** and his disciples. **St. Nicholas**, a native of Patara, became bishop here in the 4thC AD. The church dedicated to him draws both believers and standard tour groups. The well-kept edifice

Statue of St. Nicholas and children

was once used to house the Saint's relics, which were smuggled to Bari, Italy, long ago. The cast statue of St. Nicholas and children in the garden is a fine creation of modern sculpture. Every December 6 the Christian world celebrates the memory of this gentleman saint, benefactor to the needy and children, and protector of seamen. Santa Claus, or St. Nick, originated in a sunny Anatolian beach resort, just as St. Paul came from nearby Tarsus. Leaving Kale, a comfortable and scenic road winds up and down and curves around rocky small inlets on the sea front. These enjoyable small inlets have fascinating colors from turquoise to emerald green.

Spectacular Lycian rock-cut tombs and, in front, Roman theatre frieze with representations of masks

Three Byzantine apses, Church of St. Nicholas.

Below: Large theatre of Kale-Myra

Lycian rock-cut tombs representing houses of the period

Phaselis

Traveling by road through the countryside of Kemer's shores, the view to the east is the panorama of the sea. Seen from the top of the forest green, to the west is the Beydağları chain of the Taurus Mountains. In this National Park's spectacular setting, the mountains, forest, and sea shelter romantic remains under the pine-tree shades of a mini-peninsula. In addition, this well-positioned harbor made Phaselis' fortune: timber export, the main trade of the area, was the source of wealth. Legends take the settlement back to 7[th]C BC colonists from Rhodes. Like its neighbors, Phaselis was a free city-state that minted its own coins. The 6[th]C BC Persian rule was followed by Carian support and a period of freedom after Alexander the Great. Remains at the site are from the "Pax Romana", the peaceful period of the Roman Empire in the 2nd and 3[rd]C AD. During Byzantine and Turkish

A peek at the Taurus Mountains through a Roman arch

rule, it was an unimportant settlement. The main street was a large paved boulevard connecting the north harbor to another at the south. The important buildings were on both sides of the road with a monumental gate in memory of Hadrian's visit at the center. The site is well organized but has not yet been excavated. The original breakwater, theatre, baths, and aqueduct in magical surroundings are the attractions. A snow-capped mountain peak, seen from an arch of the aqueduct, is a wonderful photo opportunity.

Kemer

The Taurus mountain range is the dominant feature of the west horizon of Antalya Bay. Seen at sunset from Antalya or by the sea, the wall-shaped silhouette of dark mountains is inspiring. Viewing the scenery by day is quite different and unique in the Mediterranean world. The deep blue sea color at the shore changes sharply to forest green. The narrow shore slopes gently at first, then steep slopes rise up to blue skies. Before the rocky peak line, tones of

A beach at Kemer

green cover the slopes and cliffs and seem to pour right down to the beaches. Soft curves of shoreline permit only a few inlets and islets. The coastline, partly small pebblestone and partly sand, has undergone successful development dedicated to holiday centers. From five-star hotels to camping grounds, all are perfectly designed under the natural forestry shades of the beautiful beaches. Kemer is the chief town of the coast, only thirty scenic miles from Antalya and its international airport. After skiing or snow sports in the mountains, it is possible to swim at Kemer beaches within an hour in early spring months. During high season (March to November), the town of Kemer has all the fun of good food, nightlife, and shopping. The rest of the year it is the favorite of second honeymooners. Situated in the heart of the town, the marina is an important port for "Blue Voyage" yachts. This coastline is considered one of the Seven Natural Wonders of Turkey. From Kemer there are daily tours to nearby historical or natural wonders.

Kemer Marina and Bay

Antalya

For perfectionist travelers, traditional vacationers, beach worshippers demanding unspoiled and colorful Mediterranean nature, and beginners or old-hands seeking the richest ancient sites, there emerges at the peak, as the Mecca for all of these: Antalya. To the west, the miles-long smooth pebble beach of **Konyaaltı** and to the east the sandy **Lara Beach** are within the city limits. The endless beaches and holiday resorts within an hour's drive are truly impressive. Antalya is not only for beach holidays, but is also a very famous and unequaled center for cultural and historical activities. Nowhere else can one view so many antique ruins, such well preserved Roman theatres, and so many other fine remains of the past in such

Coastal rock formations

natural and original surroundings. Since Antalya is centrally located a short and easy distance to the ruins of ancient **Pamphylia**, it is possible to visit most of the sites in a day or two: Perge, Aspendos, Side ruins and the town of Alanya to the east; extraordinary Kemer shores and the romantic Phaselis and Chimera, site of perpetual fire, at the west; and many more sites within a few hours' distance, including Myra (town of St. Nicholas), Lymira, Arykanda and untouched Termessos, like an eagle's nest on the peak of a mountain, to the north.

Fifteen miles east of Antalya stretches the **Belek** holiday center, famous for its top-grade hotels and golf courses and surrounded by pine forests and golden sandy beaches. The early-season vegetable and flower greenhouses, the perfectly irrigated plains, tobacco and cotton production, and citrus fruit and vegetables provide important revenue. The region has wet winters

Opposite: Famous Konyaaltı Beach

Opposite: Yivli Minaret. Top: Ancient harbor. Below: Hadrian's Gate, Antalya

and dry summers; July and August are the warmest months with high humidity. Early spring and late autumn offer perfect weather for sea sports, safari and site tours. A modern international airport is 10km/6miles away, and the commercial harbor only 9km/5miles from the city center. Some of the best hotels anywhere on the Mediterranean are in the city limits or close by.

One of the most important Paleolithic excavations in Turkey took place on the lower

Karain Cave

slopes of the Taurus Mountain chain near the city. This interesting natural **Karain Cave** is a half-day visit with a twenty-minute climb on the rocks. All over Antalya's plain there are hundreds of dolmens, large stone blocks erected in the shadows of time. Rich in calcareous content, great amounts of underground and surface water left behind the excess limestone. These terrace formations end at the edge of the city, and vertical cliffs drop down to the deep sea. Built during the Pergamum Kingdom in the 2ndC BC, Attaleia remained the youngest and least important town in the history of Pamphylia. Parts of the old city wall, the monumental Gate of Emperor

Hadrian, the Roman harbor, and the **Yivli (fluted) Minaret**, a 13thC Seljuk Turkish edifice, are reminders of the past. The small harbor, once a pirate port, and the walled old city are the center for many activities. The landmark of Antalya, the Yivli Minaret, with its brick-red color, stands just above the stairs to the harbor, while the nearby clock tower marks the entrance to the old city. Narrow streets and well-restored typical old houses—now used as good hotels, cafes, and bars—add great color to Antalya. At the eastern end extends one of Turkey's best parks which includes the Hıdırlık Tower, a Roman remain right at the edge of the cliff, once used as a lighthouse. A must visit in Antalya is the modern Archaeological Museum. The impressive displays, in chronologically arranged rooms, include outstanding art objects of antiquity gathered from the excavations of nearby ruins over the last fifty years. When the sea is calm, boat tours in the Antalya Gulf are a popular way to get the best idea of the cliff formations while watching the Duden waterfalls. Inner Duden Falls at the north end of the city is another point of interest.

Sarcophagus depicting the Labors of Hercules.

Below: Inner Duden Falls, north of Antalya

Theatre

Below: Bouleuterion, Termessos

Termessos

Between two mountains, positioned on a saddle-like plateau at 1050mt/3400ft, this site is one of the best-preserved ruins of Turkey. Although no excavations have taken place yet, still the location and the fantastic remains of the past scattered around or covered by pine trees and bushes make Termessos a ruin worth viewing. After an hour's drive from Antalya and a twenty-minute climb up to the Taurus Mountain chain, one can enter the untouched world of a ghost town. Trying to discover most of the ruins is a difficult task because of the bushes and rocky paths. However, for adventure seekers it can be a fruitful try. The earlier history of the settlement before Alexander the Great is wrapped in mythological tales. Their language came from the northern neighbor, Pisidia. The fame of these brave, native warriors and the strategic location of their eagle's-nest-like city must be what stopped Alexander the Great from attacking Termessos. That was in the year 333 BC, the first historical reference to the city. The city had its brightest period in the 3rd and 2nd C BC, and rose again under the great tolerance and friendship of the Romans in the 2nd and 3rd C AD. It seems the site was abandoned during the late Roman epoch. Local guard-guides of the National Park are required for the visit to selected tombs and very rich sarcophaguses on the site. The remains worth seeing are grouped behind the Theatre, which affords a fascinating panoramic view down to Antalya plain. Hewn partly from the rocks, this 4000-capacity theatre with a Roman stage building is charming and impressive. Surrounded by the rocky peaks this might be the highest and most inspiring location for a classical drama. To the west, at the edge of the cliff, stand the ruins of two temples; the larger was the main temple of the city and dedicated to Artemis. Behind the theatre is the best-preserved structure, the Bouleuterion, with its 10mt/30ft high walls built of fine masonry. This Senate House of the city was also used for other kinds of meetings, including winter shows, as a roofed-over theatre. The agora, private houses, a colonnaded promenade, and more temples of high architectural quality are placed near an essential spot of the city: the gigantic water cisterns for dry summers. Rock-cut tombs next to sarcophaguses—some with heroic and sad memories, some decorated with reliefs or inscriptions—are other principal sites of the ruin.

Burdur and Isparta

The northern inland Mediterranean region is the lake district of Anatolia. This **Pisidia** region of antiquity has a number of fresh water lakes. At the southern shores of Burdur Lake lies the famous Neolithic settlement **Hacılar**. Burdur Archaeological Museum and the colorful İnsuyu Cave are interesting places. Within the Taurus Mountains near Isparta's

Ağlasun town, the ruins of **Sagallasos** offer a lot to discover. Isparta is the center for Turkey's rose-oil production and exports its harvest to the European perfume industry. Bass fishing at nearby Eğridir Lake is the best in the country.

Yalvaç-Antioch of Pisidia

On the hill next to town stand the ruins of Antioch of Pisidia, site of a Cybele and Man sanctuary used until the Roman period. Remains are few, but since St. Paul and Barnabas visited the site, it is important for Bible tours.

Villagers moving to higher pasture lands for the summer

Earliest multicolor pottery, Neolithic Hacılar, Burdur   Below: Wheat harvest, Isparta area

Remains of Cybele and Man Temple

Below: Arches of Roman aqueduct, Yalvaç

Perge-Aksu

Perge, Aspendos, and Sillyon, the three cities of the Pamphylian plain, are comparable in many ways: founded on a fortified acropolis, expanded to the lower plain during the Hellenistic and especially the Roman period, then in the Byzantine era driven back to the hills, and finally in decline after Arab attacks. Next to the fertile plain and a navigable river down to the nearby sea, the site had all the grandeur of a wealthy free city-state. Legends were the customary way to relate foundation stories of ancient settlements. In the myth of Perge and Aspendos, the cities' founders were the Trojan War soldiers Chalcas and Mopsos. Little is known about the history of the Pamphylian cities before the arrival of Alexander the Great. The Macedonian king was welcomed to unfortified Perge in 333 BC. There are some insignificant Byzantine remains on the acropolis. In the lower city, all remains except the walls are from Roman masterpieces. Some Hellenistic walls are still partly standing at their original height and some buildings existed at the time of St. Paul's first journey to Perge. A large theatre is the first edifice at the entrance of the ruins opposite the stadium. Partly built into a hillside, the theatre got its final shape in the 2^{nd}C AD with the addition of a stage building. This well-preserved 15,000-seat theatre had separations for gladiator fights and fine carvings of mythological scenes. When the stage building is restored, Turkey will have another complete Roman theatre. The Stadium is the second-best of its kind (next to the one in Aphrodisias) and could hold 12,000 spectators. Oval rows of seats are set over the vaulted arches of areas used as shops or stadium entrances. One of the best examples of its kind, the round-towered Hellenistic City Gate is the landmark of Perge. In front of the towers a large ceremonial courtyard was added in the 2^{nd}C AD. The smaller gate entrance to the courtyard led to a colonnaded portico and agora on the right. The left wall front was decorated with a monumental fountain and niches for statues of heroes and rulers. The entrance to the excavated Roman Baths is from this section. Because of the abundant findings, Perge is called the "field of sculptures" by authorities. These beautiful pieces are on display at the Antalya

Archaeological Museum.

In the horseshoe-shaped inner court of the Hellenistic towers, the walls were covered with marble slabs and niches filled with statues of Roman imperial figures. Passing to a wide colonnaded street, visitors can see many statue pedestals with Latin inscriptions around the gateway. Most of the inscriptions bear the name of Lady Plancia Magna, daughter of the Roman governor of Bithynia and principal magistrate and sponsor of Perge. The main street is impressive with the colonnaded and once mosaic-paved sidewalks and shops. A unique feature designed for the summer enjoyment of citizens was a canal placed in the middle of the boulevard for running water. The colonnaded street meets a similar east-west road just before the monumental fountains that provided water for the canal. The small Agora has a round temple of Hermes in the middle and many recently re-erected columns in front of the shops.

Bird's-eye view of Perge, drawing by the late Alfred Harris

OF PERGE

F Nymphaeum
  Nymphée
  Nympheum
G Church
  Eglise
  Kirchen
H Propylaeum
  Propylée
  Propylaeum
I Baths
  Bains

K Basilica
  Basilique
  Basilika
L Acropolis
  Acropole
  Akropolis
M Fortifications
  Fortifications
  Befestigungsmauer
N Palestra

Dionysius relief, theatre stage

Below: Hellenistic towers on main gate

Aspendos

Known in Turkish as the ruins of **Belkis**, this is the home of the best-preserved ancient theatre, another colossal edifice in Turkey. On the one-hour trip from Antalya to the site, the road passes by well-irrigated fertile lands for cotton and tobacco and a myriad of greenhouses. The first sight before the Theatre is the fine 13thC Turkish bridge, on the site of an earlier Roman one, which can still be used by smaller vehicles. The navigable river was used as the port of Aspendos in BC periods. The city's destiny was similar to that of its sister cities of the Pamphylian plain. Little is yet known of its history before Alexander the Great; all the ruins are after his period. Some bits of information like the Persian fleet's docking at the river harbor and the minting of coins in the 5thC BC are the earliest records. The city's name, Aspendos, similar to the name of the 8thC BC king of the Late-Hittites from southeastern Turkey, and the early local language are two proofs of its older history. Although most travelers visit the theatre there is more to enjoy on the site. Less than a mile away stands the best-preserved aqueduct in Turkey, a perfect example of Roman water engineering. For climbers there are more remains at the upper city, the acropolis. Scattered around the major remains are an agora, town hall, monumental fountain, and a basilica, all from the Roman era. A stadium and large baths were erected in the lower city. The Theatre is the highlight of Aspendos. This unique structure, constructed by a local architect under the sponsorship of two citizen brothers, has come down to us intact. Its stability, its use as a caravansary by the Turks from the 13thC on, and good luck brought the theatre to our days. The Aspendos Theatre, located next to the Acropolis, was built party over a barrel-vaulted substructure. The outer façade gives a harmonious, palace-like impression. The stage retains its original height, and its interior appearance is also fascinating. Some other striking characteristics of this theatre were the vaulted entranceways, arched galleries above upper seats, and awe-inspiring marble decorations. There was an extended timber covering of the stage for better acoustics. The theatre can hold up to 10,000 easily and is still full during festivals of classical drama or modern shows.

Bird's-eye view of Aspendos, drawing by the late Alfred Harris

Theatre exterior

Below: Theatre interior

Modern irrigation canal and remains of Roman aqueduct   Below: Turkish bridge

Side

Resting on a small peninsula, the city has taken advantage of the abundance of the sea and the surrounding natural resources since early times. Only an hour's drive down the coast from Antalya, it is a unique place offering everything for a cheerful holiday. Nowhere but in Side village can one live amidst the splendor of aesthetic ancient ruins, mingled with a vivid atmosphere of shops, pensions, good restaurants, and cafes, and yet rest peacefully in the luxurious facilities of five-star hotels along gorgeous sandy beaches stretching for miles or in the comfort of a pension within the village. Earlier settlement flourished between the 2nd and 3rd C AD as an important trading center, especially slave trade. Most of the incredible historical remains seen today are from that period. It declined in the 3rd C AD, but flourished again after becoming an important center of the Christian world of Pamphylia after the 5th C AD. Arab and pirate attacks led to the abandonment of cities along the shores by the 9th C AD. Immigrant villagers from Crete

settled in Side at the end of the 19th C. Old remains include an aqueduct through which Roman engineers brought Side's water. City walls belong to the Hellenistic and Roman periods, and the city gate was once a magnificent portal similar to the one at Perge. The museum, in the 5th C AD Agora Baths, has five sections displaying fine marble statues, sarcophaguses, and inscriptions written in the as yet undeciphered language of Side. The commercial agora, backed up against the stage building of the huge theatre, was the social and business center of the town and the place where slaves were bought or sold. The gate between the museum and the theatre dates to the 3rd C AD and the fountain and adjacent well-preserved public toilets are interesting remains of the ancient world. The gorgeous Side Theatre, one of the best in Anatolia and the largest of Roman style, was built on flat land and raised up on vaults and arches. Dating to the 2nd C AD, it underwent some changes during the following centuries and seated up to 15,000 people. The partially reconstructed Temple of Apollo near the ancient harbor, and the Temple of Athena, main goddess of the city and featured on its coins, date from the 2nd C AD. East of the Temple are the ruins of a 5th C

Christian basilica and 9th or 10thC AD additions of another smaller church. The State Agora, situated on the eastern side of the theatre overlooking the sea, consisted of a courtyard surrounded by colonnades and, on the eastern flank, three large chambers. More sections of Side still lie under the dunes of the eastern beach.

Side peninsula showing theatre and harbor, drawing by the late Alfred Harris

SIDE

Above: Theatre and State Agora. Below: Commercial Agora. Opposite: Athena Temple

Manavgat Falls

Turkey's largest waterfall, a few miles to the north of Side, is a cool and scenic location for picnics and offers a café under the age-old trees. Clear greenish waters fall only about fifteen feet (four meters) but the size of the river and the beauty of the surrounding nature are striking. An upstream dam controls the amount of running water; spring is the best season to see the greatest amount of water. The river's high-quality water is exported to Cyprus and Israel. The small farming town of Manavgat is a good departure point for small boats to explore the lower river and its exit to the Mediterranean.

Right: Summer stilt cottage near Manavgat

Manavgat Falls in spring with Taurus Mountains behind

Alanya-Coracesion

An immense reddish rocky promontory jutting out into the water with long castle walls at the top, wide sandy beaches stretching out from either side, the navy blue of the sea, and, as a background, the forested Taurus Mountains rising up to the sky with snowy heights. That is Alanya, a city in the middle of this atmosphere and surrounded by banana, tangerine, and orange gardens perfuming the air with an incredible scent. Alanya has gradually become a vacation paradise with its year-round sun, romantic boat trips, vivid nightlife, port facilities, wide range of food and hotels, interesting old buildings, and history. New churches are under construction to serve Christian visitors. The town is two hours' driving distance from Antalya and one hour from Side on a nice scenic route. Coracesium, the "rookery" as it was known in ancient times, was a pirates' lair until captured by the Romans in a sea battle in 67 BC. Only a few years later Mark Anthony presented the region to Cleopatra. From that time until the 19thC, wood continued to be an important export item for the town. Byzantines named it Karakesion and, following Seljuk Sultan Alaattin Keykubat's capture of the town in 1222 AD, it was named Alaiye, the origin of its present name, Alanya. The city was used as the Seljuk winter capital and shipyards. The beautiful and imposing Red Tower, the symbol of the city, is a 32m/100ft red octagonal brick tower on the water's edge, built to guard the city and the harbor. The citadel was first constructed by pirates and was leveled by the Romans during their invasion. The existing Seljuk walls were built in the 13thC AD on the ruins of the first ones. Two religious buildings, an 11thC AD Church of St George and the other a 16thC AD Ottoman mosque replacing the former Seljuk one, are located at the Citadel. To the west of the peninsula, the Cave of Damlataş (Cave of Dripping Stones) is another site worth seeing. This cave, below sea level and full of stalactites, was formed about 15-20,000 years ago. The cave's carbon dioxide and high humidity are believed to relieve asthma. The small Alanya Museum displays archaeological findings of the region and ethnographical artifacts. To get a good taste of the colorful small sea caves, a boat tour around the promontory is a favorite Alanya activity. Iron ore gives the reddish color to the rocky mass. The Pirates' Cave, the Lover's Grotto (a

phosphorescent cave), and nearby Cleopatra's Beach are some of the remarkable points of interest.

Cliff and walls

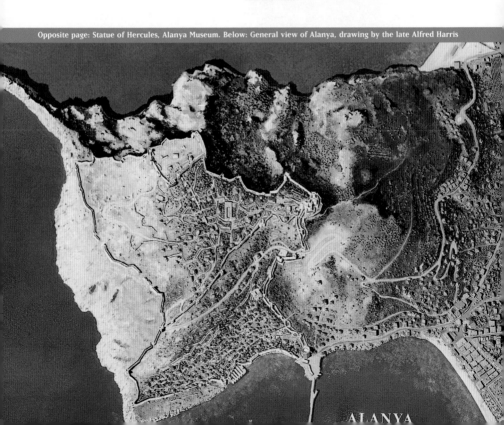

ALANYA

Alanya scenes: Above: Eastern shores   Below: Unusual morning photo opportunity   Red Tower

Anamur-Anamurium and Silifke-Seleucia of Isauria

Turkey's Mediterranean coast is divided into three geographical subdivisions, Antalya Bay to the west (Ancient Pamphylia), Mersin and Iskenderun Bays (Cilicia) to the east, and the Taşeli peninsula (Rough Cilicia) at the center. The shore road of this peninsular section is a unique scenic drive of over 150 miles up and down, following curve after curve.

The famous local banana plantations and mountains covered with dense green vegetation run parallel to the deep blue color of the sea. Mostly the jagged shoreline offers little chance for settlements but a few medieval castles exist on higher hills at the eastern part, each more interesting than the other. Situated almost midway between Alanya and Silifke, Anamur is famous and worth a stop. The historical ruins of Anamurium, the old city a few miles to the south, are spread across a slope at the shore, protected by a fortified acropolis. Sites to discover

Shoreline west of Anamur

Ruins of Anamurium

are the large Roman and Byzantine necropolis with hundreds of different kinds of tombs, remains of the city wall and high basilica walls, and the theatre. A few miles east of the ruins, right on the beach stands beautiful **Mamuriye Castle**, one of the most picturesque examples combining Roman, Crusader, and Turkish features. It stands against the waves in an excellent state of repair. Way to the east, at the end of the curving drive, is the fertile agricultural plain and the town of **Silifke**, the Seleucia on Calycandos of antiquity. This was an important port on the busy crossroads of the vast hinterland up to Konya plain until silting changed the geography. On this route, which follows the Göksu River, are some castles and the 6thC Byzantine "**Alahan**" monastery complex. Also in this range of the Taurus Mountains is "**Binbir Kilise**" (Thousand and One Churches) of 7thC AD Christians running far from Arab invasions in Asia Minor. A small local museum and the 5thC AD Hagia Thecla church are Silifke's main sights, along with some less important ruins. Little remains of an apse, but the crypt attracts believers to the Basilica of

Hagia Thecla, an early member of the community and the first female follower of St. Paul. It takes some effort to climb to the citadel. The drowning of Frederic I Barbarossa, the leader of the Third Crusade, in 1190 is another story in Silifke's history. From Silifke to Tarsus there are famous and attractive ancient ruins close to the sea front. In the same direction, but within the Taurus Mountain chain, far from the danger of sea attacks, there are dozens of castles and settlements, especially of Byzantine age, with little or no record yet known. **Taşucu**, Silifke's port, is a ferry station to Cyprus. The shores from Silifke to Mersin have been given over to numerous summer holiday resorts.

Mamuriye Castle on Anamur waterfront

Uzuncaburç-Olba-Diocaesarea

This famous ruin, 32km/19 miles north of Silifke, is at 1200m/3600 ft, an ideal elevation for local people to escape from the summer heat. Town and ruins together have seen continuous settlement since the 3rdC BC. The two ancient walled cities are two miles from each other. Because of a slender, high Hellenistic tower on the wall, the Turkish people named it Uzuncaburç (long tower). Originally established as a sanctuary to nearby Olba, Diocaesarea developed over time into another town. The Temple of Zeus Olbius (Jupiter of the Romans), the first example of Corinthian style in Asia Minor, was erected by Alexander the Great's well-known general Seleucus in 295 BC and converted into a Christian basilica in the 6thC. The remaining columns are the landmarks of the site. A temple to Fortuna, a fine three-arched entrance in the walls, attractive standing columns of the monumental

Temple of Zeus, Uzuncaburç

ceremonial gate, several rows of Roman theatre, and water reservoirs with fountains are the noteworthy sites in Diocaesarea. The huge necropolises of both settlements are striking sights. Numerous graves, sarcophaguses, or temple-shaped tombs, from Hellenistic to Byzantine epochs, have all survived to our age in good condition.

Roman tombs

Kanlıdivane-Kanytelis

In a rocky expanse of limestone, less than two miles from the coastal highway, is the site of a natural formation and a settlement of Hellenistic, Roman and Byzantine periods. Ruins are spotted around the crater-like chasm that occupies the center of the town. This large, deep hole in the rocks was carved by the underground water systems; the deep erosion caused the surface to collapse, a common occurrence in such formations within the mountain range. The locals considered this cavern sacred. A stairway and a tunnel hewn through the rocks reach the 60m/190-ft-deep bottom. Several carved reliefs adorn the walls of the formation; the one on the south wall shows six figures, probably symbolizing a ruling family. A half-collapsed 3rdC BC watchtower made of fine polygonal stones stands at the southwest edge of the sacred crater. Of five existing Byzantine basilicas at the site, two have high walls still standing. All had the same basilica plan: after the entrance corridor (the narthex), narrower side aisles border the central large nave. Some of the apses are still standing up to roof level. To the north and west of the ruin there extends a huge necropolis, the city of the dead, with burial chambers of many dates and styles.

← ◀︎
Opposite: Columns on Roman road

Cavern of Kanlıdivane

Below: One of four Byzantine churches in Kanlıdivane

Kızkalesi-Corycos

On a long sandy beach to the east of Silifke once stood two lonely but beautiful white castles watching each other, one on the shore and the other on an islet nearby. Although their appearance has not changed much, the shoreline has been overcrowded with all kinds of lodgings. Crusader and Cilician-Armenian construction of the castle dates to the 12thC. There used to be a sort of breakwater connecting the offshore castle to the mainland thus forming a safer harbor. First mentioned in the Hellenistic period, the site flourished during the Roman Empire and again in the Christian era. Churches and other monuments of the Christian period still survive. The offshore castle Kızkalesi (the Maiden Tower) was the subject of a famous legend. The land castle erected on the peninsula was built with earlier Roman materials. Among the other remains at the site, the necropolis is worth exploring.

Kız Kalesi, a beautiful medieval castle guarding city and harbor of Corycos

Cennet-Cehennem-The Caverns of Heaven and Hell

Three natural formations stand side by side to make an impressive sight. These crater-like pits are collapsed surfaces over the lower limestone levels, eroded by the underground waters. Those seeking an asthma cure favor the smallest of the three, with a modern stairway leading down. The largest of the collapsed formations, the Cavern of Heaven, has a length of about 250m/800 ft and a visible depth of 100m/300 ft. After walking partway down the stairs, the visitor discovers a small chapel dedicated to the Virgin Mary.

Farther below, in the mythological kingdom of darkness, in the territory of Typhon and his fearsome son, Cerberus, the loyal guards of the underground world, there is the noise of the rumbling underground river. North of Heaven is Hell, only 50m/150ft in diameter but over 100m/300ft in depth. It is truly a hellish-looking pit. Only experienced cave explorers should descend this steep-walled formation. Back on the main road, right at the seaside, the mosaic floor pavement of a Roman bath bears witness to a once-great complex. The mosaics of three nude figures are now protected, but the chilly spring water, mixing with the salty, warm Mediterranean, is the same as it was thousands of years ago.

Modern highway near ancient Cilician Pass

Cilician Pass before the modern highway

Mersin

From the earliest days to the Byzantine age, Silifke and Tarsus handled timber export to the Mediterranean countries and imported Cilicia's needs until the harbors silted up. In our day, the modern port facility of Mersin serves the region. For a traveler there is not much to visit within the Mersin, Tarsus, and Adana city limits. The archaeologically important artificial mounds of Mersin and Tarsus shed light on the early settlements dating back to the 4th millennium BC.

Chalcolithic and Early Bronze Age civilizations were followed by the Hittite, Hellenistic, and Roman periods, one after another. West of Mersin, the flat lands of ancient Cilicia, a well-irrigated plain named Çukurova in Turkish, is one of the most fertile lands in Turkey. This top cotton-growing farmland also produces early-season fruit, vegetables, and citrus fruit for distribution to the rest of the country. A few miles west of Mersin, at the ruins of Pompeipolis, once a large Roman settlement, there remains only a colonnade. Recently many modern apartments replaced the orange groves at the outskirts of town. There are good hotels in Mersin and Adana.

Panorama of Mersin

Tarsus

The town was and still is at the junction of important roads. The prehistoric Gözlükule tumulus is the archaeological research site of the town. Historic **Cilician Pass** (Gülek Boğazı) was the easiest route down for highlanders to reach the Cilician Plain and served as the export route for lower Mesopotamian goods to the northern countries. Tarsus was the nearest metropolis before or after crossing the pass. Hittite and Assyrian trading in the 2nd millennium BC, Persian armies marching west in the 6th C BC, the Anabasis (the Retreat of the Ten Thousand), Alexander the Great's march to the east in 333 BC, St Paul's trips to the inland, 8th C AD Arab attacks and more-all traveled through this strategic passage. Gülek Pass today is a modern highway. The memory of Anthony and Cleopatra remains in Tarsus on a part of the old wall named Cleopatra's Gate. City tours point out a Roman-period marble well aperture as the site of St Paul's home. It is likely that without the efforts of this man of Tarsus, Christianity might have continued only as a small regional belief. Other monuments, buildings, stadium and so on have disappeared except two: a 2nd C AD thick-walled Roman structure locally called Dönük Taş (turned-over stone), the function of which has never been clear; and a well-paved Roman road. A unique, gigantic 2nd C BC metal door with two panels of high craftsmanship was taken from Tarsus during the 9th C and stands at the exit of the Hagia Sophia Museum in Istanbul; such a large, decorative and beautiful door must have been used originally in a local palace or a temple. A small waterfall of the Tarsus (Cydnus) River, which is most attractive in the springtime, fascinated Alexander the Great after his arrival over the Cilician Pass. History records that a cold shower taken here sent him into a deep coma for forty days. The shoreline today is 14km/9ml to the south of the fertile plain. Colorful streets and numerous kebab restaurants are the pleasures of this farming town.

➡
Overleaf: Tarsus Falls at its springtime high water level

Recently excavated paved and colonnaded Roman road

Below: Well of St. Paul's house, Tarsus

Adana

Adana is Turkey's fourth largest city and the center of its cotton industry; Çukurova (Cilicia of antiquity) plain is a huge and well-irrigated farming area. The prosperous city does not offer much for travelers except some 15th and 16thC mosques, several buildings, and quite a rich local archaeological museum. The oldest existing edifice is the bridge (partly Roman, then altered in the

Drawing of an old mountain pass

Justinian and Turkish periods) on the Seyhan River, which flows through the center of the city. Because of the rapid extension of settlements, the international airport is within the town. The city offers high-class hotels, shopping variety, and one of the delicacies of Turkish cuisine, Adana kebab, served in many special restaurants at its best. Adana has a strategically important air base, Incirlik.

The Hittites put an end to the local Kizivatna kingdom here in 1333 BC and established their domination over the region. Six miles southwest of Ceyhan at Sirkeli there is a Hittite rock relief dating to 1286 BC. When the Hittite empire collapsed around 1200 BC, late-Hittite art, customs, and traditions continued in this region in places like Karatepe, eleven kilometers from Kadirli, and Sakcagözü. Beautiful mosaic floor pavements of Roman villas at Misis are to the east of Adana. As in the rest of the Mediterranean region, castles protected every available hilltop in Cilicia. To the original Roman and Byzantine chain of fortifications, Crusaders added more. Most of them retain the Crusaders' final repairs. About 90km/60 miles northeast of Adana, Karatepe is a significant ruin of the 8thC BC Late-Hittite site; King Asitawanda erected a summer palace that dominates the plain and river from its hill. This is the ruler mentioned early in this chapter for the name similarity with Aspendos, a city in Pamphylia. Palace remains include large basalt slabs with reliefs depicting daily life.

Highest peak of Taurus chain before Cilician Pass

Below: Roman bridge, Adana

Top: Antakya   Below: Bagras, one of the many mountaintop castles throughout Cilicia   Soteria Mosaic, wall docorat

Antakya-
Antioch on
Orantes

Issus, southeast of Dörtyol, was the battlefield (333 BC) between Alexander the Great's Macedonian army and the Persians. The shore town of Payas offers a secluded Crusader castle and a unique—for such a small settlement—16ᵗʰC Ottoman complex comprising a mosque, school, covered market, Turkish baths, and a caravansary. Founded after the victory over the Persians and called Alexandria Minor to distinguish it from its Egyptian sister, **Iskenderun** is the busiest Mediterranean port of Turkey and will become more important after the completion of the Caspian Sea oil pipeline by 2006. Turkey's largest steel mill is in this town. At Antakya's **Amik plain** there are over 180 prehistoric tumuli of which only a few have been excavated. Next to newly

Orpheus mosaic

discovered Neolithic sites, the Hittite settlement at Tel-Acana is well known for the royal palace. To the southeast of Islahiye town one of the most interesting early wonders lies on a gentle slope: **Yesemek**, the workshop site for Hittite sculpture. The local name, "field of statues", is a perfect description of the still-standing unfinished blocks of the stone quarry.

Founded by Alexander's general Seleucus Nicator, for his Syrian kingdom in 301 BC, Antioch remained for centuries one of the principal cities of the world. After the Roman conquest, the city maintained her autonomy and received much personal interest from Caesar and Augustus. Apostles in Antioch took important decisions for the future of their faith under the leadership of St. Peter, right after the crucifixion of Jesus Christ. The city's large Jewish population worshiping in Greek was the early Christians' great chance and hope. Once a prosperous city and a political, cultural, and commercial center, Antioch was surrounded by wealthy Roman citizens' large mansions. Only a few of the ancient edifices are visible today, including parts of an aqueduct, catacombs, city walls and towers at the acropolis, and many mosaic floor pavements from the villas. The **Grotto of St. Peter**, the very first hidden church of Christianity, is situated two miles east of downtown at the mountainside. Although Crusaders added the façade, this original site attracts many biblical or regular tours. For Christians the other importance of Antioch is their name: believers referred to themselves as Christian for the first time in Antioch.

Antakya's Archaeological Museum has fantastic mosaics, mostly floor decorations of the villas from **Harbiye** district. The modern displays also include other regional artifacts. Daphne, or Harbiye, district on the south outskirts of town was the site of Roman mansions and of temples. Nothing from the past can be seen but several hotels and restaurants in a romantic atmosphere on the cool hillside with lots of pools and tiny waterfalls make this a pleasant location. On this spot, according to the legend, the rejected lover Apollo transformed a young and beautiful water nymph, Daphne, into a laurel tree. **Seleucia de Pierre**, built as the harbor of Antioch, is another unique ruin in Turkey near the north of Samandağ town. St. Paul and his followers started their missionary journeys from there. It is still possible to see the artificial harbor's breakwater remains in the sea. Following the easy path through the rock-cut canal from the harbor to the east for a half-mile or so, visitors come face to face with the great creation of Roman military engineering. On the construction dedication carved onto the rock, there are the names of Emperors Titus and Vespasian (2^{nd}C AD). The 1435m/4500ft-long canal was mostly cut quite deep through the rock and at the location of the huge, hill-size rock block. The Romans dug an enormous tunnel (143x8m/450x24feet), so big that a modern train could pass through it. The heavy flash rains, which thundered through the vicinity-and still do today-were the reason for all the effort. Floodwaters silting the harbor and damaging the fleets were canalized and diverted with the help of this system. Hand-cut by the army, **Titus Tunnel** is famous as one of the Seven Historical Wonders of Turkey. Nearby remains are not yet excavated.

Interior of Mosaic and Archaeological Museum

Below: Façade of the first Christian church, Antakya

Opposite: Titus Tunnel interior   This page: Exterior views and rock-carved church

Opposite page, top: Traveling salesmen offer everything from prayer beads to knife-sharpening services

Opposite page, below: Beautiful scenery and historic tumuli are found throughout the fertile lands north of Antakya

This page, right: Dörtyol town near Antakya is known for its vast orange groves

Below: Turkish Turkeys chat in Turkey

Central Anatolia Region

Ankara

Once a small town in Central Anatolia, Ankara became Atatürk's headquarters for conducting the War of Independence, and with the declaration of the Republic in 1923, it became the capital. It is now the second largest city in Turkey. Excavations in the vicinity have revealed continuous settlement layers since the Paleolithic period. The Hittites and the Phrygians settled at the famous citadel rising on steep rocks and in the area around the Temple of Augustus on the lower plain. The keep is full of old Turkish houses and narrow streets. Pieces from Roman statues and columns installed in the city walls draw visitors' attention. The victories and deeds of the Roman emperor Augustus were inscribed in both Greek and Latin on the walls of the Augustus Temple, built on the remains of an earlier temple. The Hacı Bayram Mosque (15thC) beside the temple is one of the important mosques in the city. The outer walls

◀▪▪▪
Previous page: Panoramic view of Ankara from Çankaya

have not survived to our day, but a few remains are beneath the modern city. A big Roman bath in the classical style, the remains of a theatre, the grooved column of Emperor Julianus dating to 362 AD, and "Ankyra" coins are all reminders of those days. Ankara is also well known for its famous Angora goats, cats, and rabbits. The most important places to visit are the **Mausoleum of Atatürk (Anıtkabir)**, the Museum of Anatolian Civilizations, and the Ethnographical Museum near the inner castle. When Atatürk died in 1938, his body was first laid to rest in a temporary tomb at the Ethnographical Museum. On 10 November 1953 (the fifteenth anniversary of his death), his body was moved to the imposing mausoleum his nation built for him. After the entrance, there is a broad avenue, flanked by statues of lions, ending at the ceremonial square. Atatürk's personal possessions are exhibited in the nearby towers and the gallery sections. The large monolithic marble sarcophagus lies inside the mausoleum, above the real tomb below. After the pyramids in Giza, it is the largest monumental tomb ever erected for a leader and national hero. Housed in a beautiful 15thC Ottoman covered market building, the **Museum of Anatolian**

Citadel and interesting walls   Below: Augustus Temple, next to Haci Bayram Mosque, Ankara

Civilizations exhibits findings from all over Anatolia, from the Paleolithic to the Roman periods, in chronological order. The objects displayed in the showcases are the earliest, richest, and most unusual pieces found in Turkey. The domed section in the middle is allocated to huge stone works, and an exhibition of artifacts found in the Ankara vicinity is on the basement floor. One of the early Republican buildings of the city, the **Ethnographical Museum**, houses beautiful objects from daily life of the recent past. Gençlik Park and Çankaya Hill are places in the midst of the city where one can enjoy a leisurely stroll. Rising on a hill overlooking the city, the Kocatepe Mosque with its four minarets is a modern structure. At the crossroads of all kinds of busy transportation routes, Ankara is a bureaucratic city with many hotels, entertainment, and cultural activities.

Below: Anıtkabir, Mausoleum of Atatürk

Opposite: Interior with symbolic sarcophagus

Sights from Museum of Anatolian
Civilizations, Ankara

Opposite page, top left: Roman eagle in
the garden.

Top right: Cybele statuette from
Çatalhöyük

Below left: Copy of a room at
Çatalhöyük

Below: Twin clay Hittite bulls from
Hattuşaş

This page, right: Mother goddess Cybele
of Hacılar, Burdur

Boğazköy-Hattuşaş

The important settlement of the Hittite Empire was the capital, Hattuşaş. It is 210km/130miles from Ankara and can be seen on a day tour. Along with their heavy trading with the Assyrians, the Hittites learned cuneiform and started the written history era in Anatolia (Kültepe, 1950 BC). In Anatolia, the Hittites (17thC BC) achieved the first unification of city-states and principalities under one authority. Expanding like an empire, they became the only rival for the Egyptians. After the

Lion statue, Lion's Gate

Battle of Kadesh, the world's first peace treaty was signed between the Hittites and the Egyptians in 1270 BC. The Hittites inherited the Hatti land and culture and adopted the religious system of the neighboring Hurrians. They spoke an Indo-European language. Mentioned in Egyptian texts and the Old Testament, this advanced civilization

was brought to light with excavations started a century ago. Hattusas was settled on a hill, easy to defend from three sides, and surrounded by strong city walls. The main features of the site are the acropolis, also called the Great Fortress, including the king's palace and the state archives; the Great Temple below, surrounded by remains of storerooms; castles on every rock; and small temples. The partly visible city walls give a good idea of their original form. King's Gate, whose original is displayed at the Ankara Museum, and the Lion Gate were military gates. Two lion-sphinxes protected the entrance of a secret tunnel built under the city wall. Of the tens of thousands of clay state tablets kept in the archives, only a small number of them have been deciphered. These documents reveal previously unknown facts about the Hittite civilization, which played a leading role in the development of the Aegean World. **Yazılıkaya** open-air temple, 2km/1mile from Hattusas, is another "must-see" place. Here, in the larger gallery, a rock is inscribed

with low reliefs of numerous gods and goddesses led by the chief god Teshup and goddess Hepatu in a religious ceremony. In the narrow gallery reached by a passage, one side depicts a dagger thrust into the ground; on the opposite side is the relief of twelve gods marching in procession. On the side walls the reliefs depict kings. Carved areas in the rocks, on either side of a gorge, once held the supports of the first-ever wooden bridge, built here, east of Yazılıkaya temple and connecting it to the Great Fortress-Acropolis. In the Hittite world, civil and women's rights were highly developed. The most valuable Hatti (pre-Hittite) findings of the Ankara Museum were unearthed in the tombs of the kings at **Alacahöyük**, near Boğazköy. The ruins to be seen include reliefs at the monumental gate guarding the door, the temple, and the walls. Certain finds are also on exhibit at the nearby **Çorum** Museum.

View of the Acropolis

View of lower city and the plain

Below: Temple storage rooms

King's Gate and the walls

Below: Exit from the secret tunnel under the walls

Opposite: Secret tunnel   Above: Lion's Gate   Below: Paved main road

This page, below: Yazılıkaya
open-air temple

This page, right: Storm god of the
Hittites, Late Hittite relief,
Gaziantep Museum

Opposite page, top: Relief showing
procession of twelve gods, Yazılıkaya

Below: Sphinx Gate, Alacahöyük

Gordion

This is a magnificent site located 95km/59miles west of Ankara. It was the capital of the Phrygians, who arrived in Anatolia with migrations from the West, put an end to Troy and the Hittites, and later founded a new state (8ᵗʰC BC). Its name comes from its legendary founder-king, but the most famous of them all was **King Midas**, renowned for his golden touch and his long ears. Passing the bridge over Sakarya River (ancient Sangarios), the site called Yassı Höyük can be seen. After an easy climb to the top, one can see many tumuli, the artificial mounds built as tombs of the royal family. The excavated area is notable for its early megaron-type palace buildings, the earliest mosaic pavements, and a main gate with a strong defense system. The most famous of the thousands of tumuli in Anatolia is this one lying next to the Museum on the site. With its 300m/985ft

Ram's head situla, cermonial brass buckle

diameter, the tumulus is an earth mound 50m/164ft high. Access to the tomb chamber, surrounded by gigantic juniper logs, is from the modern gallery at the ground level. This room, surrounded by stones and pebbles, is the oldest wooden structure ever found in Anatolia. The tomb is attributed to King Midas, and its precious bronze, wood, and other materials are in the Ankara Museum. A peasant named Gordios, who tied up his cart to the temple and was named king, began the famous legend. He who could untie the knot would be the ruler of all Asia. Many centuries later, another king, in the winter of 332 BC, "loosened" the knot with his sword and continued on his way. This Macedonian king, Alexander the Great, inspired by this episode, began his "adventure" to conquer the rest of the world—an operation that lasted only ten years before his sudden death.

Main entrance to Gordion with large tumulus above   Below: Angora goats on the streets of Polatlı, near Ankara

Right: Situla, ceremonial lion buckle found at Gordion

Below: Excavations of tumuli brought to light megaron-plan buildings and the earliest-known mosaic floors.

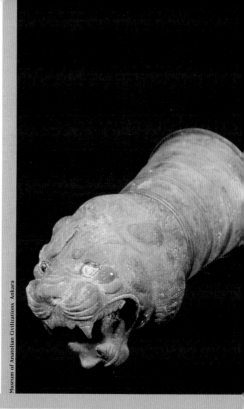

Museum of Anatolian Civilizations Ankara

Konya-Iconium

The historical city of Konya, bearing the same name as the vast Anatolian plain, is the rich granary of Turkey. This is the place where St. Paul was thrown over the high city walls. The Aladdin Mosque, erected on top of the early settlement mound at the city center, is one of the most important Seljuk works of art. The medreses (schools) in the vicinity, contemporaries of the mosque, are now used as museums. While living in Konya, **Mevlana Celaleddin-i Rumi** (1207-1273), Turkish philosopher and Islamic mystic, preached messages of unity and brotherhood and was a light of hope during the dark and difficult years of the 13th C. Every year in December, there is a festivity held in Konya, in which the whirling dervishes perform their ceremony, the "sema" dance. It is a traditional ceremony commemorating the "wedding night" of Mevlana, meaning his union with Allah. The Mevlana

Tiled dome of Mevlana complex

Museum complex, the Archaeological Museum, Koyunoğlu Private Museum, and the 16th C Selimiye Mosque are other places worth visiting. The 19th C church in the town of Sille, to the north of Konya, is cited in certain books, without any historical reference, as a building from very early periods. Konya is also known for another world famous archaeological excavation conducted in Çatalhöyük, near Çumra town, since the 1960s. The first organized town settlement ever found in the course of history is **Çatalhöyük** (7th millennium BC). There were no streets in the settlement, and houses—some of which also functioned as temples of the Mother Goddess, Cybele—were entered from the roof via wooden stairs. Deceased family members were buried under the floors. Among the most interesting artifacts are bulls' head plaster reliefs, the earliest murals on the walls, Çatalhöyük weapons made of obsidian, the first cosmetics (including lipstick), and textile samples. Excavations using the latest techniques continue at the site. On the main route, which passes through Cappadocia and ties the

Earliest examples of seals, Çatalhöyük

Below: Mosque of Alaaddin, model at Miniaturk Park, Istanbul

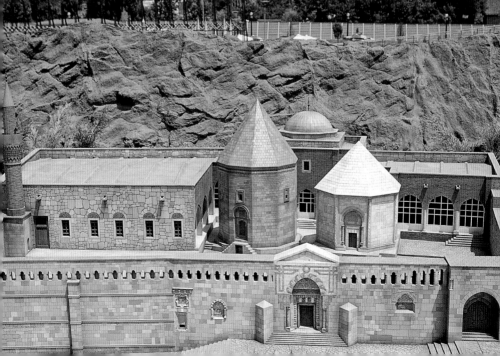

The Whirling Dervish "dance" Mevlana Complex, model at Miniaturk Park, Istanbul

İnce Minare Medrese, now a museum of stone and wood works   Below: İnterior wall tiles, Karatay Medrese Museum

Entrance to İnce Minare medrese

Below: Model of Sultanhanı

Seljuk capital Konya, to the towns of Kayseri and Sivas, is a row of caravansaries that are unique and strictly Turkish in creation. The caravansaries were a series of inns, built in the form of a castle, especially influential in encouraging safe travel and trade. The modern road to the east follows the old caravan route. On the Konya-Aksaray highway the **Sultanhanı Caravansary** has reached our days in perfect condition. It is an impressive castle-like establishment built with local white stone. Water was piped to the site from miles away. Its tower-like higher section on the roof is visible from miles away. Massive walls were installed with round pillars, and the entrance is a huge portal with classical decoration carved in marble. Similar to other 13th C edifices, it served as an inn. The open courtyard has a kiosk-like mosque, a bath, kitchens, and an arcade for the loads, camels, and horses. Another portal is the entrance to a cathedral-like roofed section. Arches and vaults support the roof. At the center is a tower-like higher section with windows for light; from the interior, it is a dome, but from the exterior, it is conical. This section was reserved for caravan travelers, who could stay up to three days without charge.

Copy of Fasıllar Hittite Monument in the garden of the Museum of Anatolian Civilizations, Ankara

Beyşehir

To the North of Beyşehir town, on the shores of the fresh water lake of the same name, stand the interesting **Eşrefoğlu Mosque** and adjacent tomb. The walled outer structure has a timber interior. Wood columns support the flat roof. The perfect timber pulpit and large prayer niche, decorated with cut tiled bricks, are originals from the 13thC.

Important Hittite monuments in the region are **Eflatun Pınar**, next to a holy spring, and **Fasıllar**, a huge uncompleted statue, which may have been part of Eflatun Pınar.

Interior wood, Eşrefoğlu Mosque, Beyşehir

Göreme Region-Cappadocia

The Göreme region, known as Cappadocia in ancient times, has one of the most spectacular vistas in the world. It is located within a triangular area surrounded by the cities of Kayseri-Aksaray-Niğde and is the geographical center of Anatolia. Natural routes that once crossed Anatolia used to pass through or meet in Cappadocia. Today Nevşehir is the provincial center and the shopping center is Ürgüp. Such a variety of enchanting formations can be found nowhere else. It is the highlight of touristic places in Turkey. The Göreme valley and a village by the same name are situated here. In order to take better photographs in the region, one should make the most of the bright and shadowy times of the day. From the high terraces, shots of the valleys below can best be taken by shielding

the lens. The famous fairy chimneys at the entrance to Ürgüp, the northern side of the Uçhisar formation, the Zelve valley and nearby formations can be photographed ideally in late afternoon hours. A flashlight is necessary to take photographs within churches and in the underground cities. Flash is not permitted while photographing the frescoes. As one comes out of Ortahisar onto the Ürgüp-Nevşehir road, there is a road heading to Aktepe, a terrace overlooking a panoramic vista. The Açıksaray (Open Palace) settlement on the Gülşehir-Hacıbektaş road is an interesting spot for its rock formations. The best time to take pictures at the last two spots is before noon. Autumn days are the ideal time for brightness. Along with its unequaled and striking scenery, Göreme is full of artistic products belonging to different civilizations. An active rural life, with all its authentic color and folklore, completes the atmosphere. Most of the churches and monks' cells are decorated with frescoes. Nowhere else do nature, history, art, and life meet in such harmony and unity as this area, one of the Seven Natural Wonders of Turkey.

The type of soil in the area is tufa, exhibiting different colors in different areas. This diversity in color is due to the variations in the metallic content of volcanic eruptions. Although tufa is hard on the surface, it is easy to carve into. Mixed with manure, it is highly productive in agriculture. Steep valley slopes, pyramidal and chimney-shaped formations have been easily carved for ages, for different purposes. The atmosphere of mystery is completed by pointed rock formations called "fairy chimneys". The fortress-like, big block formations are also hardened and accumulated natural formations. The best-known examples of these are Uçhisar and Ortahisar.

No one has yet ventured to name the Seven Wonders of Nature on this earth. The Göreme region would no doubt outshine most candidates. One cannot help feeling that some majestic sorcerer has chosen this place to perform his magical wonders. Everything started with the rise of several volcanoes around the area; for long periods, they erupted and scattered their volcanic dust,

Typical Cappadocian formations: valley erosion, flat terraces, and natural castles

ashes, lava and other remains. Accumulated in the surrounding lakes and valleys, these volcanic residues underwent successive erosions through wind, rain, and temperature changes and started to take countless forms.

Later, a series of earthquakes caused the tilting of the Göreme region toward the Kızılırmak (the Red River) basin and increased the impact of erosion. Its southern boundary is lined with table-shaped mountains and between them lies the Soğanlı Valley, adorned with a variety of formations. To the west, on the slopes of Mt. Hasan, the Ihlara Valley twists and extends as a deep canyon. Great blocks of stone and rock have tumbled from the sides. Ihlara Valley shelters a great number of churches and monastery rooms carved into the rocks.

Just beside Erciyas Mountain, which is the eastern volcano of the region, lies Kültepe (early 2nd millennium BC), a site of the Hittites, the first empire of Anatolia. Kızılırmak River (ancient Halyas), the vital artery of this empire, crosses Cappadocia from one end to the other. Other major excavation sites in the region are:

Rare twin formation   Opposite: Landmarks of the region: classic view of fairy chimneys and Mt. Erciyes volcano

Aşıklıhöyük

This was the one of the earliest settlements in Anatolia (circa 9,000 BC) and engaged in a little farming and mainly hunting-gathering activities. This unique copper-using and trading society was among the first settlements organized and ruled by its leading citizens. Its position is 25km/16miles from Aksaray, en route to the Ihlara Valley, and on the banks of the fertile Melendiz Creek. It possessed the most vital goods of its times: obsidian (volcanic formation like very hard glass) and salt mines. The settlement was divided into wards, and mud brick walls surrounded the narrow streets. The houses were entered from the roofs by wooden stairs. Aşıklı is known as the first planned and walled settlement ever and has the earliest remains of domesticated animals. The mound and its vicinity form an open-air museum area with a parking lot.

Çatalhöyük

Among the many centers in 7000-6000 BC, the most important one, situated in the middle of the Central Anatolian plain, was Çatalhöyük. The mound is near the district of Çumra, 65km/40miles southeast of Konya, and as crow flies about 160km/100 miles to Cappadocia. Among the dozens of mounds on the site, the major excavated one is that of Çatalhöyük, rising on an artificial mound by the side of a small creek. In the excavations carried out in the 1960s a small section of the mound was unearthed. Among its important features are the settlement patterns of the town, as well as the first examples of pottery, agriculture, domesticated animals, home industry, and goods imported from afar. Even more important are the murals decorating the walls of many of the dwellings, the statuettes of the first goddess of humankind (the mother goddess Cybele), and bulls' head plaster reliefs on the walls. The mud-brick houses were built side by side for easier defense. Wooden stairs descending from the flat roofs provided entrance to the houses. Its twelve habitation layers are dated between 6500-5500 BC. Systematic excavations continue in Çatalhöyük and its matchless findings are exhibited in the archaeological museums of Konya and Ankara.

Acemhöyük

Acemhöyük is located atop an artificial mound rising from the plain in the Yeşilova district of Aksaray. Here, rich findings from Early Hittite and Assyrian trading colonies (2000-1750 BC) were unearthed. In recent years, archaeological excavations brought to light the remains of the largest palace complex ever found in Anatolia, with more than forty chambers. The mound was the seat of one of the Hittite principalities, as were Kültepe and other important centers for trade with Mesopotamia.

Kültepe

Situated 20km/13miles to the east of Kayseri, Kültepe is one of the most important Hittite settlements of the Early Bronze Age. The town of Kaneş, the central mound where the Hittite princes lived, and the nearby colony of Karum, where the Assyrians lived, provide the richest findings of this period in Anatolia. Thousands of clay cuneiform tablets, rich ceramic finds, statues and metal artifacts, kings' palaces, shops and warehouses have been excavated at this site and colony town. These finds are exhibited in the Kayseri Museum and the Anatolian Civilizations Museum in Ankara. The city developed after 2000 BC. Its name in the Hittite language was Nesha. The age of written history in Anatolia starts in this city and its contemporaries, with the discovery of cuneiform tablets. The Hittite Confederation's principalities, led by Kültepe and Hattusas, founded the first state in Anatolia (1650 BC).

Roman Eagle at the peak of Mt. Erciyes, statuette from author's private collection

Typical Cappadocian village   Erciyes volcanic mass in spring (below) and in winter (above right)

Below:Orta Hisar town center

Each valley has its own spectacular shapes, created by erosion

Byzantine and Turkish Periods

Anatolia is a natural bridge connecting Asia to Europe. It has, therefore, always been the target of invasions from both the East and the West. Cappadocia functioned as a shelter for Anatolian people seeking refuge during times of chaos. Many tribes in danger found lodging for long periods in these hidden shelters, and underground cities were dug under those mysterious formations that aroused fear in the enemies. Local Cappadocian princes, who gained wide fame for their thoroughbred horses, governed the region until the Roman invasion in 17 AD. There is no sign of a monastic way of life in Anatolia during the early Christian period, but a great many people adopted it in Egypt (Thebaid) and in the Holy Land. After Islamic Arabs conquered these lands, many Christian groups took refuge in the interior of Anatolia and continued their monastic way of life in accordance with their religious

The castle-like Uçhisar formation and snow-white canyon are well worth visiting

beliefs (7^{th}C). In Binbir Kilise (1001 Churches) on the Taurus Mountains in the south, in Heraklia (near Miletus) on Bafa Lake in the west, at Uludağ in Bursa, and finally in the Cappadocia region there was an expansion of monastic life. The mosaic and fresco arts of the Byzantine Empire were practiced in the churches, drawing on Biblical stories. In the capital, artists produced these frescoes, whereas in the provinces, mainly monks practiced the art. Thus the majority of the Cappadocian church frescoes reflect a comparatively primitive provincial style. The Cappadocian churches had to obey the rules of the Iconoclastic Era during the years 726-842. In the rock churches of the Göreme region, simple forms and cross motifs can be seen on naked walls or under deteriorating fresco plasters. Some claim that these motifs belong to the Iconoclastic Period, but they do not. It is quite clear that these churches, dug into rocks, were built according to the principles of their day. Many of the pillared churches in the Göreme region are in a Greek cross plan (four-pillar type), a style which first appeared in the Byzantine capital in the 10th-11^{th}C. Churches built according to this plan must have spread from the capital to the provinces in the

11th-12^{th}C, when the Empire was at its peak of political and artistic activity. In a rather uncreative religious community such as Cappadocia, the use of these plans could be no earlier than this period. It is clear that the walls of churches carved into rocks are according to a plan that originated well after the Iconoclastic period. Therefore the motifs on the walls, claimed to be of Iconoclastic Period, cannot belong to this era. At the end of the 11^{th}C, most of Anatolia came under the rule of the Seljuk Turks. Christians cherished their wide freedom under the tolerant Turkish governments. Some of the Cappadocian churches were built and painted with frescoes during this Turkish period. The Mongolian invasion of the 13^{th}C finally hindered these and other activities. One of the most important national and religious institutions established during the spread of Turkish influence in Anatolia was in the small village of **Hacı Bektaş**, in Cappadocia.

Single-nave and simple vaulted churches are the earliest examples of rock churches in Cappadocia, dating from the 7th-8th centuries. The churches with pillars, domes, and other rock-carved architectural elements are from the 11th-13^{th}C. None of the monasteries, dormitories, refectories, monks' cells, or churches had exposed doors or windows. They were carved into the rock, hidden from the eyes of hostile powers, with no easy access. What are visible today are the remains after extensive damage and collapses of later times. The narrow doors and passageways were equipped with millstone-like, rolling security doors carved on the spot. The ventilation chimneys and windows were disguised. There are unknown numbers of underground cities in the region. Acıgöl, Özkonak, Derinkuyu, Kaymaklı, Mazı and others are open for visitors. These seven- to eight-story cities go meters deep with large and small chambers, halls, churches, and ventilation systems carved out and used by different peoples at different times. Originally the rock-carved settlements were much vaster than what is visible today.

Eastern Christianity embraced an isolated life, with entire families in communal monasteries. As an isolated region, Cappadocia enabled them to lead a spiritual and less dangerous communal life. The limited population had plenty of room in small valleys and vast plateaus. The many graves of children show that families lived all together in big communities. The monks' small, single cells carved into the fairy chimneys are also numerous. The most famous monastic center among the many in these valleys is Göreme, ancient Korama.

The rock formations, suitable for lodging and storage, were easily carved with simple tools. The temperature in the caves is almost the same all year round. Today these rock-cut cavities function as houses, hotels, storage areas, and stables, and are also used for refrigerating apples and citrus fruits. Some of them were recently turned into nightclubs.

Kayseri is the biggest city in the region. Göreme is 100km/70miles from the Kayseri airport. The distance between Ankara and Nevşehir is approximately 300km/190miles. Transportation by bus is also available from Nevşehir to many cities. The local airport has only summer service. The most suitable time for traveling in the region is between early April and late November. The wintertime in Göreme is very cold but also has a striking beauty. The continental climate provides hot days and cool nights during the summer. A rich variety of flowers fills the fields and roadsides in springtime. The most colorful times in Cappadocia are the long and bright autumn days.

Potatoes, onions, and beans are among the most famous agricultural products. Dried apricots and tasty wine are other specialties. Among handmade goods, regional carpets play the leading role.

Tours start from Nevşehir, Ürgüp, Avanos, and other centers, continue on the Nevşehir-Ürgüp highway, passing through this magical panorama with its vineyards, and arrive first at Uçhisar. At the tip of the high plateau, Uçhisar stands in all its glory like a majestic fortress, with myriad openings on its façade due to former collapses. Just outside the small town, on the outskirts of the fortress, is a picturesque little rock hotel. There is an extraordinary view from the ridge just next to this hotel, with an outstanding panorama right at one's feet. Yellow, pink, and gray valley slopes are full of dovecotes with their tiny windows.

After the pause in **Uçhisar**, tours descend into Göreme village. But first, after a short walk, one reaches a panoramic spot with an unequaled view no words can accurately describe. The chief cause of all these formations, the Erciyes volcano, rises in the east with all its grandeur, and can be observed from all the terraces in the region. On the left side of the road descending into Göreme lies the snow-white canyon that starts from Uçhisar, suddenly deepens, and opens to the Kızılırmak valley. The lower sections of these valleys and every available piece of land on their banks are cultivated. A short distance away appears the typical Cappadocian village of Göreme, formerly known as Maçan-Avcılar. The village carries the same name as the region. Today, some of the old houses carved into the rock pyramids are used as restaurants, pensions or hotels. From this spot one reaches the open-air museum of churches and monasteries.

A small burial chapel to the west of Göreme village

Pre-Roman or Roman period rock-carved tomb in the center of Göreme village

380

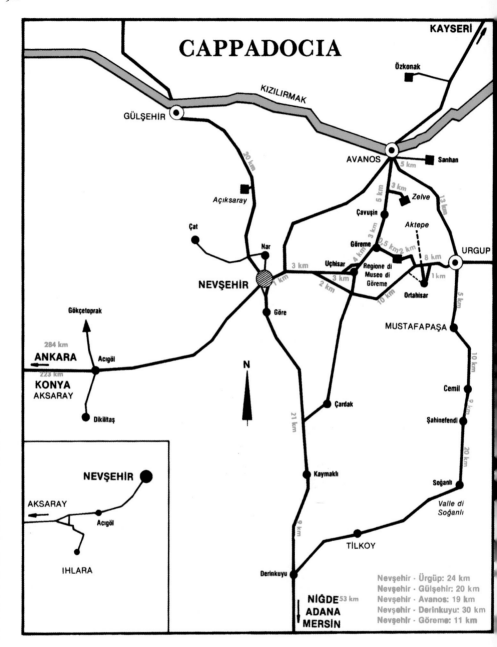

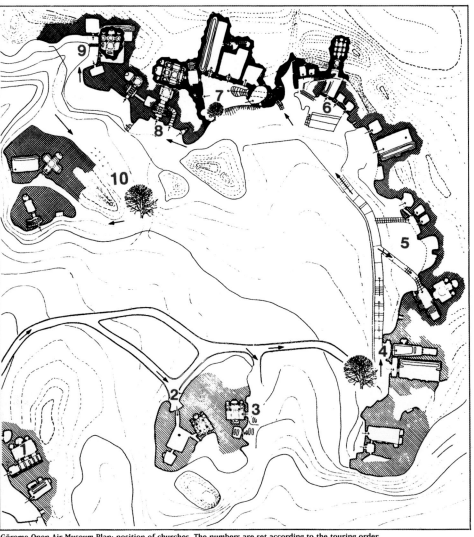

Göreme Open Air Museum Plan: position of churches. The numbers are set according to the touring order.

1 - An unnamed church
2 - The Elmalı church
3 - Church of St. Barbara
4 - The Yılanlı (Serpent) church
5 -6 Refectory and monasteries
7 - The complex of Dark church
8 - An unnamed church
9 - Çarıklı (Sandal) church
10- The Convent

and provincial in style; those of the new church date to the late 10[th]C, in the rare capital style. The frescoes here are of high artistic quality and unique in the region with their dominant blue color and iconographic characteristics. The main and side apses and arch piers give a majestic appearance to the church.

Tokalı (Buckled) Church

The largest church in the valley can be seen on the left, a couple of hundred meters before the parking lot of the Göreme Open-Air Museum. The arched entrance hall is known as the old church, whereas the wider inner one, vaulted over the large nave, is known as the new church. The frescoes of the older church are from the early 10[th]C, rather primitive

Rock-Carved Churches in the Göreme Open-Air Museum

The pillars, vaults, and domes of the

Tokalı church, west wall frescoes

Formation known as the Convent, at the entrance of the museum grounds

churches are completely carved into the rock. The chambers and the refectories of the monasteries here are typical of the whole region. The frescoes on the walls are dated to the 11th and 12th centuries. Their decorations are similar, using traditional themes and subjects, but the tones of color used in them are different. To identify the persons and scenes depicted, artists have written the appropriate names next to the figures. On the big panels, saints are shown life size; in the medallions, smaller bust portraits appear.

Elmalı (Apple) Church

The entrance is from the inner court through a narrow corridor, proceeding through the narrow gateway, into the church. This domed, four-pillared, cruciform church is carved into the rock with all its architectural elements within a square plan. A window, opening out into the valley, illuminates the interior. From under the deteriorating frescoes earlier monochrome red geometrical and cross motifs are seen here and there.

Saint Barbara Church

Saint Barbara Church is located on the backside of the rock in which the Apple Church is located. It is carved out of the rock with only two pillars. Adorned only with simple, primitive decorations drawn right onto the walls, this 11ᵗʰC church was mistakenly described by some sources as an example of the Iconoclastic Period. As mentioned above, this is not possible.

Yılanlı (Serpent) Church

Yılanlı (Serpent) Church is a small vaulted burial chapel. The apse is on the left wall. On it can be seen St. George and St. Theodore killing the Dragon. The figures on the left are Emperor Constantine the Great and his mother, Helena, holding the true cross. The upper ridge of the Serpent Church contains many carved rooms and dining halls.

Karanlık (Dark) Church

Karanlık (Dark) Church is in fact a complex. On the lower level is a dining hall (refectory) and on the upper, a dormitory, the facade of

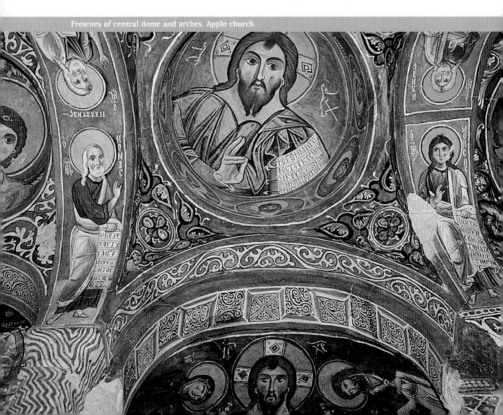

Frescoes of central dome and arches, Apple church

which has collapsed. After the narrow entrance, one climbs up several steps into the narthex of the Dark Church, a classic example of the four-pillared, cruciform, domed type. It has one small window. Due to lack of sunlight, the colors of the frescoes have stayed very bright. The depiction of Jesus on the dome, the birth of Jesus on the left-hand wall, and the transfiguration above the entrance are well-preserved, typical examples. The fresco on the narthex vault depicting the Ascension of Jesus is unique. These frescoes are highly artistic works of art in the capital style and differ from the ones in the other churches of the vicinity.

Çarıklı (Sandals) Church

This domed, cruciform-plan church has two freestanding pillars. The other two pillars and the corner bays are not carved out. Ascended by a flight of stairs, this church is well illuminated via the entrance. Its frescoes, like others in the area, are greatly damaged. The church is named after the footprints carved into the ground.

Transfiguration, Apple church fresco

Red motifs in St. Barbara church

Zelve

One of the most interesting fairy-chimney formations of the region can be seen here. Paşabağ, a couple of kilometers before the valley of Zelve, has twin, triple, and other fairy chimney formations offering a wonderful opportunity for photographers, especially in the afternoon hours. The pyramidal rock formations that rise from among the vineyards or apple and apricot orchards are characteristic of Cappadocia. Zelve consists of two canyons, extending side by side in a deep and narrow valley. The rock formations in this valley have a distinctive pink color. Just beside the museum entrance, there is an oasis-like, cool picnic ground under the old trees. Zelve village, once located in the valley, was moved in the 1950s to the nearer plain, due to erosion threat. Some of the valley slopes are filled with caves and openings caused by collapses.

Opposite page: Crucifixion, Dark church fresco

Below: Paşabağ formations on the way to Zelve valley

Opposite: Single formation with a small chapel   Above and below: Zelve valley at different hours

Avanos

Formerly called Venessa, Avanos is a charming little town situated to the north of Göreme. Anatolia's longest river, Kızılırmak (ancient Halys), passes through the town. Avanos attracts great attention for its locally produced red earthenware pots and jugs, which can be seen in workshops. Their red color comes from the earth of this district. Old houses, hand-woven Turkish carpets, vases, and souvenirs made of onyx and alabaster are other tourist attractions. There is a range of hotels on the other side of the river, in the "new" town. The **Saruhan Caravansary**, situated at the fifth kilometer of the Avanos-Ürgüp road to the east, is a fine example of 13[th]C Seljuk architecture.

Ürgüp

The capped fairy chimneys lining the Nevşehir-Ürgüp road are a "must-stop-and-see". Famous for its wines, Ürgüp is located on a fortress-like

Formations in a valley north of Uçhisar

Gallery and frescoes of St. Theodore church, Yeşilöz village

slope rising from the plain. Because of erosion, the houses on the slope were abandoned. The town is the shopping center of the Göreme region. About 20 km from Ürgüp, on a narrow village road that turns off from the main route to Kayseri, the largest rock church of the Cappadocia region, the Tagar Church, is located in Yeşilöz village. It is a four-pillared, domed church with a gallery, the only one in the region, surrounding its upper level. Dedicated to St. Theodore, the church and frescoes are from the 11th-13th centuries. It receives light from its partially collapsed dome. Ürgüp town has a full range of accommodation.

Ortahisar

At both sides of the junction with the main road are many old and new rock-carved storehouses. Locally produced potatoes and apples, as well as lemons and oranges brought from the Mediterranean region, are kept in these natural cool storerooms for long periods. Ortahisar has developed around a large, fortress-like block formation.

The fortress, used as a settlement throughout the ages, has holes and openings on the façade due to successive collapses. Coming out of Ortahisar in the Ürgüp-Nevşehir direction, there is a road heading north to Aktepe, location of one of the most beautiful and panoramic views in the region, starting from Kızıl Çukur (Red Cavity) and stretching out to Uçhisar on the horizon. The best time to take pictures here is before noon on clear days.

Region's only Byzantine building, now a mosque, Çardak village

Soğanlı Valley

Passing through typical Göreme vistas and crossing over hills and valleys, the Ürgüp-Soğanlı road extends far into the distance. Mustafa Paşa (Sinasos) town is six km from Ürgüp. There is a variety of formations in the Soğanlı valley, which is located on the southern end of Göreme between table-shaped mountains. A great many churches and monasteries, many decorated with frescoes, are situated in the valley and on the slopes.

A church in the Soğanlı valley ➡

Fresco detail

394

Hacı Bektaş

Originally called Sulucakarahöyük, the town has been settled since the Hittite period. In the 13th C it was a small village with only seven houses. The place developed and gained importance when Hacı Bektaş, the founder of the Bektaşi order, eventually settled here. During the severe conditions of the 13th C, he spread his humanistic belief, based on social and religious principles, from this place. The foundation stone of his belief was (divine) love. In the excavations carried out in Sulucakarahöyük since 1967, settlement layers from the Hittite, Phrygian, Roman, and Byzantine periods were revealed. Some of these findings are on exhibit at the Hacı Bektaş Museum, together with ethnographical pieces. There are ample hotels in Nevşehir.

Nevşehir

Settled since the Hittite Period, Nevşehir (New City) is located near a hill with an Ottoman fortress. The 18th C mosque complex built by Damat İbrahim Paşa is a fine example of Turkish architecture. Son-in-law and Grand Vizier to the Sultan, İbrahim Paşa contributed to his birthplace and built this complex with a mosque, theological school, imaret (soup kitchen for the poor), baths, and a library. The Archaeological and Ethnographical Museums are at the city center. **Açık Saray** (Open Palace), a rock-carved settlement on the Gülşehir-Hacıbektaş road, is an interesting spot with its churches and monastery complexes. They differ from the works in Göreme Valley in their decorated façades.

Kaymaklı

Kaymaklı Underground City is in a small town 20km/12miles to the south of Nevşehir. The entrance to the largest and most famous underground city of the region is through the slope of a low hill in the center of the town. The eight-story underground city has been cleaned,

illuminated, and provided with safety measures for the protection of visitors. Kaymaklı, like other underground cities in the vicinity, was designed and built over many generations as shelter against threats and invasions in both the pre-Christian and Christian eras. Ventilation chimneys supplied fresh air to these self-sufficient, relatively safe shelters. Narrow passages separated by round, millstone-like doors connected the stories. The niches for storage jars, the round doors, rooms, the basilica, the meeting room, and the graves are all of major interest.

Derinkuyu

Another underground city 10km/6miles to the south of Kaymaklı, Derinkuyu has a distinguished place among the many well-known underground cities in the region. Some Hittite works and the "Eagle on the Summit" statue symbolizing the Roman conquest were found here and put on display in the museum as evidence of pre-Christian settlement in the region. The Derinkuyu Underground City developed at the bottom of an 85m/280ft-deep shaft. There are dwellings and rooms around the shaft and, at the bottom, a wide semicircular hall used as a meeting hall and church.

Aksaray

The verdant town of Aksaray is located at the Cappadocia turnoff from the main Ankara-Adana route, and offers a rich collection of Turkish historical works. There are large, modern rest stops at the highway junction. By the side of the road leading to Cappadocia, there are three Seljuk Turkish caravansaries, one of which is well preserved, while the other two are in ruins. The 13[th]C **Ağzıkarahan Caravansary**, built with local pink stone in the classical plan, is one of the best examples of typical old Turkish castle lodgings formerly used throughout the Turkish empires. All had monumental portals, open courtyards with surrounding galleries, and small, central mosques built like kiosks. The kitchen, Turkish bath, and quarters for personnel are on one side of the courtyard; the colossal covered section (reminiscent of a cathedral) on the other side offered lodging to travelers up to three days free of charge.

Hasan Dağ volcano and Aksaray in spring

Hüdavent Hatun, a classic example of 14ᵗʰC Seljuk tombs, Niğde. This perfectly balanced and well decorated edifice of local pink stone has an octagonal shape. The interior dome appears pyramidal from the exterior. The city of Niğde, south of Nevşehir, has a citadel and other important historical Turkish monuments and nearby rock-carved churches with frescoes. ⮕

Ağzıkarahan Caravansary, east of Aksaray

Above: Interior of Ağzıkarahan Caravansary

Below: three views of spring color in Cappadocia

Village girls with Hittite hairstyle

The Ihlara Valley-
Peristrema

The Ihlara valley, which completes the Cappadocian sights and tours, differs from the Göreme and Soğanlı valleys. Over thousands of years, the torrential waters flowing from Mt. Hasandağ (3254m/10510ft) and the Melendiz Mountains into the Salt Lake on the Central Anatolian plain formed a deep canyon with innumerable twists. Many large blocks of rocks have tumbled down and filled the slopes of the U-shaped canyon. The valley's depth can hardly be appreciated until one approaches the slopes. At the bottom of the valley, the Melendiz Stream was a source of life for the Christian monasteries and the churches on the wall-like slopes. Selime village, on the northern exit of the canyon, is located among the fairy chimneys at the skirts of the slope of a table-like flat hill. The 16km/10mile-long Ihlara Valley has more than 100 rock-carved churches of various plans and styles, along with innumerable monasteries and chambers. Pürenliseki, Karanlık, Kokar, Ağaçaltı, Yılanlı, and Sümbüllü are the local names of some of the churches close to the stairway descending into the valley. Tours visit a few easily reached churches with the latest frescoes found in the region, from the end of the 13thC. St George is depicted between a man and a woman dressed in the typical Turkish style of that time. The name of Turkish Seljuk Sultan Mesud is inscribed beside that of Byzantine Emperor Andronicos. This is an example of the tolerance shown to Christian subjects by the Turkish state of the time.

Ihlara valley is 16km/10 miles long and has more than 100 rock-carved monasteries and churches. The painting technique and colors of the frescoes here differ from those in the Göreme region. Water from the Melendiz and Hasandağı mountains reach the Salt Lake via this valley's river.

402

Güzelyurt

Güzelyurt (Gelveri) is a village 15km/9miles from the Ihlara Valley and 45km/28miles from Aksaray. One of the highlights of Cappadocia tours, it is renowned for its location and the beautiful examples of 19thC houses. St. Gregory of Nazianus chose this spot for his missionary activities to spread Christianity. Here, the High Church and

Monastery, Red Church, Anargyros Church, Ram and Ahmatlı Churches are open for visits. Another interesting building in the village is the church built in 1891, now used as a mosque.

Interesting rock formations in Selime village at the entrance of Ihlara valley

Kayseri, an important industrial and trading city, has beautiful walls and historic Turkish edifices

Kayseri-
Caesarea

Kayseri had strategic importance for centuries because of its location at the crossroads of Anatolia. It is situated on the northern skirts of Mt. Erciyes (Argeus), an extinct volcano and Turkey's second highest peak (3917m/12.846ft). The archaeological site of Kültepe, 20km/12miles east of Kayseri, was an important trade center in ancient times. A very rich Hittite archive of precious cuneiform clay tablets unearthed here has added greatly to knowledge about the period. This and other finds are exhibited in Kayseri's Archaeological Museum. Kayseri, renowned in the region even before the Roman period, is now a developed trade and industrial center especially famous for its hand-woven silk and wool carpets. The city, which was invaded by the Sassanids and Arabs many times during the 8th and 9th centuries, has almost no remains of the Roman period. The name of the city is a Turkish adaptation of its Roman name, Caesarea. It is famous for Seljuk and Ottoman works. The most important of these are the numerous medreses (schools), türbes (tombs) and the Ulu Camii (Great Mosque), all from the 13[th]C. The Byzantines built the inner walls of the city. Later the Seljuks reconstructed them with additions. The inner castle forms the core of the city today and still has its original shape and character. The new, modern city spreads towards the plain. The Hunad Hatun complex, constructed in 1238, is a typical example of Seljuk architecture with its mosque, medrese (theological school), bath, and türbe. The Çifte Medreseler was the most famous medical school of its time. Among the most important Turkish style tombs, called kümbet, are the Döner Kümbet, the Sırçalı Kümbet, and the Çifte Kümbet. The biggest caravansary in Anatolia, on the Kayseri-Sivas highway, is Sultanhanı, constructed in the classical style in 1236 and still in very good condition. Trade, hand-woven carpets, pastırma (pastrami), and winter skiing

facilities are Kayseri's trademarks. Sinan the Great, Turkish architect of the 16th C, was born in Ağırnas, a small village near Kayseri where there are still traces of houses from that period. The city has a busy airport and a few nice hotels.

Opposite page: Kızılırmak (ancient Halyas), the longest river in Turkey, runs north of Kayseri province

Right: Full-size bronze Roman bathtub, Kayseri Museum

Below: 13th C Alaca Kümbet on the main street of Kayseri

Important Kültepe Hittite settlement east of Kayseri. Excavations on the site are continuing

Museum of Anatolian Civilisation, Ankara

◀▦ Ivory, nude female statuette.
Kültepe 18th c B.C

Sivas

At an altitude of 1275m/4182ft Sivas is the highest and most mountainous city of the Central Anatolian Region. This uneven land of many peaks has sheltered various tribes from the earliest ages. Situated at the junction of the Silk Road and Mesopotamian caravan routes, this was once a busy commercial center. Sebastea was the Roman name of this city. Sivas became a cultural, educational and transportation center during the Turkish Seljuk Empire (12th-13thC). Izzeddin Keykavus Sifahanesi (1217), a former hospital decorated with colorful tiles, is beautiful. Gök Medrese and Buruciye Medrese, both built in 1271, are fine examples of wonderful Seljuk artistic works, while the Ulu Mosque, another significant historical monument, reflects a different style. The Çifte Minareli Medrese is also noteworthy with its twin minarets rising elegantly on both sides of its ornate portal.

Stone-carved decoration with rich baroque detail, Divriği Ulu mosque

During the War of Independence, the National Congress took the decision in Sivas in 1919 to fight for the liberation of Turkey. The school building used then is now the Atatürk and Congress Museum. The iron ore center of Turkey, Divrigi (165km/102miles southeast of Sivas), is also well known for the Ulu Mosque portal of 1229, a unique edifice in Turkish Baroque style, a real masterpiece of stonework. This monumental building has been declared by UNESCO to be one of the prominent cultural heritages of the world. Balikli Kaplica, in the town of Kangal, is an interesting thermal spring filled with tiny fish living in the hot waters, providing a different type of cure for skin complaints. Another special characteristic of this town 68km/42miles south of Sivas are the world famous Kangal dogs. These hardworking sheepdogs are very loyal and friendly. Sivas is an important cereal-producing area at the junction of several railways and highways and linked by air with Istanbul via Ankara. Hotel accommodations are modest.

➠
Next page: Nemrut Dağı, part of the Southeast Taurus chain

⬅ Çifteminareli Medrese, Sivas   Poplar trees in winter

Gaziantep

An important crossroads in every period, the fertile lands of Upper Mesopotamia have housed continuous settlements. Various cultures dominating the region produced rich works of art. The Southeastern Anatolia Region stretching to the east of the city is called the "**Fertile Crescent**" and was the home of the earliest civilizations. Recent excavations provide the world of archaeology with brand-new information from sites uncovered for the first time. The fortress rising on the tumulus at the center of Gaziantep has survived to our time with repairs from the Turkish period. The Archaeological Museum is famous for its collection of Roman mosaics unearthed in **Zeugma**. Orchards yielding pistachio nuts of matchless taste surround Gaziantep, a city well known for its world-famous baklava, in which pistachios are used in abundance,

View of Gaziantep

Medieval castle in city center

Below: Gaziantep's famous pistachio trees

and for its delicious kebabs. The typical old houses with courtyards are protected by preservation laws and have been renovated for new functions. One can find exquisite handmade copperware and inlay work in Gaziantep's vivid markets. A stone quarry dating back to the time of the Hittites (about 3500 years ago) and a unique workshop with many complete and incomplete statues can be visited in the **Yesemek** open-air museum near the town of İslahiye. The tumulus settlement of Sakçagözü near the same town has layers dating from the Chalcolithic Period to the Byzantine Era, but its richest findings are from the Late-Hittite period (8thC BC). The local museum exhibits mosaics and frescoes from Roman villas, innumerable customhouse cargo seals, and other precious finds brought to light during excavations in **Zeugma**, to the east of Gaziantep on a slope of the lake formed by the dam built on the **Euphrates River**. Many more remains await archaeologists in this easternmost trading and military center of the Roman Empire. Gaziantep is a leading, modern industrial city of Southeastern Anatolia where accommodation at all comfort levels is available.

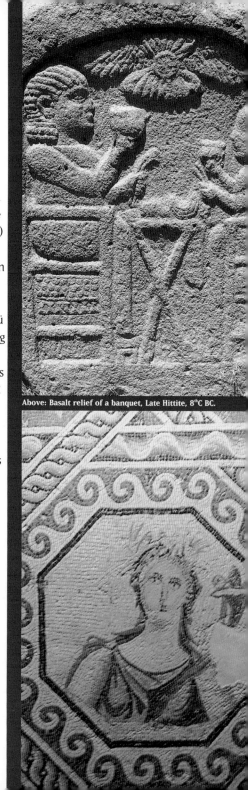

Above: Basalt relief of a banquet, Late Hittite, 8thC BC.

Above and below: Three mosaics from Zeugma, Archaeological Museum, Gaziantep

Şanlı Urfa-Edessa

This is the land of the Prophets mentioned in the holy books. The is the place where King Nimrod threw **Abraham** from a castle into a burning fire, and the fire was miraculously transformed into a pool of fish. Two pools full of holy fish under cool shade trees are still an important and colorful place to visit. The towel on which the face of **Jesus Christ** appeared is also another legend peculiar to this city. Şanlı Urfa is near the Euphrates River, on the hottest plain in the country. With the completion of dams and irrigation canals over the river (the "**GAP**" or Southeastern Anatolian Project), the Harran plain will have the capacity to yield three irrigated harvests a year. Şanlı Urfa's main attractions are the citadel on the acropolis, two columns from the Roman Period, the mosques and pilgrimage places near **Balıklı Göl** (the Pool of Abraham), the restored old houses, the local museum, and the bazaars and hans. Other famous charms of the city are the covered bazaar and the typical teahouses at the hans in the vicinity, the local men's weekly music and conversation gathering called the **sıra gecesi**, chili/red pepper, and çiğ köfte (minced uncooked mutton). Glimpses of the past survive today in the town's mosques from different centuries, narrow streets, and historical beliefs. All along the main road, nearly every rural settlement is located on the slope of a tumulus waiting to be uncovered. **Harran** (Altınbaşak), a settlement 50 km/33miles from Şanlı Urfa, was inhabited from the 3000s BC. It is also the place where Abraham is supposed to have lived (18^{thc} BC !). The excavations conducted in the ancient city have not yet revealed the well-known temple of the moon-god Sin, but remains of the first mosque in Anatolia and its surroundings were unearthed. The minaret with a square plan, a single gate remaining from the city walls and the inner castle are the remains surviving to our day. Harran has become an important and rich agricultural region, owing to its irrigated plain. Old village houses with conical dome-like roofing are interesting to see; this widely used style system provided protection from the extreme summer heat.

Views of Urfa citadel and two Roman columns

Right: Urfa's narrow streets

Far right: Small but colorful
covered bazaar

Below left: Abraham's Pools
filled with sacred fish

Below right: Old coffee shops

Many of the old shops specializing in traditional crafts are disappearing today

Author in a namesake village at Harran plain

Three views of Harran

Nemrut Dağı- Mt. Nemrut- Commagene

One of the most striking monumental works of the ancient world is on this mountaintop near **Adıyaman** and **Kahta** town. From the peak it seems as if one is standing on the top of the world, at a spot where it meets the dome of the skies. The panoramic view is purely amazing. This site is considered one of the Seven Historical Wonders of Turkey. Part of the lake of a dam built on the Euphrates River can be seen down to the east. Looking toward the flat south is a completely different view; this is the first high peak away from Mesopotamia. This is a rocky world: the mountain, the artificial hill, and the colossal statues made from the rocks. With eagles as their only companions, these statues have guarded the mound for over 2,000

Nemrut Dağ's peak, an artificial burial mound, can be seen for many miles

Eastern terrace statues on their thrones

years. Heavy snow covers the peaks in this part of Turkey, so tours to Mt. Nemrut monuments are seasonal from late April to November. The Commagene independent local kingdom was from the early 1stC BC until 72 AD, when the region was annexed to the Roman Empire. A family ruled in this part of the Fertile Crescent, the upper Mesopotamia, the land of earlier Late Hittites, and declared their ancestors to be descended from Persian and Macedonian origins. Near Mt. Nemrut at the west are the remains of **Arsameia** town and one of the best-preserved single-span arched

Roman bridges still in use, the **Cendere Bridge**, dating from the 200s AD. Tree columns were erected to the south of a nearby tumulus, a burial mound for the women of the royal house. Up from the temple-mausoleum (hierotheseion) of **King Atiochos** I of Commagene there is an overall view of these and more. His choice of burial place was at a 2150 m/6500-foot altitude. The starting point of the visit is after a twenty-minute climb from the parking lot to the eastern terrace of the site. The stepped altar in the center and huge statues at the back are the first sight. The artificial burial mound (50m/160 feet) is made of piled-up fist-size rocks. This simple construction was used to avoid future pillaging. If a lower stone is removed, many more will fall from above. Seated on their thrones thirty feet high (10m), five colossal sculptures were guarded and flanked by a lion and an eagle. The heads of four statues (all except Fortuna, goddess of fertility) were toppled and now are lying on the ground. Like the other statues of the western terrace, all have noble features on idealized, late Hellenistic style handsome faces. Seated on their thrones are Hellene gods who were adopted and mixed with the Eastern equivalents, and the king wearing a diadem and a tiara in the Persian fashion of the period. The influence of Eastern and Western cultures is clearly reflected. Facing the statues, from left to right they are Apollo, Fortuna, Zeus, King Antiochos, and Herakles, all looking toward the eastern horizon. The pedestals were engraved with inscriptions about cult ceremonies and laws of the country. Walled with upright stone slabs, the north and south sides of the terrace were decorated with reliefs depicting King Antiochos' ancestors. The narrow north terrace was used as a processional way to the western terrace, which has better-preserved colossal statues lined up in the same order. The mound contains a horoscope carved on a dark stone slab featuring a lion with a crescent, nineteen stars and tree planets. It gives the date July 7, 62 or 61 BC, the coronation date of King Antiochos. Climbing the artificial mound is not permitted. Some tours prefer to watch the beautiful sunrises or sunsets way below the mountaintop. Tours start in the city of Adıyaman and Kahta town. The city of Diyarbakır is another easy alternative, with tours starting in the morning, taking the ferryboat at the lake, and returning in the late afternoon by the same route.

Opposite page, top: Head of Apollo with eagle.

Below: High relief on stone blocks with horoscope lion in center

Diyarbakır

Situated on the tip of a plateau that falls steeply down to the **Tigris River** valley, Diyarbakır is a peerless, magnificent city surrounded by city walls built of local basalt stone. It has been an important center since ancient times because of its location at trading crossroads. Its historical city walls, stretching over five kilometers, are considered the best example of their kind. Built originally in the

Street seller with cold sherbet drink

Roman Period, the city walls received additions partly in the Roman Period and mostly during Turkish administrations. Yet they failed several times to prevent the capture of the city by states reigning in the region. The facades of some of the imposing wall towers are decorated with inscriptions from different periods; the two most important towers (12ᵗʰC AD) can be seen at the southwestern side. All four main gates have survived to our

day. The partially circular inner side of the wall is full of crowded and vivid streets and alleys, with examples of religious and civilian Turkish architecture. The oldest mosque in Anatolia surviving to the present day is the **Ulu Cami** (11ᵗʰC). Columns and capitals from the Roman period, exquisite Seljuk inscriptions, fountains, and a pyramidal-roofed portico for latecomers decorate the vast courtyard. The wooden roof of the rectangular-plan mosque rises on the pillars inside. The Şeyh Matar Mosque, built around 1500, is the only one with a minaret rising on four columns. The keep, on the eastern side of Diyarbakır, is separated from the city by high walls. The old hans (large commercial buildings), the caravansary, the small covered bazaar, hamams (baths), and churches continue to function. Some of the old houses with courtyards are now used as museums. The Archaeological Museum and the museum dedicated to a great Turkish intellectual, **Ziya Gökalp**, are places of interest. The **Bridge** with ten arches (11ᵗʰC) over the Tigris and the **Atatürk Kiosk** on the slope (15ᵗʰC)

Old Turkish bridge over the Tigris with city walls behind

Below: City view

are among the symbols of this rapidly expanding city, which has spilled well beyond its city walls. Highlights are two 12ᵗʰC monuments—the **Ulu Camii** in the town of **Silvan** in the east and the huge single-span **Malabadi Bridge**, one of the most beautiful bridges of antiquity—and the cave settlements in the town of **Eğil**. Today Diyarbakır is also famous for another reason: the earliest example of a village settlement has been discovered in the caves near the Neolithic settlement of **Çayönü**, located near the town of Ergani in the north. Çayönü, in addition to

other sites uncovered recently in the region, has gained fame in the world of archaeology for its planned quarters, the first agricultural activities and domestication of animals, and the earliest pottery finds. Diyarbakır is also famous for its very big watermelons and other honey-sweet melons, grown on the sandy banks of the Tigris. Hotels in all categories are available in the city.

Previous page: Southwestern walls of Diyarbakır

Below left: Southeastern walls, overlooking Tigris River.

This page, top: Roman capitals and column, probably from a theatre, reused in Ulu Mosque courtyard.

Below right: Square minaret of Ulu Mosque

Top: Minaret on four columns

Typical old street

Detail of Behram Paşa Mosque

Below: Atatürk Köşk and another typical residence

◄▬ Çayönü excavations   Above: Malabadi Bridge   Below: Silvan Ulu Mosque

Left: In the summer heat in Diyarbakır, any cool place can be right for a nap.

Right: Villager posing with his sheep

Below left: At a coffeehouse, watching the world go by

Center: Preparing homemade bread

Right: Karacadağ village girl checking the boiling wheat cauldrons

Mardin

Included on the World Heritage list, Mardin is a unique town where time has stopped. The endless Mesopotamian plains halt here on a hill with an unconquerable acropolis-citadel, and the town runs down the narrow streets on the slopes. The local creamy-white limestone has been used in its architecture and worked like embroidery. Looking down from the terraces or the restaurants to the south of the main street, one can watch the plain take on different colors at various times of the day. Here church belfries stand among the minarets. The mosque, medrese (school), and the other monuments are outstanding pieces of architecture, unique to this surrounding. The **Jakobids** (Syriacs living in this region) were the first tribe to accept Christianity; their historical monastery, **Deyruz Zafaran**, is an important site to visit. **Hasankeyf**, at the slowest running section of the river Tigris, is of particular interest because of the

current controversy over a planned dam that may leave this site under water, as well as for its broken Roman/Turkish bridge, old cave dwellings, and a unique Turkish tomb on the plain. The cliff rising up from the river was the location of 13[th]C rulers' residences. Diyarbakır, equipped with all the facilities of a metropolis, is just an hour away.

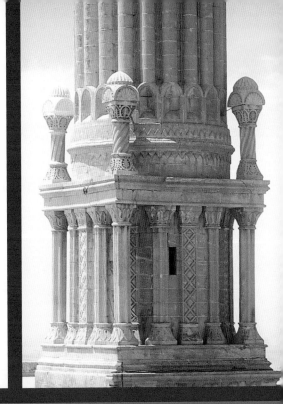

Below left: View of Mardin from the plain

Right: Typical minaret of the region

Below right: Cliffside houses of Mardin

View of Mesopotamian plain from the city

Below: Minaret and belfry side by side

Deyruz Zafaran monastery

Below: "No comment!"

Above: Few ox carts are still in use   Above right: Tent residences for semi-nomadic villagers

Below: Village life: Threshing, spinning, and preparing bulgur

Eastern Anatolia Region

Malatya

It lies in a fertile plain watered by a tributary of the Euphrates and is surrounded by high ranges of the eastern Taurus Mountains. The modern town was founded in 1838 near two earlier settlements. The ancient Hittite city of Malitiya, where the earliest settlement dates back to 4000 BC, is 6 km/4miles north on the site of present-day **Arslantepe**. Its successor, the Roman and medieval city of Melitene, now called Eski (Old) Malatya, is 10km/6miles northeast.

Malatya was an important road junction of the Roman Empire's eastern frontier. The Seljuk Ulu Cami "Great Mosque" and the caravansary both date from the 13thC. In 1515 the city was incorporated into the Ottoman Empire. The Archaeological Museum displays important local findings. Inönü University was founded at Malatya in 1975. The city is the regional market for agricultural goods and a busy industrial center. Malatya's dried apricots are tasty and world famous. This green city has some nice new hotels and daily flights to Ankara and Istanbul.

←▥

Previous page: Akdamar Island, Lake Van

Malatya's famous dried apricots

Bitlis

This small city, ideal for a brief stopover, lies midway between Diyarbakır and Van in a narrow gorge that offered easy control of the strategic curving pass. Bitlis, named after one of Alexander the Great's generals, has a medieval castle and a few historic mosques. The district is a center for quality tobacco production. The city's masonry monuments were built with the local dark stone. **Tatvan** on the western shore of **Lake Van** has a passenger and train ferry service to and from city of Van. **Nemrut Dağı** (Mt. Nemrut), with a deep crater lake bubbling with volcanic hot springs, is to the north of town. The ruins of **Ahlat**, 44km/27miles north of Tatvan on the west shore of Lake Van, are the remains of an important Seljuk Turk city of art and culture. In the 12thC this city was the capital of the Turkish state that ruled the Van basin. Several mausoleums are among the best examples of Seljuk funerary architecture and decoration. In the Seljuk cemetery there are beautifully inscribed monumental tombstones from the 12thC.

Van-Tuşpa

Railroad and partial highway transportation to Iran is possible via this border city. Lake Van is the biggest lake in Turkey, and there are regular ferryboat services between its two shores, from Tatvan to Van. Eastern Anatolia's greenest and bluest panorama can be found here. To the north, **Mt. Süphan** (4058m/13,310ft), an extinct volcano with a huge crater, dominates the view. The ruins of the former city, which was demolished in the local turmoil during World War I are is to the south of Van Castle (the former Urartu Acropolis) with its 2-km-long walls erected at lakeside, on the top of a huge rock formation. On the cliffside, tomb chambers, temples, cuneiform inscriptions, and a secret tunnel, with a thousand steps reaching the cisterns in the plain, are remains of the Urartians, who reigned in the region in the 10th-6thC BC. The remaining Ottoman monuments of **Old Van** are mud brick walls rising on the rocks, the remains inside the citadel, the two beautiful mosques and the twin türbes to the south of the acropolis.

Urartu and old Van citadel on shores of Lake Van

Below: Citadel and ruins of old Van

Of special interest in this region are the fertile plains by the lake, early trade routes of strategic importance, and the prehistoric carvings in the surrounding caves. Toprakkale, and, 24km/15miles to the east, **Çavuştepe** (open for visit) are fine examples of high Urartian castle-settlements. Their heritage also includes good examples of hydraulic engineering (water channels), excellent metal objects, city and temple planning, and masterworks of masonry. Some of these finds are exhibited in the local museum of Van and the Anatolian Civilizations Museum in Ankara. To the east of the city, 65km/40 miles away, two Turkish monuments, the **Hoşap Castle** rising on the former Urartian fortress and the bridge in front of it, create a beautiful vista. The town of Ahlat located on the opposite shore of the lake and **Gevaş**, situated at the south, are important places to visit with their Seljuk cemeteries and türbes (monumental tombs). Reached by motorboat from near Gevaş, **Akdamar Island**, housing a 10th C church, welcomes visitors. This Armenian "Church of the Holy Cross", with a cruciform plan and a dome covered with a conical roof, has beautiful stone carvings. The interior is decorated with frescoes. Biblical scenes, reliefs of royal figures, floral decorations, and animals are depicted on the exterior of this famous and well-preserved church of East Anatolia. The water of the lake is alkaline and a few kinds of small fish live in it. Van is also very famous for its beautiful kilims, herb cheese, and the unusual Van cats, known for their eyes of different colors and their love of swimming. There are some nice hotels in the city and direct flights to/from major cities.

16th C mosque in old Van

Van cat

➠ **Next page: Lake Van and Süphan Dağı volcano**

Akdamar Island: spring scene; Folkdancers welcome visitors; Church façade

Çavuştepe Urartu ruins

Above: Hoşap Castle

Below: Tombs in Gevaş and Ahlat

Erzurum

Some of the mounds in the vicinity are from the Chalcolithic Period and others yield finds from the Urartians. Rising on a high plateau surrounded by mountains, this historical city was at an important crossroads. From the Roman Period until the beginning of the 19thC, it was significant as a strategic border town and customs post. The Silk Road coming from Asia stopped at this point, where goods were bartered. Erzurum changed hands a few times between Russia and Turkey until the end of World War I, and was badly damaged in the meantime. Today it is a growing trade and winter sports center. It spreads towards the plain from the slopes of the mountain and contains a large and well-established university. The outer walls of the Old City no longer exist, but the inner walls have survived to the present day. The Tepsi minaret and Ulu Cami (the Grand Mosque), erected on 40 pillars with a flat roof, are both from the 12thC. Çifte Minareli Medrese (the Twin Minaret theological school) is a

Çifte Minareli Medrese in Erzurum

monumental example of the open courtyard style. Next to its magnificent portal are twin brick minarets decorated with blue tiles, but now only half their original height. Students' rooms on two floors surround the courtyard across from a large türbe. Üç Kümbetler (Three Tombs), one of the symbols of the city, is behind the medrese and is typical of monumental Turkish tombs of the 12th-13th centuries. Yakutiye Medrese (14th C), at the crossroads of the city center, is a fine example of a medrese with a covered courtyard and four vaulted halls. With its richly decorated portal and two minarets, one tiled and both lacking their top half, this medrese functions as an ethnographical museum. The 16th C caravansary, Taşhan, is now a shopping center for handmade goods. Oltu taşı, the locally mined black amber, is used in silver jewelry and the famous prayer beads. In Erzurum nature turns white during the long winters. With full modern facilities, plus long ski tracks, nice hotels serve winter ski guests just 6-7 km from the city center. Findings from the region are exhibited in the Archaeological Museum. Javelin (Cirit) on horseback is an old sports tradition of this district.

Next to the Erzurum-Arvtin highway stands the great Georgian Church of

Öşk-Vank in Çamlıyamaç village. This 10ᵗʰC cathedral is in quite good condition and the central dome is still in place. Scattered farther north throughout the mountain ranges, there are a dozen or more churches of the same period.

Opposite page: Taşhan, an old caravansary, is today a market

Above: Üç Kümbetler (Three Tombs)

Below: Yakutiye Medrese

Ağrı Dağı-
Mt. Ararat

At any season when the sky is clear, Mt. Ararat (Ağrı Dağı)'s conical mass offers a fascinating view. This panorama compares favorably with other great world mountains and is one of the Seven Natural Wonders of Turkey. To the east of Great Ararat (Büyük Ağrı), which is 5165m/16,945ft high, is Lesser Ararat at 3896m/12,778ft. Neither of these inactive volcanoes has craters. Beyond 4000m/13,000ft, Mt. Ararat, the highest mountain in Turkey, is covered with snow all year long. The biggest glacier is also here, and its northern side may be the longest uninterrupted slope in the world. Visitors need permission to climb the mountain. The fertile **Iğdır Plain** on the south side of the mountain has a very different climate; here Mediterranean crops are grown. To the south, the plateau of Doğubeyazıt is well known for its cold climate. The busiest border gate of the historical transit highway to and from Iran is here, in Doğubeyazıt. The mountain can be viewed even

Ağrı Dağı in August (below) and in early April (opposite)

better from this side. According to the Old Testament, **Noah's Ark** landed on Mt. Ararat but according to the Koran, it was on Cudi Mountain in the south. One of the lava formations close to the summit looks just like a huge boat. The mind-boggling question, "What happened to the waters that rose to 5000m/15,000ft during the flood?" is still unanswered.

İshak Paşa Palace

Climbing to the southern slopes of the mountain, the road from the town of Doğubeyazıt reaches an 18thC palace complex, resembling an eagle's nest. The breathtaking vista could inspire a novelist or moviemaker. Following the classical layout of Turkish palaces, buildings surround the courtyards. The stonework is a blend of Seljuk, Persian, and Indian styles. The selamlık (official part), the mosque, the harem (ladies' quarters), the kitchen, and the türbes (tombs) of the complex are quite remarkable. Recently copper roofing replaced the long-gone originals.

Ishak Paşa Palace from a distance. Opposite: Inner courtyard with mosque and tombs

Rural scenes of Eastern Turkey

One small village, eleven kids, six hair colors

Below A village wedding ceremony near Sarıkamış

Kars and Ani

Kars is another important border city of Turkey. On a high plateau covered with grasslands, a citadel-acropolis stands atop a steep hill above a creek with the same name as the city. In the course of history it has changed hands many times. The spacious grid plan of the city and some of the stone buildings date from the time of the Russian occupation. Although the 12thC citadel seems intact, there are few remains of the city walls. The 10thC Apostles' Church was converted for use as Kümbet Mosque. The economy depends on cattle dealing, and Kars is also very famous for its cheese. The winter is long and hard. The Archaeological Museum displays local findings. **Sarıkamış**, a nearby town surrounded by pine forests, is a world-class winter resort. There are two ski-resort hotels with ideal skiing tracks.

Citadel of Kars

Opposite: Kümbet Mosque | Above: Village near Kars in winter

Ani

Located right on the Turkish-Armenian border, on the upper plains of a canyon to the west of Arpaçay River, Ani is a ghost ruin protected by a splendid city wall on the north and a deep valley to the west. Research at its citadel-acropolis has dated the earliest settlements back to the 4000s BC. The visible architectural remains are from the Armenian, Arab, and Turkish periods between the 10th-13th centuries, and are noted for their fine stonework. Armenian Bagratid Kingdom remains include the Cathedral in the center of the town; the Tigran Honentz Church, decorated with frescoes and set on the slopes of Arpaçay River; the Maiden's Church on another terrace; a nearby half-ruined, round-plan church dedicated to Jesus Christ; and others either intact or visible only at foundation levels. The remains of the bridge, certain mosques, a caravansary, part of the city walls, and a palace are from the Seljuk period. The ruins at Ani are 45km/28miles from Kars.

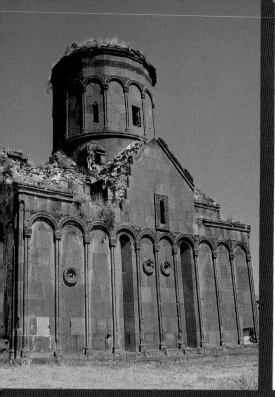

Left: Well-preserved Tigran Honentz Church

Below: Main cathedral of Ani, in the center of the city

Opposite: Rotunda-plan Church of the Redeemer

⯈
Overleaf: Remains of old Turkish bridge on the Arpaçay River

Black Sea Region

476

The **Black Sea region** is a unique place in the world with its green shores, a reflection of the deep green forests rising above the shoreline. The richest and most extraordinary flora, not only in Turkey but in all the Middle East, the Mediterranean coasts and this climatic zone, are seen along these shores. From the Bosphorus strait along the coast to the eastern border with Georgia, one first encounters the deciduous

forests and beyond that the hazelnut groves, providing 70% of the world's production. Then comes the tobacco cultivation in the plains, and going farther east, cornfields and tea plantations on the slopes. Dense endemic forests start to appear as one travels farther inland. Bare peaks of high mountains rise behind the shore. Historical routes descending from East Anatolia first meet the high green pastures, and as they pass the clouds and descend into the valleys, they reach the spruce, red pine, chestnut, and other types of forests. The richness of the

The Southernmost heights above the tree line of a Black Sea valley

Alpine flora and fauna cannot be expressed in words. While all kinds of flowers and insects enrich the multicolored valleys, rivers flowing through these valleys reach the Black Sea with their white, frothy, roaring, and wildly running waters. The slopes above the clouds are the temporary summer pastures and houses of the people living in the villages below. The atmosphere of **Rize** and **Artvin** provinces is matchless, and each valley is a world in itself. Chains of fortifications, castles, settlements, 9th-10thC **Georgian churches**, and opportunities for mountain trekking attract many visitors. The river Çoruh is a well-known rafting spot in spring. Among the many monasteries and churches, the Georgian Oşk-Vank Basilica is the largest and in good condition. **Kaçkar Mountain** is the favorite region for a few days of trekking. A planned series of dams on the district's rivers will change the view, but will add more electric power to meet the country's needs. Every June the **Kafkasor yayla** (summer settlement) near Artvin hosts a unique bullfighting spectacle. Crowds of visitors, as well as all the locals, enjoy this bloodless event in which the bulls fight until one gives up and runs away. Artvin

Uzungöl, Trabzon

Below: A valley and a village

Köknar village, east of Trabzon

A vegetable garden at every house

Below: Typical valley near Rize

is on a mountain with an almost vertical slope and commands a beautiful view of the deep and narrow **Çoruh River** valley. Just next to the city, a large dam will add more color to the green slopes. Tea is an important industry on the Black Sea coast. Turkey's **Sarp village**, customs gate to Georgia, is in this province. Accommodations in Rize are better than in Artvin.

Above: Gathering winter grass for cattle

Below: Two river and bridge scenes

Two of the Eastern Black Sea region's many Georgian churches: Öşk Vank (far left) and Rabat (left)

Below left: Hawks are commonly used for hunting in this region

Right: The rich flora includes mushrooms (some, like these, are poisonous)

Below: Coastal road along the Black Sea, near the Georgian border

Left: Preparation for fishing

Below left: Local bread varities

Right: Market day in a coastal town

Below: Beautiful alpine flowers
in the forest

Right: Tea plantation

Far right: Cutting and carrying
tea is women's work

Below: Tobacco for cigars

Below right: Drying, cleaning, and
inspecting hazelnuts

Overleaf: Downtown Trabzon
and harbor
⠀➡

Trabzon-
Trebizond

Trabzon is the most important port city among the coastal towns that have survived to our day. In *Anabasis:The Return of the Ten Thousand* (403 BC), Xenophon described the mountain passes, routes, and local customs in great detail. Sinop and Samsun in the west were settlements of equal importance in history. Silk Road caravans loaded their goods onto ships in Trabzon, and the port is still important today. The old city rests on a flat terrace, flanked by deep valleys. It first appeared in history as a colony of Miletus, along with other colonies founded in 7th-6thC BC. The Roman city walls have survived to our day thanks to repairs in the Byzantine period. After the Fourth Crusade seized and sacked Constantinople, the imperial family of the Comnneni founded a kingdom here. The historical monuments and

Roman walls of old Trabzon

Opposite: Atatürk Museum

the works of art from this period, and those from after the Turkish conquest, are the treasures of the city. The Hagia Sophia Museum on a terrace overlooking the sea, 13thC churches converted into mosques, later mosques, the Atatürk Kiosk, and Boztepe, the panorama hill of the city, are places worth visiting. Fish caught in the Black Sea, especially turbot and anchovy, are very tasty. This busy commercial town has a large university. The **Sumela Monastery**, founded on a dark rock above a narrow valley 45km/28miles to the south of Trabzon, is renowned

Interior and exterior of Hagia Sophia Museum, Trabzon

as the easternmost monastery of Byzantium. The first records of the monastery are from the 13[th]C, but like other holy places, it is shrouded in legends dating back to the 3rd and 4th centuries. It is an important site to visit, and the difficult, steep, and narrow path winding up to the monastery can be traveled partially by motor vehicle today. A cave was converted into a church and decorated with frescoes. The monastery building and other rooms have been restored. This valley, with its precious historical works, is the most frequently visited in the region and is one of the Seven Natural Wonders of Turkey. With its airport and hotels, Trabzon is an ideal starting point for excursions to the magnificent valleys, unique forests, high plateaus, and mountains lying to the east. Seafront cities, towns, and villages lie very close to each other to the west. **Giresun** and **Ordu** are small, modern, and picturesque cities with few memories of the past.

Friday noon service in summer, İskender Paşa Mosque, Trabzon

Sumela Monastery interior and (opposite) exterior

Palovit Falls near Zilkale, Rize

Below: Ayder yayla houses, Rize

Forest roads of a valley, east of Trabzon

Below: So many beautiful flowers, never enough film!

Opposite page:

Above: Kaçkar Mt. peaks, Artvin

Below: Pokut yayla settlement, Rize

This page:

Left: Three girls with local hair covers, Rize

Below: East of Kaçkar Mt. upper Barhal river, Artvin

Samsun-Amisos

Amisos was a 7thC BC colony of Miletus of Ionia. Between two very fertile plains, Samsun today is a commercial city with a full range of accommodations and an airport. On **19 May 1919**, Atatürk landed at this harbor to organize the Independence War. Turkey celebrates this date by honoring Turkey's youth and commemorating Atatürk. His elegant statue on horseback is a landmark of Samsun. **İkiz Tepe**, 55km/30miles to the west and situated on the Bafra plain, is the oldest known ruin of the Black Sea coast. It was settled from the 4th millennium BC until the Hellenistic period. Rich metals, high-quality textiles, and burial offerings found in the excavations are on display in Samsun's Archaeological Museum. No marble or stone was used in this site because of the abundant forests.

➠
Next page: Black Sea coastline, west of Sinop

Ikiztepe excavation site

Opposite: Atatürk statue, Samsun

Sinop

This city, settled on a strategically important peninsula, is the only safe natural harbor of the Black Sea region. Beautiful seashores offer miles-long sandy beaches, and green mountain ranges rise along the interior. Sinop is a small and pleasing city with few remains of the past. Downtown Sinop is on an isthmus connecting the peninsula to the mainland. According to legend, the **Amazons** founded Sinope, naming it after their queen, Sinova. The first recorded settlement was the 7thC BC colony of Miletus. It ultimately became the most flourishing settlement and naval base on the Black Sea. The **philosopher Diogenes** (famous for carrying a lantern in Athens in daytime to search for a honest man and for living in a barrel) and the 2ndC BC Pontic kings were natives of this city. The Roman general Lucullus captured the seaport in 70 BC, and the city

Downtown Sinop, fortifications, and harbor

was nearly destroyed by fire. Sinop's existing monuments include a ruined ancient citadel, rebuilt during Byzantine and Seljuk periods; remains of a Temple; a Byzantine basilica; some towers at the city walls; and the Aladdin Mosque (1214), whose religious school now houses the local museum. Sinop links to Samsun in the east via a nice highway. A curving road following the coastline to the west leads to **Amasra**, a lovely summer resort on a peninsula, and to **Zonguldak**, the center of Turkey's coal mining industry. Fish restaurants by the harbor and several hotels add to the town's appealing ambiance.

Hamsilos Fjord, 11km/6 miles to the west, is the only fjord in the country. Gerze, situated on a peninsula 40 km southeast of Sinop, has fine beaches, meadows, restaurants, and parks.

Hamsilos, Turkey's only fjord, west of Sinop

Western Black Sea: A typical beach   Above: West of Cide, Gideros cove   Below: Historic Amasra

510

Amasya

With its natural setting and historical monuments, Amasya is a charming little settlement in the narrow valley of Yeşil Irmak (Green River). The fertile fields of this area, and

Gök medrese

the city's position on an ancient busy road to the Black Sea, were the advantages of ancient Amaseia, homeland of the famous geographer Strabo. The ruin of a citadel over the rocky facade shelters the valley and bridges. On the steep facade there are impressive rock tombs of the Pontus kings. The kingdom reached its zenith under **Mithradates VI Eupator** (c.115-63 BC). A struggle with Rome made this king the very first national hero of a twenty-five-year independence war. After his army's victory, Julius Caesar sent the famous message from here to Rome: "Veni, vidi, vici", that is, "I came, I saw, I conquered". Well-preserved Turkish

edifices include the 13thC Seljuk Burmalı Mosque, the 15thC Yıldırım Bayezid Mosque and complex, the 14thC Bimarhane (mental hospital) with lovely reliefs around its portal, the amazing octagonal Kapi Aga Medrese, the Torumtay Mausoleum, the Gök Medrese, and traditional mansions. Amasya was much favored by the early Ottomans; crown princes often served here as governor for their first official experience. The Archaeological Museum of Amasya has an interesting collection.

◄ Previous page: Kurucaşile Beach and winding roads of the western Black Sea coast

► Pontus kings' rock-cut tombs and medieval acropolis above traditional Turkish houses on the Yeşil Irmak River

INDEX

A

Abdülmecid : 150, 160
ablution fountain : 96, 103, 170, 176, 178
Abraham : 53, 416
Abraham's Pools : 418
Acemhöyük : 371
Achaeans : 184
Achaeminian rule : 54
Acıgöl : 377
Acroterium : 242
Açıksaray : 366
Adana : 325, 330
Adıyaman : 27, 29, 64, 424, 426
Aegean : 46, 143, 220, 226
Aegean cities : 53
Aegean culture : 54
Aegean islands : 253
Aegean region : 6, 14, 55, 204
Aegean Sea : 10, 14, 92, 200
Aegean shores : 253
Aegean world : 82, 183, 348
Aeneas : 47
Aeolian immigrations : 53
Aesculapium : 195, 196
Aesculapius (god of medicine) : 195
Afrodisias : 6, 231
Afyon : 239
Agora Baths : 306
agricultural products : 84, 378, 448
agriculture : 52, 180, 367, 370
Agaçalti : 400
Agirnas : 405
Aglasun : 296
Agri Dagi : 7, 30, 460
Ahlat : 449, 451
Ahmet III, fountain of : 108
Ahmet III, library of : 113
aircraft carrier : 146
airline fleet : 80
airports : 30, 246, 405, 493, 500
Aizanoi : 6, 239
Aizanoi Temple : 242
Akdamar Island : 448, 451, 455
Akhisar : 207, 208
Aksaray : 7, 40, 364, 366, 370, 371, 396, 397, 402
Aktepe : 366
Alaattin Keykubat : 312
Alaca Kümbet : 405
Alacahöyük : 43, 48, 53, 349, 354
Alaçati : 201
Aladdin Mosque : 359, 505

Alahan monastery complex : 317
Alaiye : 312
Alanya : 4, 7, 258, 288, 312, 314, 316
Alasehir : 208
Alexander the Great : 43, 49, 50, 54, 55, 106, 186, 192, 200, 206, 210, 211, 223, 229, 284, 295, 299, 302, 326, 333, 356, 449
Alexander the Great, Sarcophagus of : 104
Alexandria Minor : 333
Alexandria of Egypt : 213
Alexandria Troas : 6, 186, 187
Allied fleet : 180
Allom, Thomas : 4, 11, 15, 209, 211
Alparslan : 60
alphabet reform : 57
alphabets : 60
Alpine fauna : 477
Alpine flora : 34, 477
Amaseia : 48, 510
Amasra : 505, 507
Amasya : 7, 510
Amazons : 504
ambassadors : 140
ambo (pulpit) : 102
Amik plain : 333
Amisos : 500
Anabasis : 47, 55, 326, 490
Anadolu fortresses : 142
Anamur : 7, 316
Anamurium : 316
Anargyros Church : 402
Anatolia : 6, 7, 10, 30, 40, 43, 46, 47, 49, 50, 52, 53, 54, 55, 57, 61, 70, 80, 82, 183, 192, 205, 206, 229, 242, 296, 344, 348, 356, 366, 368, 370, 371, 375, 376, 390, 403, 404, 412, 414, 416, 428, 446, 451
Anatolian cities : 56
Anatolian civilizations : 43, 106, 270
Anatolian Civilizations Museum in Ankara : 4, 42, 47, 50, 297, 342, 347, 348, 358, 364, 371, 406, 451
Anatolian culture : 55
Anatolian dress : 183
Anatolian Fortress : 148
Anatolian hairstyle : 183
Anatolian Mother Goddess : 242
Anatolian navigation equipment : 183
Anatolian people : 375
Anatolian plain : 359
Anatolian treasure : 185
Anatolian weapons : 183
Anaxagoras (physicist) : 47
Anaximander : 226
Anaximandros : 47

Anaximenes (philosopher) : 47, 226
anchovy : 492
ancient citadel : 505
ancient cities : 201
ancient coins : 104
ancient ruins : 306
ancient settlements : 299
ancient sites : 288
ancient societies : 226
ancient statues : 104
ancient theatre : 302
Ancient Theatre, Bodrum : 246
ancient times : 428
ancient walls : 253
ancient world : 142, 204, 306, 424
Andronicos (Byzantine Emperor) : 400
Anemurium : 316
angels : 102, 136
Angora cats : 342
Angora goats : 342, 357
Angora rabbits : 342
Anitkabir : 344
Ani : 469
animal husbandry : 52
Ankara : 22, 57, 80, 130, 152, 200, 342, 343, 347, 348, 356, 357, 377, 409, 448, 451
Ankyra : 342
Antakya (Antioch) School of the Roman Age : 98
Antakya : 7, 49, 52, 332, 333, 339
Antalya : 6, 18, 19, 47, 52, 258, 285, 288, 292, 293, 295, 302, 306, 312
Antalya Bay : 285, 292, 316
Anthemios : 99
Anthony and Cleopatra : 326
Antioch : 7, 49, 333
Antiochos, King : 425, 426
Antiphellus, ruins of : 274
antiquity : 195, 213
Anzac (Australian and New Zealand) troops : 180
Aphasa : 210
Aphrodisias : 1, 6, 55, 231, 234, 299
Aphrodisias school of sculpture : 232
Aphrodite : 183, 184, 231, 232
Apollo : 46, 229, 270, 334, 426
Apostles : 333
Apple Church : 384
apricot : 378, 387, 448
apse : 102, 103, 382
aqueduct : 160, 238, 285, 302, 306, 334
Arab attacks : 56, 299, 306, 326
Arab conquests : 56
Arab invasions : 317

Arab siege : 135
Arab world : 59
Arabia, deserts of : 80
Arabic calendar : 56
Arabs : 50, 174, 403, 469
arch of triumph : 140
archaeological artifacts : 104
archaeological collection : 160
archaeological excavations : 40,
89, 192, 210, 226, 359, 371
archaeological findings : 192, 266,
313
Archaeological Museum : 104, 106,
178, 201, 208, 270, 292, 359, 371,
412, 428, 448, 458, 467
archaeological remains : 190
archaeological research : 40, 200,
211, 232, 326
archaeological sites : 14, 18, 82
archaeological treasures : 167, 231
archaeology : 184, 185, 186, 412,
432
Argonauts : 47
Arkadiane : 214
Armenia : 10
Armenian Bagratid Kingdom : 469
Armenian Church of the Holy Cross
: 451
Armenian period : 469
Arpaçay River : 469, 470
Arsameia : 425
Arslantepe : 448
art events : 83
art historian : 9, 167
Artemis : 46, 215, 219, 270, 295
Artemis temple : 210
Artemis temple in Ephesus : 82
Artemis temple in Sardis : 82
Artemisia (Queen) : 245, 247
Artemision : 55, 133, 216, 219
artificial mounds : 325, 356, 371,
426
Artvin : 7, 477, 481
artworks : 88
Arykanda : 288
Ascension of Jesus : 385
Asia : 10, 49, 59, 60, 80, 375, 457
Asia Minor : 40, 46, 55, 56, 184,
190, 205, 226, 229, 236, 245, 270,
272, 317, 319
Asian peoples : 50
Asian shore : 115, 141, 148, 149, 180
Asian side : 91
Asitane : 91
Asitawanda (King) : 330
Aslantepe, Malatya : 53
Aspendos : 4, 7, 288, 299, 302,
303, 330
Assos (Behramkale) : 186

Assos acropolis : 187
Assyrian trading colonies : 371
Assyrians : 53, 54, 326, 348, 371
Asikli Höyük : 40, 52, 370
Atatürk and Congress Museum :
409
Atatürk Cultural Center : 118
Atatürk Kiosk (Atatürk Kösk) :
428, 435, 492
Atatürk Museum : 490
Atatürk statue : 118, 158
Atatürk statue, Samsun : 500
Atatürk, Mustafa Kemal : 56, 57,
59, 60, 102, 140, 152, 180, 201, 242,
342, 500
Athena : 183
Athena temple : 186, 224, 308
Athens : 47, 48, 55, 184, 185, 211,
504
Athens Acropolis : 211
Atiochos I of Commagene : 425
Atlantis : 274
Attaleia : 292
Attalus III : 192
Augustus (Emperor) : 192, 333, 342
Augustus Temple : 342, 343
Avanos : 378, 390
Ayasofya : 99
Ayder yayla houses : 496
Aynalikavak Kasri : 134
ayran : 70, 71
Ayse Sultan : 208
Ayvalik : 6, 197
Azerbaijan : 10, 84

B

Babel, tower and hanging gardens
of : 54
backgammon : 66, 69
Bafa Lake : 230, 376
Bafra plain : 500
Baghdad Avenue (Bagdat Caddesi)
: 158
Bagras : 332
Bagdat Kiosk : 115
baklava : 61, 70, 71, 73, 412
Balat : 129, 226
Balikli Göl (Pool of Abraham) : 416
Balikli Kaplica : 409
Balkan Wars, monuments of : 169
Balkans : 139
Balyan, Karabet : 150
Balyan, Sarkis : 154
banking activities : 46
banking center : 210
barbarian invasions : 50
Barhal river : 499
Bari : 280

Barnabas : 296
baroque detail : 407
basalt : 27, 50, 330, 414, 428
basilica : 56, 99, 103, 214, 223, 232,
302
Basilica Cistern : 103
basilica plan : 99, 321
bass fishing : 296
bath : 55, 59, 118, 167, 186, 195,
204, 206, 213, 227, 242, 272, 285,
302, 364, 404
Bath of Faustina : 227
Bath of Hadrian : 186, 232, 233
Battle of Kadesh : 348
Battle of Manzikert (Malazgirt) :
50, 57
battlefield : 333
Bayezid : 148
Bayezid II : 56, 167
Bayezid Mosque : 118
Bayrakli : 200
bazaars : 416
beaches : 160, 163, 186, 197, 201,
204, 220, 258, 274, 285, 306, 317,
505, 507
beauty contest : 46
beer : 46, 70
Behram Pasa Mosque : 435
Behramkale (Assos) : 6
Belbasi : 52
Beldibi : 52
Belek holiday center : 288
belfry : 442
Belgrade Forest : 160
Belkis : 302
Bellini : 56
belly dancers : 61, 141
belly dancing : 50, 69
Bergama : 6, 190
Berlin : 185, 195
Berlin Museum : 194, 227, 228
Bes : 104
Besiktas : 66, 152
Beyazıt Square : 118
Beycesultan, Denizli : 52
Beydaglari chain : 284
Beylerbeyi : 160
Beylerbeyi Palace : 149, 160
Beysehir : 7, 18, 365
Bias (philosopher) : 47, 223
Bible : 135, 190
Biblical interests : 238
Biblical scenes : 451
Biblical stories : 376
Biblical tours : 186, 205, 238, 296,
334
Bilge Khan : 60
Bimarhane (mental hospital) : 510
Binbir Kilise : 317, 376

Birgi : 208
Bishops' Palace : 232
Bithynia : 174
Bitlis : 7, 449
Blachernae Palace complex : 138
black amber : 458
Black Sea : 10, 40, 47, 84, 92, 142, 143, 148, 149, 180, 226, 477, 483, 492, 504, 510
Black Sea coast : 34, 160, 481, 500, 510
Black Sea coastal motorway : 80
Black Sea countries : 11
Black Sea region : 7, 10, 34, 476, 504
Black Sea valleys : 476
Blegen : 185
Blue Cruise (Blue Voyage) : 220, 250, 252, 253, 258, 262, 274, 285
Blue Flag : 220
Blue Mosque : 95, 96, 110
boat safari : 270
boat tours : 197, 274, 292, 312
boats : 89, 149, 163, 310
Bodrum (Halicarnassus) : 55, 133, 223, 244, 245, 246, 249, 251, 253, 256
Bodrum yacht : 251
Bogaziçi : 142
Bogazköy : 7, 53, 348, 349
Book of Revelation : 238
Bosphorus (Bull's Pass) : 11, 47, 62, 80, 84, 88, 89, 90, 91, 110, 115, 128, 141, 142, 143, 146, 148, 149, 150, 152, 154, 155, 476
Bosphorus Bridge : 81, 91, 143, 160
Bouleuterion : 223, 225, 227, 294, 295
Boztepe : 492
Bögü Khan : 60
Brancihds oracle family : 229
brass buckle : 356
British Museum : 245, 247, 270
British soldiers : 158
British troops : 180
bronze : 94, 103, 246, 356, 405
Bronze Age : 53
Bronze Age settlement : 55
bronze baldachin : 115, 124
Buda Pest : 57
Bulgaria : 10
Bulgarian church : 134
bulgur : 64, 70, 445
bullfighting : 477
bulls : 186, 229
bulls' head plaster reliefs : 359, 370
Burdur : 6, 40, 297, 347
Burdur Archaeological Museum : 296

Burdur Lake : 296
Bursa : 6, 11, 47, 175, 176, 178, 376
Buruciye Medrese : 407
bus transportation : 80
Büyükada : 79, 163, 165, 166
Byzantine : 317
Byzantine age : 318, 325
Byzantine apses : 282
Byzantine basilica : 208, 270, 274, 321, 505
Byzantine chapel : 214
Byzantine church : 109, 206, 232, 322
Byzantine edifice : 237
Byzantine Empire : 56, 376
Byzantine era : 160, 299, 414
Byzantine family tomb : 175
Byzantine period : 88, 160, 176, 223, 237, 321, 375, 490, 505
Byzantine remains : 206, 299
Byzantine renaissance : 135
Byzantine rule : 284
Byzantine works of art : 106
Byzantines : 174, 192, 231, 312, 404
Byzantium : 43, 56, 57, 89, 91, 139
Byzas : 89

C

Caesar : 333
Caesarea : 403, 404
café : 126, 135, 163, 237, 292, 306, 310
calcium oxide : 235
calendar reform : 57
Caliphate : 57
Caliphate, abolition of : 60
caliphs : 109
calligraphic inscriptions : 103
calligraphy : 176
camel wrestling : 14
Can Hasan, Karaman : 52
candied chestnuts : 176
canyon : 220, 368, 375, 378, 387, 400, 469
capital style : 382
capitals : 428
Cappadocia : 359, 366, 368, 370, 375, 376, 377, 387, 400, 402
Cappadocian church frescoes : 376
Cappadocian village : 372
car manufacturing : 176
Caracalla : 206
caravan route : 52, 364
caravan travelers : 364
caravans : 49, 490
caravansaries : 49, 57, 59, 167, 302, 333, 364, 404, 428, 448, 458,

459, 469
Caravansary Hotel : 169
Caretta caretta turtle beach : 262
Caretta caretta turtle nests : 258
Caria : 55, 231
Carian fleets : 55
Carian kingdom : 245
Carians : 245
Caribbean-style crowds : 253
carpet : 50, 73, 75, 95, 98, 160, 378
Carthage colony : 54
Cascading formations, Pamukkale : 15
Caspian Sea : 34, 59
Caspian Sea oil pipeline : 30, 333
Cassandra : 47
castle : 54, 201, 239, 246, 253, 258, 274, 312, 316, 317, 318, 323, 330, 332, 348, 364, 404, 413, 416, 449, 477
catacombs : 334
cathedral : 459, 469
cattle : 61, 481
cattle dealing : 467
Caucasus : 34, 80, 84
cauldrons : 439
cave dwellings : 41, 52, 441
cave settlements : 432
Cavern of Heaven : 324
Cavern of Kanlidivane : 322
caves : 52, 313, 377
ceilings : 150
celadon : 111
Celsus, Library of : 213
cemeteries : 62, 122, 135, 158, 237
Cendere Bridge : 425
Cennet-Cehennem (Caverns of Heaven and Hell) : 324
center : 306
Central Anatolia : 342
Central Anatolian language : 52
Central Anatolian nomadic or village cultures : 53
Central Anatolian plain : 370, 400
Central Anatolian Region : 7, 22, 407
Central Asia : 80
Central heating : 152
centralized plan : 96
ceramic : 73
ceramic finds : 371
ceramic ware : 95
Cerberus : 324
cereal : 409
Ceyhan : 330
Chalcas (Trojan War soldier) : 299
Chalcolithic Age civilizations : 325
Chalcolithic Period : 52, 414, 457
chariot race : 92, 99
Children's Day : 85

chili/red pepper : 416
Chimera : 288
Chinese : 114
Chinese porcelain : 111
Chora monastery : 135
Christ : 135
Christian church, Antakya : 335
Christian Ecumenical Council : 56, 158
Christian faith : 43
Christian history : 238
Christian monasteries : 400
Christian period : 192, 323
Christian visitors : 312
Christian world : 280, 306
Christianity : 56, 192, 219, 326, 402, 440
Christianity, first hidden church of : 334
Christians : 49, 56, 174, 317, 333, 334, 376
churches : 49, 59, 99, 102, 135, 197, 205, 237, 280, 307, 312, 359, 366, 368, 376, 378, 381, 383, 400, 428, 440, 451, 455, 492, 493
cigars : 486
Cilicia : 316, 325, 330, 332
Cilician Gates (Gülek Pass/Bogazi) : 49
Cilician Pass : 324, 326, 331
Cilician Plain : 326
circumcision : 61, 129
Circumcision Room : 115
cistern : 94, 103, 449
Cistern of a Thousand and One Columns : 94, 95
citadel : 31, 169, 183, 201, 239, 312, 318, 342, 343, 440, 449, 450, 467, 510
citrus fruit : 18, 280, 288, 325, 377
city walls, Iznik : 175
city weddings : 61
civil rights : 349
civilizations : 40, 50
Civilizations of Anatolia and Neighboring Countries : 106
classical Turkish architecture : 95
clay cuneiform tablets : 371
clay Hittite bulls : 347
clay seals : 52
clay state tablets : 348
Cleopatra : 55, 192, 312
Cleopatra's Beach : 313
Cleopatra's Gate : 326
cliff formations : 292
climate : 10, 220
climatic conditions : 40
clock tower : 176, 201, 203
clocks : 115, 152

coal mining industry : 505
coastal sites : 82
coastal towns : 490
coastline : 14
coins : 46, 54, 205, 284, 302, 306, 342
Cold War years : 60
colonies : 46, 226
colonists : 284
Colonnaded Roman Road : 237
Colophon : 48
Colossus : 46
Commagene local kingdom : 425
commercial agora : 213, 306, 308
Comnneni, imperial family of : 490
Constantine Porphyrogenetus (Emperor) : 93
Constantine the Great (Emperor) : 56, 94, 99, 103, 117, 384
Constantinople : 91, 117, 167, 175, 490
Constantius (son of Constantine the Great) : 99
Coracesion : 7, 312
Coracesium : 312
Corinthian style : 319
Corycos : 323
Cos : 48
Cotton Castle : 235
Covered (Grand) Bazaar : 73, 121
covered bazaar : 88, 118, 120, 176, 416, 418, 428
covered market : 121, 167, 333, 342
crater : 321, 449, 460
crater lake : 449
crater-like pits : 324
Crete : 53, 306
Crimean War : 91, 158
Croesus (King) : 49, 205, 208
Crown Prince : 152, 510
Crucifixion : 387
crucifixion of Jesus Christ : 333
cruise companies : 220
cruise lines : 82
cruise ship : 258
cruise ship port : 190
Crusade, First : 56
Crusade, Fourth : 56, 93, 490
Crusade, Third : 318
Crusader castle : 333
Crusaders : 174, 175, 317, 323, 330, 334
crying rock of Niobe : 208
crystal chandelier : 50, 152
Cudi Mountain : 462
cuisines : 70
cult buildings : 52
cult ceremonies : 426

cult of emperor worship : 232
cultural activities : 140, 288
cultural center : 333
cultural exchange : 59, 134
cultural heritages of the world : 409
Cunda Island : 197
cuneiform : 47, 348
cuneiform clay tablets : 104, 371, 403
cuneiform inscriptions : 449
cuneiform writing : 40, 53
currents : 128, 253
Cybele : 46, 206, 215, 231, 296, 298, 347
Cyprus : 106, 310, 318
Cyrus (Persian ruler) : 205

Ç
Çakir Aga Mansion : 208
Çamlica : 91
Çamlica Hill : 143, 155
Çamliyamaç village : 459
Çanakkale : 6, 64, 180
Çarikli (Sandals) Church : 381, 385
Çatal Höyük : 40, 41, 43, 52, 347, 359, 360, 370, 371
Çavdarhisar Roman temple (Temple of Zeus) : 242
Çavustepe Urartu ruins : 456
Çayönü : 40, 41, 52, 432, 437
Çemberlitas (Column of Constantine) : 117
Çesme : 201, 204
Çiragan Palace : 152, 154
Çirali : 47
Çifte Kümbet : 404
Çifte Medreseler : 404
Çifte Minareli Medrese : 407, 409, 457
çig köfte : 416
Çoruh : 477
Çoruh River valley : 481
Çorum Museum : 349
Çukurova : 18, 325, 330
Çumra : 359, 370

D
dagger : 114, 115, 349
Dalaman : 258
Dalyan : 6, 186, 258, 262
Dalyan River : 263
Dalyan see also Alexandria Troas*
Damlatas Cave (Cave of Dripping Stones) : 313
Daphne : 334
Dardanelles : 11, 84, 92, 143, 155, 180

Dark Age : 53
Dark Church : 381, 385, 387
Datça Peninsula : 258
Davutlar beach : 220
Dawn Ceremony : 180
Dead Sea : 252, 267
declaration of the Republic : 59, 342
Delian Confederation : 55
Demeter : 46
Democratic Party : 57
Demre : 280
Denizli : 66, 236, 238
Derinkuyu : 377
developed countries : 84
Deyruz Zafaran : 440, 443
diadem : 426
dialects : 60
Didim (Didyma) : 220, 229
Didyma's temple of Apollo : 82
Didymaion : 229
Diesis mosaic : 99
dignitaries : 223
Dikili : 190
Dil promontory : 163
Dilek National Park beach : 222
dining hall (refectory) : 384
dining room : 152
Diocaesarea : 319, 321
diocese seat : 223
Diogenes (philosopher) : 48, 55, 504
Dionysus (Bacchus) : 46
Dionysus relief : 301
Dionysus, altar of : 223
Dionysus' Temple : 192
Directorate of Foundations (Vakiflar) : 98
Discovering Turkey through the Lens : 9
Divrigi : 409
Divrigi Ulu mosque : 407
Diyarbakir : 7, 26, 27, 40, 41, 130, 426, 428, 432, 433, 439, 441, 449
documented history : 53
dog : 52, 253
Dogubeyazit : 460, 462
Dolmabahçe : 50
Dolmabahçe Mosque : 143
Dolmabahçe Palace : 142, 149, 150, 152
dolmens : 292
domestication of animals : 52, 432
Domitian (Emperor) : 237
Domitianus statue : 217
Domitianus, gate of : 237
Dorian colonists : 245
Dormition : 136
döner kebab : 70, 71

Döner Kümbet : 404
Dönük Tas : 326
Dörpfeld : 185
Dörtyol : 333, 339
Dragon : 384
Duden Falls : 292, 293
Dursunlu, Konya : 52

E

Early Bronze Age : 371
Early Bronze Age civilizations : 325
early Christian period : 375
Early Hittite trading colonies : 371
Eastern Anatolia : 61, 449, 476
Eastern Anatolia Region : 7, 30
Eastern Anatolian civilization : 54
Eastern Anatolian sites : 52
Eastern Black Sea region : 483
Eastern Christianity : 377
Eastern civilizations : 88
Eastern cultures : 426
Eastern Mediterranean coast : 55
Eastern Roman Empire : 43
Eastern Turkey : 464
economy : 192, 205
Ecumenical Council : 56, 158, 214
Ecumenical Council meetings : 175
Edirne : 6, 49, 59, 61, 132, 167, 169
Efes (Ephesus) : 6, 210
Eflatun Pinar : 365
Egypt : 52, 53, 56, 106, 192, 226, 375
Egyptian civilization : 52
Egyptian gods : 195
Egyptian Obelisk : 92, 93
Egil : 432
Egridir Lake : 296
electrum : 54
elementary schools : 85
Elmali (Apple) Church : 381, 383
Emerit, Catherine (Austrian peasant) : 214
Eminönü Square : 118
endemic forests : 476
entertainment : 88
environmental protection : 11, 18
Ephesus (Efes) : 48, 55, 133, 205, 210, 211, 214, 219, 220
Ephesus ruins : 211
Ephesus' theatre : 213
Eratosthenes (mathematician and philosopher) : 48
Erciyas Mountain : 23, 368, 378
Ergani : 432
Erim, Prof. Dr. Kenan T. : 231, 232
Erzurum : 7, 457
Eski (Old) Malatya : 448
Eski Camii (Old Mosque) : 167

Eşen River : 46
Esrefoglu Mosque : 365
Ethnographical Museum : 342, 344, 458
Etruscans : 53
Eumenes II : 192, 236
eunuchs : 110
Euphrates : 26, 52, 448
Euphrates River : 414, 416, 424
Euromos city : 230
Europe : 10, 18, 50, 78, 80, 82, 103, 113, 152, 375
European (Sea) tribes : 53
European architectural styles : 150
European artists : 150
European shore : 128, 149
European side : 149, 155
Exodus : 53
Eyüp Mosque : 129, 135
Eyüp Sultan, mosque and mausoleum of : 135
Eyüp-el-Ensari : 135

F

Far East : 113, 152
Fasillar Hittite Monument : 364, 365
Fatih Bridge : 146, 148
fauna : 10, 220
Fener : 128, 134
Fenerbahce peninsula : 158
ferry services : 201
ferry station : 79, 318
ferryboats : 149, 178, 180, 426, 449
Fertile Crescent : 52, 412, 425
Fethiye (Telmessus) : 6, 258, 266, 267
Fethiye Bay : 266
Fethiye-Kalkan road : 272
fez making factory (Feshane) : 135
Fikirtepe, Istanbul : 52
Florence Nightingale Hospital : 158
flower market : 126
forests : 34, 160, 178, 197, 284, 476, 485, 493, 497, 500
Fortuna : 426
Forum Tauri (Square of the Bulls) : 118
Fossati brothers : 102
four-wheel ox carts : 53
Frederic I Barbarossa : 318
French soldiers : 158
French troops : 180, 384, 385, 387, 400, 414, 451, 469, 493
Friday noon service : 62, 493

G

Galata Bridge : 118
Galata district : 115
Galata hills : 90
Galata Tower : 122, 141
Galatians : 195
Gallipoli : 11
Gallipoli Peninsula : 180, 182
GAP (Southeastern Anatolian Project) : 416
Gate of Emperor Hadrian : 292
Gate of Felicity (Bab-üs Saadet): 113
Gate of Salutation (Bab-üs Selam): 110
gates : 139, 174
Gaziantep : 7, 26, 412, 413, 414
Gaziantep Archaeological Museum : 26, 354, 415
Gelibolu (Gallipoli) Peninsula : 180
Gençlik Park : 344
Genoese fortress : 160
Georgia : 10, 476, 481, 483
Georgian Church of Ösk-Vank : 458, 477, 483
Georgian Church of Rabat : 483
German Fountain : 94
Gerze : 505
Gevas : 451
Gideros cove : 507
Gilgamesh Epic : 53
Giresun : 493
Giza, pyramids in : 342
glacier : 460
goddess of fertility : 231
goddess of love : 231
goddess of nature : 231
goddesses : 47, 54, 183, 349
gods : 47, 48, 54, 183, 349
golden apple : 183
Golden Fleece : 47
Golden Gate : 140
Golden Horn : 57, 64, 89, 90, 115, 121, 124, 128, 129, 130, 134, 135, 138, 139, 141, 154, 163
golden touch : 48, 356
Gordion : 7, 48, 54, 356, 357, 358
Gordios : 48, 356
Goths' Column : 117, 118
Göbekli Tepe : 52
Göcek : 266
Gök Medrese : 407, 510
Gökova Bay : 254, 258, 260, 261
Göksu River : 317
Göktürk script : 60
Göktürk state : 60

Göreme (antique Cappadocia) region : 7, 22, 24, 366, 376, 378, 379, 390, 400
Göreme Open Air Museum : 381, 382
Göreme valley : 366
Gözlü Kule, Tarsus : 52, 326
Grand National Assembly : 57
Great Ararat (Büyük Agri) : 460
Great Palace : 92, 98
Great Wall of China : 59
Greece : 10, 14
Greek : 333, 342
Greek alphabet : 43
Greek and Bulgarian borders : 167
Greek cross plan : 376
Greek island : 258
Greek language : 56, 184
Greek period : 160
Green Mausoleum : 178
Gregorian churches : 477
grid city planning : 226
Grotto of St. Peter : 334
Grotto of the Seven Sleepers : 214
group tours : 82
guesthouses : 160
guide book : 4, 9, 266
Guides' Guild of Istanbul : 9
Gülek Pass : 326
Gülhane Park : 118
Güllübahçe village : 223
Gülsehir : 366
Gümüskesen : 246
Gümüskesen Mausoleum, Milas : 244
Güzelyurt (Gelveri) : 402

H

Hacı Bayram Mosque : 342, 343
Hacı Bektas : 366, 376
Hacı Bektas complex : 130
Hacılar, Neolithic settlement : 40, 52, 296, 297, 347
Hacivat : 178
Hadrian (Emperor): 167, 192, 195, 211, 213, 272
Hadrian's Gate, Antalya : 291
Hadrian's granary storage : 272
Hadrian's temple : 212
Hadrian's visit : 285
Hadrianopolis : 167
Hagia Eirene : 108, 109
Hagia Sophia Museum : 88, 99, 174, 326, 492
Hagia Sophia Museum, Trabzon : 492
Hagia Thecla : 317, 318
Halaf and Ubeyd cultures : 52

Halicarnassus : 48, 245
Halicarnassus Mausoleum : 223
Haliç (Golden Horn) : 89
Haliç Bridge : 129
Hamsilos Fjord : 505
Harbiye district : 334
Harem : 110, 115, 129, 150, 152, 160, 462
Harpy tomb : 270
Harran (Altinbasak) : 53, 416, 422
Hasankeyf : 440
Hatti : 43, 106
Hatti city-states : 53
Hatti civilization : 40, 53
Hatti land and culture : 348
Hatti period : 160
Hattusas : 347, 348, 371
Haydarpasa Railroad Station : 158, 159
Hector : 47
Hecuba (King Priam's wife) : 47
Helen : 184
Helena : 384
Hell : 324
Hellas : 55
Hellas city states : 55
Hellene gods : 426
Hellenes, city states of : 48
Hellenic : 47
Hellenic cities : 94
Hellenic civilization : 43, 55
Hellenic language : 55
Hellenistic age : 227
Hellenistic epochs : 238
Hellenistic period : 43, 55, 186, 204, 223, 232, 236, 299, 306, 321, 323, 325, 500
Hellenistic theatre : 270
Hellenistic world : 192, 206
Hellespont : 185
helmet : 114
helva (made from sesame seeds) : 61, 73
henna : 61
Hepatu : 349
Hera : 183
Herakleia : 244, 376
Herakleitos (philosopher) : 48
Herakles : 426
Heraklia ruins : 230
herb cheese : 451
Hercules, Labors of : 293
Hereke : 73, 77
Hereke, silk and wool carpets of : 152
Hermes : 300
Hero : 155
Herodotus : 48, 55, 245
Heybeliada : 80, 163, 164, 165

518

Hezarfen Ahmet Celebi : 141
Hidirlik Tower : 292
Hippocrates : 48
Hippodamos (architect) : 226
Hippodrome : 92, 93, 94, 99, 138
Hisarönü Bay : 262
Hittite archive : 403
Hittite civilization : 200, 348
Hittite Confederation : 371
Hittite Empire : 40, 50, 53, 330, 348
Hittite language : 371
Hittite monuments : 365
Hittite period : 160, 325
Hittite principalities : 371
Hittite rock carvings : 208, 330
Hittite sculpture : 333
Hittite settlements : 333, 371
Hittite sites : 54
Hittite sources : 183
Hittite world : 349
Hittites : 47, 48, 50, 53, 55, 106, 210,
229, 326, 330, 342, 348, 356, 368,
414, 448
Holy Land : 56, 375
Homer : 47, 54, 183, 184, 185
Homeric heroes : 183
Homo erectus : 52
Homo sapiens : 52
Honaz (Colossae) : 6, 238
Hosap Castle : 451, 456
hot and cold drinks : 69
hot and cold running water : 67
hothouse vegetable farming : 266
House of Bronzes : 206
House of the Virgin : 214
Humann, Carl (railroad engineer)
: 192
Hun Empire : 59
Hunad Hatun complex : 22, 404
Hurrians : 348
hydraulic engineering (water
channels) : 451

I - İ

Ibrahim Pasa, Palace of : 92, 94
Iconoclasm : 175
Iconoclastic Era : 376, 384
Ida : 47
Igdir : 57, 460
Ihlara Valley : 368, 370, 400, 402
İkiz Tepe : 53, 500
Iliad : 47, 54, 183
Ilion : 6
İlyas Bey Mosque : 226
Imperial Gate (Bab-i Hümayun) :
109
Imperial Palace : 92
Imperial Roman Era : 56

Imperial Roman taste : 55
Imperial Rome : 67
Imperial Turkish architecture :
208
İnce Minare Medrese : 362, 363
İncirlik air base : 330
Independence battle : 242
Independence War : 243, 500
India : 113, 114
Indo-European language : 348
İnönü, Ismet : 57
Inscribed Pillar : 270
Insuyu Cave : 296
Ionia : 55, 184, 210, 223
Ionia, natural philosophers of : 48
Ionian alphabet : 55
Ionian and Roman worlds : 215
Ionian cities : 43, 55, 211, 220
Ionian city-states : 54
Ionian culture : 55
Ionian immigrations : 53
Ionian philosophers : 226
Ionians : 229
Ionic capitals : 206
Ionic colonnade : 1
Ionic columns : 232
Iran : 10, 46, 56, 59, 114, 449, 460
Iraq : 10
Iron Age : 53
Isa Bey Mosque : 219
Ishak Pasa Palace : 462
Isidoros : 99
Iskender kebab : 178
Iskender Pasa Mosque, Trabzon :
493
Iskenderun Bays : 316
Islahiye : 333, 414
Islam : 56, 57
Islam, adoption of : 59
Islamic art : 94
Islamic manuscripts : 50
Islamic world : 109
Isparta : 6, 296, 297
Israel : 310
Issus : 333
Istanbul : 6, 11, 49, 50, 52, 56, 57, 59,
61, 64, 72, 73, 74, 79, 80, 81, 82, 88,
89, 90, 91, 94, 100, 106, 109, 111, 115,
117, 118, 121, 122, 126, 128, 130, 135, 139,
141, 143, 148, 149, 152, 155, 158, 167,
169, 174, 175, 178, 180, 200, 214, 216,
247, 270, 360, 361, 409, 448
Istanbul Archaeological Museums
: 104
Istanbul Festival of Arts : 148
Istanbul harbor : 83
Istanbul International Music Festival
: 109
Istanbul-Baghdad railway : 158

Italy : 47, 53, 54, 201, 280
İzmir (Smyrna) : 6, 14, 186, 190,
200, 203, 204, 205, 208
İzmir International Fair : 201
İznik : 64, 106, 174
İznik tiles : 96, 128, 174
İzzeddin Keykavus Sifahanesi :
407

J

Jakobids (Syriacs living in this
region): 440
Janissary Band (Mehter) : 140
Japanese porcelain : 111
Javelin (Cirit) on horseback : 458
jeep safaris : 267
Jericho : 52
Jerusalem : 4, 56
Jesus Christ : 56, 99, 385, 416, 469
Jewish population : 333
Jews of Spain : 56
John the Baptist : 99
Judaism : 56
Judas trees : 143
Julianus : 342
Julius Caesar : 510
Justinian (Byzantine Emperor) :
56, 99, 102, 103, 175, 214
Justinian I : 103
Justinian period : 330

K

Kabatas Pier : 163
Kaçkar Mountain : 477, 498, 499
Kadesh war : 53
Kadiköy : 118, 155, 158
Kadifekale : 200
Kadirli : 330
Kafkasor yayla : 477
Kahta : 424, 426
kahvehane : 69
Kale : 6, 274, 279, 280
Kalkan : 274
Kanes : 371
Kangal : 409
Kangal dogs : 409
Kanlica : 148
Kanlidivane (Kanytelis) : 7, 321
Kapi Aga Medrese : 510
Karaca Ahmet Cemetery : 91, 155
Karacadag : 439
Karagöz : 178
Karahayit village : 238
Karain : 52
Karain Cave : 292
Karakesion : 312
Karanlik (Dark) Church : 384, 400

Karatay Medrese Museum : 362
Karatepe : 330
Kargamis : 47
Kariye Museum (St. Savior in Chora) : 135
Kars : 7, 467
Karum : 371
Karun Treasury : 243
Kasimpasa : 134
Kas (Antiphellus) : 6, 83, 274, 276
Kaunos : 258, 263
Kaymakli : 377
Kayseri (Caesarea) : 7, 22, 77, 364, 366, 371, 377, 391, 403, 404, 405, 406
Kayseri Archaeological Museum : 403
Kaz Dagi : 47
kebabs : 69, 71, 414
Kekova Bay : 279
Kekova island : 274
Kemer : 6, 18, 19, 284, 285, 288
Kemer Marina : 286
Kemeralti : 201
Kerpe : 161
Keskin Color archive : 4
Khalkedon : 158
Khazar Turks : 56
Kinaliada : 164
Kinik (Xanthos) : 50, 270
Kiz Kulesi (Leander's Tower) : 155
Kizilirmak (ancient Halys) : 368, 390, 405
Kizkalesi (Corycos) : 7, 323
kilim : 98, 451
Kilyos : 160, 161
King's Gate : 348, 351
Kings Road : 54
Kizivatna kingdom : 330
Knidos : 258
knife-sharpening services : 339
Knights of Rhodes : 245
Knossos : 53
Kocatepe Mosque : 344
Koç family : 134, 160
kokoreç : 69
Konstantiniye : 91
Konya (Iconium) : 40, 57, 359, 364, 370, 371
Konya Archaeological Museum : 371
Konya plain : 22, 317
Konyaalti : 18, 288
Korama : 377
Koran : 178, 462
Korfmann, Professor : 186
Koyunoglu Private Museum : 359
Köknar village : 479
Kufi characters : 60

Kuleli Military School : 149
Kurucasile Beach : 510
Kusadasi : 6, 18, 210, 220, 221, 222
Kusadasi gulf : 220
Kusadasi marina : 220
Kültepe, Kayseri : 49, 53, 348, 368, 371, 403, 406
Kümbet Mosque : 467, 469
Kütahya : 6, 239, 242
Kütahya, citadel walls of : 241

L

labyrinth : 121
lahmacun : 70
Laodicea (Pamukkale-Denizli): 205, 238
Lara Beach : 288
Lascarid Principality : 175
late Hellenistic style : 426
Late Hittite period : 302, 330, 414, 425
Late Hittite relief : 354
Late Hittite site : 330
Latin : 342
Latin alphabet : 60
Latin culture : 43
Latin inscriptions : 300
Latin invasion : 92, 103
Latin plunder : 56
latrines : 204
laurel tree : 229, 334
Lausanne Treaty : 59
Leander's Tower : 91, 149, 155
Lebanon : 52
Lelegs : 245
leopards : 10, 220
Lesbos Island : 186
Lesser Ararat : 460
Leto : 270
Letoon : 270
Letoon sanctuary complex : 272
Letter to the Colossians : 238
Lucullus (Roman general) : 504
Lycia : 40, 270, 272
Lycian acropolis : 270
Lycian confederation : 270
Lycian edifices : 274
Lycian language : 270
Lycian rock tombs : 258, 263, 266, 267, 279, 280, 283
Lycian sarcophagus : 104, 274
Lycian tower tombs : 270
Lydia : 40, 49, 53, 54, 205
Lydian art objects : 243
Lydian burial mounds : 208
Lydian kingdom : 208
Lydians : 200, 205, 210
Lymira : 288

Lysimachos (general of Alexander the Great) : 174, 192

M

macaroni : 69
Macedonian army : 333
Macedonians : 106, 425
Maçan (Avcilar) : 378
Maglova Aqueduct, Istanbul : 130
Malabadi Bridge : 130, 432, 437
Malatya : 7, 448
Mamuriye Castle : 317, 318
Man sanctuary : 296
Manavgat : 310
Manavgat Falls : 310
Manisa (Magnesia ad Siplus) : 15, 208, 209
Marcus Aurelius : 227
Mardin : 132, 440, 441
Mark Anthony : 55, 192, 312
Marmara : 10, 57, 85, 89, 92, 139, 140, 142, 158, 163
Marmara Island : 85
Marmara Region : 11, 86
Marmaris : 253, 258, 259, 260, 262
Marmaris Gulf : 259
Marsias : 104
Martyrium of St. Philip : 237
masks : 280
Mausoleum : 55, 133, 135, 176, 178, 246, 247, 449
Mausoleum of Atatürk (Anitkabir) : 130, 342
Mausoleum of Halicarnassus (Bodrum) : 46
Mausolus (King) : 245, 247
Mazi : 377
Meander plain : 230
Mecca : 288
Medina : 56
Mediterranean : 10, 30, 34, 57, 83, 84, 220, 226, 292, 310, 324
Mediterranean basin : 40
Mediterranean climate : 14
Mediterranean coast : 316, 476
Mediterranean flora : 274
Mediterranean region : 6, 18, 296, 330
Medusa head : 229, 231
Megara : 89
Mehmet II (Fatih) : 56, 57, 90, 106, 118, 148
Mehmet the Conqueror, signature of : 60
Mehter band : 140
Melendiz Creek : 370, 400
Melendiz Mountains : 400
Melitene : 448

Memmius, monument of : 211
Mersin : 7, 316, 318, 325
mesir macunu : 208
Mesolithic : 52
Mesopotamia : 52, 53, 54, 226, 371, 424
Mesopotamian caravan routes : 407
Mesopotamian civilization : 52
Mesopotamian goods : 326
Mesopotamian plain : 440, 442
Mesud : 400
Metochites, Theodore (scholar and statesman) : 135
Mevlana Celaleddin-i Rumi : 57, 359
Mevlana Museum complex : 359, 361
Meyisti, Greek island of : 274
mezes : 70, 91
Midas : 48, 54, 356
Middle Ages : 148
Middle East : 46, 52, 80, 476
Milas : 230, 246, 256
Milet (Miletus) : 6, 48, 99, 220, 223, 226, 229, 490
Miletus agora : 228
Miletus of Ionia : 500
Miletus, alphabet of : 48
Miletus, colony of : 504
Miniature : 50, 94, 110
Miniaturk Park : 130, 132, 134, 216, 247, 360, 361
Ministry of Tourism and Culture collection : 4
Minoan Palaces : 53
Misis : 330
Mithradates VI Eupator : 49, 510
Mohammed, Prophet : 56, 135
Mongolia : 60
Mongolian invasion : 376
Mongols : 50, 57
Monks' Mount : 176
Mopsos (Trojan War soldier) : 299
Mosaic Museum : 98
Moses : 53
Mosque of Alaaddin : 360
Mosque of Selim II in Edirne : 57
Mother Goddess : 43, 206, 208, 242, 347, 370
Mother goddess Cybele worship : 52
Mother Leto : 46
Mother Nature : 226, 253
Mount Ararat : 7, 30, 46, 460, 462
Mount Uludag : 11, 176
mountain ranges : 30, 40, 459, 504
mountain trekking : 267, 477
mountains : 22, 26, 30, 47, 183,

208, 214, 284, 295, 316, 457
Mt. Erciyes (Argeus) : 371, 403
Mt. Hasandag : 368, 400
Mt. Ida (Olympus) : 183
Mt. Nemrut (Commagene) : 27, 29, 424
Mt. Nemrut monuments : 425
Mt. Pagos : 200
Mt. Süphan : 449
Municipal Museum of Istanbul : 152
Muradiye complex : 178
Muradiye Mosque : 176, 208
Museum of Paintings and Sculpture : 152
Museum of Stone and Wood Works : 362
Museum of the Ancient Orient : 104, 106
Museum of Turkish and Islamic Arts : 92, 94, 176
musical instrument museum : 134
Muslims : 78, 135
Mustafa III : 114
Mycale : 55
Myra : 288

N

Nahcivan : 10
Nasreddin Hoca : 49
National Congress : 409
NATO : 57, 60
NATO Summit : 50
Neanderthal man : 52
Neanikomedia in Thessaly : 52
necropolis : 236, 272, 279, 321, 323
Nemrut Dag : 7, 409, 424, 449
Neolithic age : 40, 41, 52, 160, 206
Neolithic sites : 333
Nereid Monument : 270
Nesha : 371
Nevali Çori, Sanli Urfa : 52
Nevsehir : 23, 130, 366, 377, 378
New Testament : 238
New York's Metropolitan Museum : 243
Nicaea : 175
Nightingale, Florence : 91
Nigde : 366
Nika revolt : 99
Nikaia : 174
Nilüfer Hatun Imaret (Archaeological Museum): 174
Nimrod (King) : 416
Niobe : 208
Niobe, crying rock of : 208
Noah's Ark : 46, 462
Nomadic life : 52, 54

nomadic Turkish tribes : 59

O - Ö

obsidian : 46, 52, 359, 370
Odyssey : 47, 54
Olba : 319
Old Testament : 348, 462
oleander trees : 237
olive : 14, 72, 174, 180, 197, 204
olive oil : 70, 197
olive oil press : 46
Oltu tasi : 458
Olympus (Mt. Uludag) : 176
Olympus : 47, 183
opium : 239, 243
oracle : 89, 183, 219, 229
Ordu : 493
Orient Express : 82
Orpheus mosaic : 333
Orta Hisar : 366, 367, 373
Ortaköy : 118, 149
Ortaköy Mosque : 146
Orthodox Patriarchate : 128, 134
Orthodox seminary : 163
Osman : 57
Osman Hamdi Bey : 104
Ottoman architecture : 106
Ottoman court : 185
Ottoman Empire : 57, 91, 109, 110, 114, 167, 448
Ottoman Empire state archives : 50
Ottoman Empire, decline and fall of : 57
Ottoman monuments : 449
Ottoman rule : 90, 106, 200
Ottoman rural areas : 59
Ottoman sultans : 150
Ottoman times : 176
Ottoman Turkish monuments : 176
Ottomans : 59, 174, 510
ox cart : 49, 444
Öküzini : 52
Ölü Deniz (Dead Sea) : 266, 267
Ölü Deniz see also Dead Sea*
Özal, Turgut : 57
Özkonak : 377

P

Paleolithic excavations : 292
Paleolithic period : 52, 342, 344
Palestine : 52, 106
Palovit Falls : 496
Pamphylia : 288, 292, 306, 316, 330
Pamphylian cities : 299
Pamphylian plain : 299, 302
Pamukkale (Hierapolis) : 235, 238

Panghia Kamariotissa : 165
Panionian Confederation : 55, 223
parchment : 192
Paris : 47, 183, 184
Parthenon : 55
pasture lands : 18, 61, 296, 476
Pasabag : 387
Patara : 272, 274, 280
Patara, beaches of : 273
Pax Romana : 56, 284
Payas : 333
Pekmez Höyük, Aphrodisias : 55
Pergamum (Bergama) : 6, 55, 192, 200, 205, 211
Pergamum acropolis : 190
Pergamum Kingdom : 55, 190, 236, 292
Pergamum monarchy : 192
Perge (Aksu) : 4, 7, 288, 299, 300, 306
Pericles : 55
Persia : 54, 56, 205
Persian armies : 326
Persian domination : 245
Persian Empire : 205
Persian fashion : 426
Persian fleet : 302
Persian governors (Satrap) : 55
Persian rule : 284
Persians : 50, 55, 94, 106, 205, 211, 226, 229, 270, 333, 425
pestil (mulberry or grape syrup paste) : 61
Peter and Paul martyred : 56
phaeton : 80, 163, 166
Phaselis : 284, 288
Philadelphia (Alasehir) : 205, 208
Philetairos : 192
philosophers : 55
Phoenicians : 54
Phrygia : 40, 54
Phrygian rock-cut burial chambers : 239
Phrygians : 342, 356
Pierre Loti Café : 135
Pirates' Cave : 313
Piri Reis map : 57
Pisidia : 295
pistachio nuts : 71, 412, 413
Plancia Magna (daughter of the Roman governor of Bithynia) : 300
Pliny the Younger : 174
Polatli : 357
Polio Monument : 211
Pompeipolis : 325
Pontic kings : 504
Pontus : 49
Pontus kings' rock-cut tombs : 510

Porcelain Collection : 111
Poseidon : 186
Poseidon, Altar of : 223
Potuk yayla settelement : 498
Praxiteles : 258
prayer rug : 73
prayers : 62, 205
Priam (King) : 47, 185, 186
Priene : 6, 47, 220, 223
primary school : 258
Princes' Islands : 79, 80, 91, 155, 163
Proclus : 92
prophetess Pytia : 229
Prusias : 176
Prussian architectural style : 158
Prytaneion : 211, 223
public latrine : 211, 212
Pürenliseki : 400
pyramidal rock formations : 387
Pyramids : 53
Pytheos (architect) : 223, 245

R

Raki : 70
Red Court : 190, 195
Red Tower : 312, 314
Republican era : 84, 152
Retreat of the Ten Thousand : 47, 55, 326, 490
Revelations of St. John : 205
Rhodes : 46, 258, 284
River God : 218, 227
River Meander : 223
River Pactolus : 205
River Tigris : 440
River Xanthos : 270
Rize : 7, 36, 477, 480, 481
rock-carved monasteries : 400
rock-cut canal : 334
rock-cut Lycian monumental tombs : 266
rock-cut tombs : 253, 295
Roman and Byzantine ages : 206
Roman and Byzantine chain of fortifications : 330
Roman and Byzantine city walls : 174, 178
Roman and Byzantine necropolis : 317
Roman and Byzantine periods : 321
Roman and Byzantine ruins : 236
Roman and early Byzantine palaces : 138
Roman Empire : 50, 56, 59, 90, 174, 210, 211, 226, 284, 323, 414, 425, 448

Roman era : 92, 104, 204, 213, 223, 302
rose-oil : 296
Rotunda-plan : 470
Royal Road : 46, 205
Rumeli fortress : 142, 146, 148
Rüstem Pasa Mosque : 122, 128

S

sacred relics of early Christianity : 118
sacred relics of Islam : 113
Sadberk Hanim Museum : 160
Sagallasos : 296
Saint Barbara Church : 384
Saint Peter's Castle : 245
Saint Sophia see also Hagia Sophia*
Saint's relics : 280
saints : 383
Sakarya River (Sangarios) : 356
Sakcagözü : 330, 414
Salamis : 55
Salt Lake : 22, 400
Samandag : 334
Samos : 220
Samsun (Amisos) : 490, 500, 505
Samsun Archaeological Museum : 500
Sanctuary of Apollo Delpinion : 227
Santa Claus : 280
Sarayburnu : 118
Sarcophagus of the Mourning Women : 104
Sardis : 54, 205, 208
Sardis burial mounds : 208
Sarikamis : 31, 466, 467
Sariyer : 118, 120, 160
Sarp village : 481
Sart (Sardis) : 204
Sart Cayi (Pactolos River) : 208
Saruhan Caravansary : 390
Sasanid Empire : 56
Sassanids : 403
Satan's Table : 197
Satan's Throne : 190
Satrap sarcophagus : 104
savory pastries (börek) : 70
Sayda (Sidon), royal necropolis of : 104
Saydan King Tabnit, family of : 104
Schliemann, Heinrich : 184, 185
Scholastikia : 211
Sebastion : 231, 233
Sedir (Cleopatra) Island : 258, 261
selamlik : 160, 462

Selçuk : 214
Selçuk Museum : 217, 218, 219
Seleucia de Pierre : 334
Seleucia on Calycandos : 317
Seleucus (Alexander the Great's general) : 319, 333
Selim I : 57
Selim I Mosque : 174
Selim II : 167
Selim III : 113
Selime village : 400, 402
Selimiye Barracks : 91, 158, 159
Selimiye Mosque : 15, 49, 132, 167, 169, 359
Seljuk : 364
Seljuk and Ottoman ceramics and tiles : 106
Seljuk and Ottoman Empires : 59
Seljuk and Ottoman works : 404
Seljuk architecture : 390, 404
Seljuk artistic works : 407
Seljuk Burmali Mosque : 510
Seljuk carpets : 95
Seljuk cemeteries and türbes : 449, 451
Seljuk funerary architecture : 449
Seljuk inscriptions : 428
Seljuk period : 57, 160, 469, 505
Seljuk Turks : 376
Seljuk Ulu Cami : 448
sema : 359
Serpent Column : 92, 94
Seven Churches of Asia Minor : 49, 55, 190, 200, 205, 208, 210, 238
seven geographical regions of Turkey : 9
Seven Historical Wonders of Turkey : 334, 424
Seven Natural Wonders of Turkey : 235, 285, 367, 460, 493
Seven Sages of Antiquity : 223
seven towers : 140
Seven Wonders of Nature : 367
Seven Wonders of the Ancient World : 46, 55, 219, 223
Seyhan River : 330
sheep : 61, 439
Sheep's intestines (kokoreç) : 64
sheepdogs : 409
sherbet : 428
shish kebab : 64, 70
sira gecesi : 416
Sirçali Kümbet : 404
Side : 4, 7, 288, 306, 307, 310, 312
Side Museum : 19
Silifke : 316, 317, 318, 319, 323, 325
silk and wool carpets : 73, 152, 403
silk carpets : 69, 77, 150
Silk Road : 80, 407, 457, 490

Sille : 359
Sillyon : 299
Silvan Ulu Mosque : 437
Simit : 62
Sinan : 57, 102, 122, 128, 155, 167, 208, 405
Sinan, tomb of : 122
singers : 141
Sinop : 7, 490, 500, 504, 505
Sipil Dagi National Park : 208
Sirkeli : 330
Sivas : 364, 404, 407, 409
Smyrna : 200, 211
Smyrna grapes : 208
Smyrna-Ephesus road : 204
Socrates : 55
Soganli Valley : 368, 400
Sokullu Mosque : 11
soldiers : 184
soothsaying : 229
Soteria Mosaic : 332
soup kitchen : 167, 208
Southeast Taurus chain : 409
Southeastern Anatolia Project (GAP) : 26, 84
Southeastern Anatolia Region : 7, 26, 412
spacious grid plan : 467
Spanish Jews : 57
Spice Bazaar : 72, 74, 118, 121, 126, 128
spices : 70, 126
Spoon Maker's diamond : 113, 114
St. Barbara, Church of : 381, 385
St. George : 384, 400
St. George, Church of : 312
St. Gregory of Nazianus : 402
St. John : 238
St. Nicholas : 272, 280, 288
St. Nicholas, Church of : 282
St. Nick : 280
St. Paul : 55, 186, 210, 213, 226, 272, 280, 296, 299, 318, 334, 359
St. Paul's trips : 326
St. Peter : 333
St. Peter, Castle of : 246, 249
St. Theodore : 384
Stavropolis : 231
Steam engine train tours : 82
Storm god of the Hittites : 354
Strabo (geographer) : 48, 510
straits : 10, 142, 180
strategic importance : 148
Street of the Curetes : 211, 213
streets : 428
Stuffed mussels : 256
subtropical climate zone : 10
subway station : 118
sucuk (prepared with grape syrup

and whole nuts) : 61
sugar : 70
suicide attack : 50
Sultan Ahmet (Blue) Mosque : 88, 92, 95, 98
Sultan Ahmet Square : 92
Sultan Mehmet the Conqueror Bridge : 91
Sultanhani : 363, 404
Sultanhani Caravansary : 364
Sumela Monastery : 492, 494
Sumerian cuneiform writing : 52
sunken city : 274, 279
Süleyman the Magnificent : 57, 208
Süleymaniye : 57
Süleymaniye Mosque : 50, 88, 122, 124
Sümbüllü : 400
Süphan Dagi volcano : 451
sweet pastries : 70
synagogue : 59, 204, 206, 208
Syria : 10, 49, 52, 106
Syrian kingdom : 333
Sale Kösk : 153
Sale Pavilion : 152
Sanli Urfa : 7, 26, 52, 416
Semsi Pasa Mosque : 155
Seyh Matar Mosque : 428
Sile : 160, 161, 162
Sisli : 118

T

Taksim : 118
Tarsus : 55, 280, 318, 325, 326, 327
Tarsus Falls : 326
Tas Han : 458
Taseli peninsula : 316
Tasucu : 318
Tatvan : 449
Taurus Mountains : 18, 49, 235, 253, 274, 284, 285, 292, 295, 296, 310, 312, 317, 318, 331, 376, 448
tea : 62, 481
tea cultivation : 34, 476, 486
teahouses : 62, 69, 416
Tekfur Palace : 138
Tel-Acana : 333
Telmessus : 266
Temple of Aphrodite : 232, 234, 258
Temple of Apollo : 237, 272, 306
Temple of Apollo in Delphi : 94
Temple of Artemis : 55, 206, 208, 219
Temple of Artemis in Ephesus : 14, 46
Temple of Artemis in Sardis : 205,

229
Temple of Athena : 187, 192, 223, 306
temple of Athena in Assos : 106
Temple of Athena, Priene : 186
Temple of Augustus : 342
Temple of Didyma : 229
Temple of Domityanus : 211
Temple of Hadrian : 213
Temple of Serapis Allom : 190
Temple of Solomon : 54
temple of the moon-god Sin : 416
Temple of Trajan : 190, 192
Temple of Zeus : 223, 230
Temple of Zeus Olbius (Jupiter of the Romans) : 319
Temple of Zeus, Aizanoi, Çavdarhisar : 242
Temple of Zeus, Euromos : 245
Temple to Fortuna : 319
temple-mausoleum (hierotheseion) : 425
temples in Letoon : 270
temples of the Mother Goddess, Cybele : 359
temple-shaped tombs : 321
Tepsi minaret : 457
Termessos : 6, 288, 294, 295
territory of Typhon : 324
Teshup (chief god) : 349
Tetrapylon : 232
Thales (physicist-mathematician) : 47, 226
theatre and stadium, Aizanoi : 243
theatre of Kale-Myra : 282
Thebaid : 375
Theodosius : 167
Theodosius I : 56, 92, 118
Theodosius I, obelisk of : 92
Theodosius II : 56
Thousand Tumuli : 54
Thrace : 10, 167
Thrak tribes : 167
Thyatira (Akhisar) : 205, 207, 208
Tiberius Portico : 232
Tigris : 26, 52, 428, 429, 433
Tiled Pavilion : 104, 106, 107
Titus Tunnel : 334, 337
tobacco : 14, 18, 34, 256, 288, 302, 449, 476, 486
toilets : 213
Tokali (Buckled) Church : 382
tomato paste : 69, 70
Tomb of Eyüp : 134
tombs in Gevas and Ahlat : 456
tombs of Süleyman the Magnificent and his wife Roxelana : 122
Topkapi : 150

Topkapi Dagger : 114
Topkapi Palace : 50, 88, 104, 106, 109, 110, 115, 118, 124, 129
Toprakkale : 451
Torba : 6, 204
Torumtay Mausoleum : 510
tour agencies : 149
tourism : 80, 155
tourist guides : 82
Touristic Excursions : 6
Tours in Turkey : 525
towel : 176, 236
Tower of St. Peter's Castle : 244
Tower of Justice : 110, 172
Trabzon : 7, 34, 477, 479, 486, 490, 493
trains : 80
Trajan : 174
Trajan Fountain : 211
Tralles : 99
trans-European motorways : 80
Transhumance: 18
travel : 49
travel agencies : 82
travertine deposits : 235
trekking : 477
tripe soup : 69
Troad : 185
Trojan affair : 180
Trojan treasures : 185
Trojan war : 53, 54, 186
Trojans : 184
Troy (Ilion): 6, 40, 45, 47, 50, 53, 180, 182, 183, 184, 185, 186, 200, 356
Troy II city wall : 185
Troy, fortifications of : 186
tufa : 367
tumulus : 54, 106, 339, 356, 412, 416, 425
turbot : 492
Turkey : 2, 4, 6, 9, 10, 34, 50, 57, 59, 60, 61, 70, 73, 78, 80, 82, 84, 88, 134, 142, 162, 167, 176, 210, 220, 226, 231, 235, 236, 243, 253, 258, 266, 270, 295, 339, 359, 425, 457, 467, 505
Turkic language group : 60
Turkic world : 56
Turkish administrations : 428
Turkish Airlines : 82
Turkish architecture : 155, 167
Turkish art : 109, 152
Turkish Baroque architecture : 113
Turkish Baroque style : 409
Turkish bath (hamam) : 67, 333
Turkish bridge : 302, 305, 429, 470
Turkish caravansary : 226
Turkish carpets : 95

Turkish coffee : 70
Turkish conquest : 102, 492
Turkish cuisine : 330
Turkish culture : 60
Turkish delight : 61, 69, 73
Turkish economy : 34
Turkish folk dance groups : 83
Turkish folklore : 50
Turkish governments : 376
Turkish houses : 178, 342, 510
Turkish independence wars : 57
Turkish Language : 6, 78
Turkish life : 95
Turkish nation : 59
Turkish palaces : 462
Turkish period : 88, 330, 375, 469
Turkish population : 78
Turkish Republic : 57, 60
Turkish restaurant : 70
Turkish Seljuk and Ottoman periods : 43
Turkish Seljuk art : 219
Turkish Seljuk Empire : 407
Turkish shadow theatre : 178
Turkish social life : 61
Turkish soldiers : 180
Turkish state : 59, 400, 449
Turkish tiles and ceramics : 175
Turkish tourism world : 9
Turkish tribes : 59
Turkish turquoise coasts : 220
Turkish wines : 70
Turkish works of art : 103
Turkish world : 49
Turkish-Armenian border : 469
Turkish-Islamic period : 167
Turkmenistan : 84
Turks : 6, 9, 43, 50, 57, 59, 60, 70, 99, 192, 245
turtle beach : 258
Tuspa : 54
Tünel : 118
türbe : 404, 449, 462

U - Ü

Uçhisar : 366, 367, 375, 378, 390
Uighur alphabet : 60
Ulu Cami : 404, 428, 457
Ulu Camii, Silvan : 432
Ulu Mosque : 176, 178, 407, 409, 433
Ulu Mosque, Erzurum : 30
Uludag : 47, 178, 376
Uludag National Park : 178
underground cities : 366, 377
underground metro system : 80
educational institutions : 60
universities : 40, 118

university education : 85
university libraries of Istanbul :
50
Unknown Soldiers' Monument : 180,
182
Upper and Lower Egypt : 52
Upper Mesopotamia : 412, 425
Ural-Altaic language family : 60
Urartian castle-settlements : 451
Urartian fortress : 451
Urartians : 449, 457
Urartu : 40, 106, 450
Urartu Acropolis : 449
Urartu art objects : 54
Urartu horses : 54
Urartu inscription : 31
Urartu period : 160
Urfa : 418
Urfa citadel : 417
Usak : 6, 243
Usak Archaeological Museum : 243
Usak handmade carpets : 243
Uzuncaburç : 7, 319
Uzungöl : 477
Üç Kümbetler : 458, 459
Üç Serefeli Camii : 167
Üçagiz : 274
Ürgüp : 64, 366, 378, 390
Üsküdar : 91, 118, 138, 143, 149, 155,
158, 160

V

Vakiflar Carpet and Kilim Museum
: 98
Valide Mosque : 126
Van : 31, 54, 449
Van cat : 451
Van Lake : 30, 54, 448, 449, 450,
451
Vatican : 214
vaults : 306, 364, 382
veal : 70
Vedius Gymnasium : 214
Venessa : 390
Veni, vidi, vici : 510
ventilation chimneys : 377
ventilation systems : 377
Venus : 232
Vespasian (Emperor): 334
Vikings : 50
village wedding ceremony : 466
vineyards : 174, 208, 378, 387
Virgin Mary : 99, 135, 210, 324
Virgin Mary, Church of the : 214

W

war chariot : 47, 53

War of Independence : 201, 342,
409
Western Aegean architecture : 55
Western Aegean philosophy : 55
Western Aegean society : 55
Western Aegean world : 48
western Anatolia : 49, 55, 205
Western Anatolian towns : 53
Western Black Sea : 507
Western calendar, adoption of :
60
Western civilization :40, 46, 88,
183,210
Western culture : 48, 226, 426
Western languages : 40
Western lifestyle : 60
Western motifs : 60
Western sources : 155
Western world : 184
Westernization : 59
wheat : 64, 297, 439
wheels : 46
Whirling Dervishes : 359, 361
white cheese : 70
Wilhelm II (Emperor): 94
Wilusa : 183
windsurfing : 201
wine : 46, 70, 204, 378, 390
winter sports : 11, 457
wolfram ore : 178
woll carpets : 76
Women's Beach : 222
women's rights : 349
World War I : 57, 59, 106, 180,
200, 449, 457
World War II : 57, 60, 185
wrestling : 61
written history era : 348

X

Xanthos : 50, 270
Xanthos River (Esen Çay) : 272
Xanthos ruins : 272
Xenophon : 47, 48, 55, 490

Y

yacht cruising : 266
yachts : 163, 258
Yakutiye Medrese : 458, 459
Yalova : 178
Yalvaç : 7, 66, 296, 298
Yarimburgaz, Istanbul : 52
Yassi Höyük : 356
Yatagan : 256
Yazici, Erdal : 4
Yazilikaya : 348, 349, 354
Yedikule (Seven Towers) : 140

Yeni (New) Mosque : 118, 126
Yesemek : 333, 414
Yesil (Green) Mosque : 174, 176
Yesil Irmak : 510
Yesil Türbe (Green Mausoleum) :
176
Yesilova : 371
Yılanlı (Serpent) church : 381, 384
Yılanlı : 400
Yıldırım Bayezid Mosque : 510
Yıldız Palace : 151, 153, 154
Yıldız Palace Museum : 152
Yivli (fluted) Minaret : 291, 292
yogurt : 69, 148
Yümüktepe, Mersin : 52

Z

Zelve valley : 366, 387, 389
Zeugma : 26, 412, 414, 415
Zeus : 183, 222, 242, 270, 426
Zeus Altar in Pergamum : 46, 130
Zeus, Altar of : 192, 194, 195
Zigana : 34
Zilkale : 496
Ziya Gökalp : 428
Zonguldak : 505

SUGGESTED TOUR ITINERARIES

Tours may begin and end in Istanbul. Rental car services are available at all major airports. Travel agencies can organize private or group tours, and official guides are available for any tour. Ideal touring seasons are from March to November for Western Turkey and from late April to October for the Central and Eastern regions.

For adequate time to visit Istanbul's monuments, museums, and markets and to take boat trips on the Bosphorus and to the Princes' Islands, it is ideal to allow 3-4 days in the city.

Five-Day Tour from Istanbul to Ephesus

1st Day: Depart from Istanbul, cross to Asian side of the Dardanelles, visit the famous ruins of Troy. Overnight in Çanakkale.

2nd Day: Morning visit to Bergama/Pergamum acropolis, Red Basilica, museum. Depart to Kuşadası for overnight.

3rd Day: Ephesus ruins, museum, St. John's Basilica, site of the Artemision, Virgin Mary's house. Shopping or swimming in Kuşadası and overnight.

4th Day: Depart to Bursa; afternoon visit to its beautiful Turkish monuments: Green Mosque and Tomb, Ulu Mosque with Covered Bazaar, Muradiye Mosque and tiled tombs; view the city from Tophane terrace. Bursa has old and new thermal baths. Overnight in Bursa.

5th Day: Drive to Istanbul via İznik/Nicaea; drive by the lake and view the Roman city walls, original gates, basilica of Hagia Sophia, Green Mosque, and local museum. Return to Istanbul.

One-Day Tour from Istanbul to Ephesus

Depart with an early flight to İzmir. Drive to Ephesus in an hour. After full visit of site (as above), fly back to Istanbul in late afternoon.

Five-Day Tour from Istanbul to Göreme Region (Cappadocia)

1st Day: Depart from Istanbul to Bursa. Visit Green Mosque and Tomb, Covered Bazaar, Ulu Mosque and other fascinating old Turkish monuments such as the Muradiye complex, tombs of founders of Ottoman Empire. Overnight in Bursa with the possibility of a thermal bath.

2nd Day: Depart for Ankara via Gordion, the site of legendary King Gordios, King Midas, and the cutting of the Gordion knot by Macedonian King Alexander the Great. Visit the amazing archeological dig of the second largest tumulus in Anatolia, local museum and the excavation site. Arrive in Ankara for overnight.

3rd Day: Drive to Nevşehir-Göreme region to discover one of the Seven Wonders of Turkey, full of astonishing natural formations, Byzantine rock-carved churches with frescoes, Turkish edifices, and an active rural life. Overnight in Göreme area.

4th Day: Depart for other marvels of the area: Uçhisar, Ortahisar, Göreme, Avanos and Ürgüp town for shopping, churches in the open-air museum, underground city of Kaymaklı, and perhaps dinner with local wine and a show in a local rock-carved nightclub. Overnight in Göreme area.

5th Day: Early departure for Ankara for a city sightseeing tour including Atatürk's Mausoleum and the Museum of Anatolian Civilizations. Depart for Istanbul.

Twelve-Day Aegean-Mediterranean and Central Anatolia Tour

1st Day: Istanbul to Gallipoli, cross the Dardanelles to Çanakkale; visit ruins of Troy. Overnight in Çanakkale.

2nd Day: Visit Bergama/Pergamum: the acropolis, Red Basilica, healing center Aesculapium, museum. Drive to İzmir/Smyrna for overnight.

3rd Day: Depart to view İzmir from the citadel. Continue to Efes/Ephesus ruins. Visit the largest excavated archaeological site, museum, and St John's Basilica. Overnight in Kuşadası.

4th Day: Priene-Miletus-Didyma are the three jewels of Ionian heritage in Asia Minor. The cities, temples, fertile lands, and people in their villages are the day's highlights. Late afternoon return to Kuşadası.

5th Day: Drive east along the Meander River to Afrodisias/Aphrodisias through olive, orange, and famous fig orchards. After visiting the site dedicated to the Mother Goddess (Aphrodite in this area), see the best preserved stadium, largest temple remains to this deity, a local museum difficult to leave, and the fascinating remains of the local sculpture school in breathtaking surroundings. Late afternoon in Pamukkale/Hierapolis, one of the Seven Wonders of Turkey. Overnight in Pamukkale area.

6th Day: Theatre, museum, other ruins, and the cotton-like formations on the cliff of Pamukkale. Depart to Antalya for city sightseeing and museum. The Antalya coast has the newest and best hotels of the Mediterranean. City hotels and Kemer or Belek holiday resorts offer different ambiances for a perfect holiday. Overnight in Antalya area.

7th Day: Ancient Pamphylian sites—Perge, Aspendos and Side—with matchless ruins such as theatres, stadiums, aqueducts, agoras, and museums. Lively surroundings and beaches are available for the rest of the day. Overnight in Antalya area.

8th Day: Free day for sea sports, personal activities, or a visit to Alanya. Overnight in Antalya area.

9th Day: Early departure to cross the Taurus Mountains to the Central Anatolian plain and the city of whirling dervishes, Konya. Visit Mevlana complex, İnce Minaret and Tile Museum. Drive to Cappadocia, stopping at Sultanhanı Caravansary on the way. Overnight in Cappadocia.

10th Day: Visit the marvels of this area: Uçhisar, Ortahisar, Göreme, Avanos and Ürgüp town for shopping, churches in the open-air museum, underground city of Kaymaklı, and perhaps dinner with local wine and a show in a local rock-carved nightclub.

11th Day: Depart for Boğazköy/Hatuşşaş, capital of the Hittite Empire. Interesting remains, city walls with gates, temples with storage buildings, acropolis, Yazılıkaya open-air sanctuary, and local museum. Drive to Ankara for overnight.

12th Day: City sightseeing tour including Atatürk's Mausoleum and the Museum of Anatolian Civilizations. Return flight to Istanbul in late afternoon.

Twelve-Day Tour of Eastern Turkey

1st Day: Fly to Trabzon. Visit the highlights. Overnight in Trabzon.

2nd Day: Depart to Altındere National Park, where beautiful Black Sea forests cover the valley slopes. Ascend to the Monastery of Sumela. Continue to Erzurum for sightseeing and overnight.

3rd Day: After completing the tour of Erzurum, depart for Kars to discover her monuments, view the acropolis, and visit the local museum.

4th Day: Visit the ruins of Ani, a ghost site at the Armenian border. Drive to Doğubeyazıt and see the spectacular Ağrı Dağı/Mt. Ararat and İshak Paşa palace. Continue to Van for dinner and overnight.

5th Day: Visit the famous Akdamar Island and Armenian church, Old Van and acropolis, Urartu site Çavuştepe, and city museum. View the unusual sunset over Lake Van.

6th Day: Early departure to Diyarbakır. Visit the fantastic basalt walls, one of the Seven Historical Wonders of Turkey, as well as Ulu Mosque and the old bridge on the Dicle/Tigris River. Overnight in Diyarbakır.

7th Day: Visit Mardin, old city resting on the slopes of a high acropolis, and Darel Zafaran Jakobid monastery. Return to Diyarbakır for strolling the downtown streets.

8th Day: Depart from Diyarbakır to Şanlı Urfa, city of prophets; visit city sights and ruins of Harran. Overnight in Şanlı Urfa.

9th Day: Depart very early for Nemrut Dağı/Mt.Nemrut, Commegene kingdom mountaintop temple-mausoleum, one of the Seven Historical Wonders of Turkey. Drive to Malatya for overnight.

10th Day: Depart for Cappadocia, visiting Kültepe Hittite site and Kayseri en route. Overnight in Ürgüp area.

11th Day: Full day visit to the marvels of one of the Seven Natural Wonders of Turkey: churches carved into the rock formations, frescoes, fantastic formations of eroded valley slopes, castle-like settlements, underground cities, villages and towns in a stunning landscape.

12th Day: Drive to Ankara via Ağzıkarahan Caravansary. City sightseeing in Ankara including the Museum of Anatolian Civilizations and Atatürk's Mausoleum. Return flight to Istanbul.

Four-Day Tour of Southeastern Turkey

1st Day: Fly to Diyarbakır and spend a colorful day seeing the basalt city walls, local people, Anatolia's oldest mosque, and the bridge over the Dicle/Tigris River. Overnight in Diyarbakır.

2nd Day: Drive to Mardin to visit the medieval settlement, mosques and churches, and Darel Zaferan Jacobid monastery. Return to Diyarbakır in late afternoon for overnight.

3rd Day: Early departure for the small ferryboat on Atatürk Dam lake beyond Siverek town. Ascend Nemrut Dağı/Mt. Nemrut for the temple-mausoleum of Commegene King Antiochus. Fantastic mountaintop location with gigantic sculptures of gods and goddesses. Drive to Şanlı Urfa for overnight.

4th Day: Visit Şanlı Urfa, historical city of prophets, old streets, cool Abraham's Pools, and Harran village and ruins. Return flight to Istanbul.

Blue Cruise Tours

For information on these voyages on the turquoise and navy blue waters of Turkey, see page 253.

THE RECOMMENDED TOURS ABOVE ARE JUST A FEW EXAMPLES. THERE ARE A GREAT MANY CHOICES FOR TAILOR-MADE TOURS OF TURKEY. PLEASE CONTACT YOUR TRAVEL AGENCY FOR DETAILED INFORMATION..